T0290170

HEROICS & HEART BREAK

HEROICS

TWELVE MONTHS WITH THE ALL BLACKS

& HEART BREAK

JAMIE WALL

ALLEN&UNWIN
SYDNEY•MELBOURNE•AUCKLAND•LONDON

First published in 2019

Text © Jamie Wall, 2019
Photography as credited on page 368

Allen & Unwin
Level 2, 10 College Hill, Freemans Bay
Auckland 1011, New Zealand
Phone: (64 9) 377 3800
Email: auckland@allenandunwin.com
Web: www.allenandunwin.co.nz

83 Alexander Street
Crows Nest NSW 2065, Australia
Phone: (61 2) 8425 0100

A catalogue record for this book is available from the National Library of
New Zealand.

ISBN 978 1 98854 732 9

Design by Kate Barraclough
Set in Garamond Premier Pro
Printed and bound in Australia by Griffin Press, part of Ovato

1 3 5 7 9 10 8 6 4 2

For Amie G

CONTENTS

INTRODUCTION   11

PART ONE A YEAR OUT

01 SYSTEMS CHECK COMPLETE   17
02 WE HATE DISNEYWORLD   29
03 INFLUENCERS   37
04 HAIRY HANDS HYPNOTISM   42
05 THE NEW BOYS   47
06 PUB TRIVIA   52
07 LONDON'S DRIPPING   56
08 MITCH'S JOURNEY   63
09 HAKA HEADLINES   69
10 RUGBY'S CATHEDRAL   73
11 EVERYONE'S A WINNER   83
12 DUBLIN'S CALLING   87

13 **UNSMILING GIANTS**   **91**

14 **EYES OF ICE**   **96**

15 **OUT-PASSIONED**   **101**

16 **FAVOURITISM**   **105**

17 **OFF THE RECORD**   **109**

18 **REGULATION HIDING**   **113**

19 **HANSEN'S ANNOUNCEMENT**   **119**

PART TWO THE LEAD-UP

20 **BIGGER THAN RUGBY**   **124**

21 **THE HARDEST POST MATCH**   **128**

22 **RESHUFFLING THE
    NORTHERN DECK**   **132**

23 **THE UNLUCKIEST BREAK**   **137**

24 **A TALE OF TWO HALFBACKS**   **144**

25 **SUPER RUGBY OUT
    OF THE WAY**   **148**

26 **THE FIRST NAMING**   **153**

27 **THE BLACK CAPS GRAB
    THE LIMELIGHT**   **158**

28 **A DAY AT THE MUSEUM**   **162**

29 **PUBLIC RELATIONS**   **167**

30   **FIRST TEST OF THE YEAR**   **175**

31   **BAG BOYS**   **180**

32   **THE OLD ENEMY**   **184**

33   **THE WORST CROWD EVER**   **192**

34   **HELL IS OTHER PEOPLE**   **197**

35   **CRAIG THE UBER DRIVER**   **203**

36   **THE RED CARD**   **208**

37   **BACK TO SQUARE ONE?**   **214**

38   **THE PRESSURE**   **218**

39   **WHAT HAPPENS WHEN YOU MAKE THE ALL BLACKS ANGRY**   **224**

40   **'NOT ON MY WATCH'**   **228**

41   **THE BIG DAY**   **232**

42   **THE CITY OF THE FUTURE**   **237**

43   **THE STATE OF THE UNION**   **243**

PART THREE THE CUP

44   **WE ARE WHERE OUR FEET ARE**   **252**

45   **HOME AWAY FROM HOME**   **262**

46   **THE COMPANY MEN**   **268**

47   **THE RISING SUN MELTS THE EYES OF ICE**   **273**

48   **HAKA, REVISITED**   **278**

49   **THE SAD PARADE**   **281**

50   **GODZILLA ROAD**   **286**

51   **NOT SO HEAVY SITS THE CROWN**   **292**

52   **THE TYPHOON**   **299**

53   **WRITERS ON THE STORM**   **305**

54   **CRUNCH TIME**   **310**

55   **HEART BREAKERS, DREAM TAKERS**   **315**

56   **FANS WITH KEYBOARDS**   **325**

57   **SWITCHEROO**   **330**

58   **FLASHBACK**   **334**

59   **DOWNFALL**   **338**

60   **THE BITTER END**   **345**

61   **FALLOUT**   **350**

62   **THE HALF-EMPTY ROOM**   **353**

63   **VULNERABILITY**   **358**

EPILOGUE: SAYONARA, DOMO ARIGATO   **362**

ACKNOWLEDGEMENTS   **367**

INTRODUCTION

THIS IS THE STORY OF a team, a goal, and a country's expectations.

It's about players, coaches, journalists, administrators and officials—the relationships that formed between them and the obstacles that they all faced. From an on-field point of view, it's about a system of winning rugby games that was tested, tinkered with and massively challenged. From an off-field one, it's about making sense of the public's mood and how it affected the team that means the most to New Zealand.

We, as the rugby media, live in a bubble—one in which a guy getting poked in the eye at training is treated like some kind of state secret, or where the biggest issue on your mind is who will be doing the goal kicking on Saturday night. Every now and then you get blasted back to reality, but for the majority of our existence it's a constant stream of plane trips, media boxes, eating whatever food is closest to a stadium and desperately trying to figure out who will be named on a team sheet the day before its release.

This was the year that the All Blacks, arguably the most dominant team in sports history, would finally be able to put a definitive line under that claim. A World Cup win in 2019 would mean a decade of being champions, after the breakthrough 2011 win and nonchalant defence four years later.

It's difficult to really put a label on a book about following the

All Blacks for a year. Part sports bio, part psychological analysis, part travel blog. Twelve months of watching expressions change on players' faces, of feeling the creeping pressure build until all you wanted was to get to Japan and see it unleashed on the field. It crept and crept, until it grew so heavy it almost shattered the careful foundations the All Blacks had built.

Yokohama to Yokohama—at least, that was the plan. We had no idea what was going to happen in between the All Blacks' first visit to the World Cup venue and the projected second in a year's time. As it turned out, that first game against the Wallabies was the most assured performance the All Blacks would put on until well into the next season.

This is also an examination of the opponents the All Blacks would face during the World Cup, and the unbelievably high level of Kiwi connections that pervaded both the playing and the coaching stock. Of the motivations of men who would have grown up only ever wanting to play for a team (some indeed became All Blacks themselves) they now desperately wanted to defeat. It's about the difference in culture between rugby communities around the world, the people who go to watch, and how they react to wins and losses.

Most of all, this is a personal account. Being so close to a team you've idolised as a kid changes the way you think about them. The All Blacks are effectively our workmates, whether they like it or not. We often like to joke about how being part of the inner workings of the All Blacks is like getting put off sausages because you get to see how they're made. While there's certainly an element of truth to that analogy, it is still hard to believe I get to do this for a job. Walking into some of the most impressive stadiums in the world and having them as your office for the day is something you never get sick of.

The journey for the All Blacks to the Rugby World Cup in 2019 was at times dramatic, at times hilarious and quite often surreal. It's also one I got to go on, and I count myself damned lucky to be able to say that.

PART ONE

A YEAR OUT

01
SYSTEMS
CHECK
COMPLETE

**Yokohama International Stadium, 27 October 2018
(328 days to the Rugby World Cup)**

ALL BLACKS	**37**
WALLABIES	**20**

WE'RE STANDING IN THE MEDIA holding room of Yokohama International Stadium, Yokohama. Kick-off between the All Blacks and the Wallabies is about an hour away. Up the hallway, past two security guards with menacing looks on their faces, is a door that opens out to brilliant sunshine and a view halfway up the first deck of the 73,000-seat stadium. It's the biggest fortnight for Japanese rugby in a long time; after this test their national side will take on the All Blacks next weekend. But right now, all we care about is the fact that no one has thought to provide us with more than some convenience-store snacks to get us through the game.

'We' being the New Zealand contingent of media that have been assigned to cover the end-of-year tour. Half a dozen of us are here in Tokyo for a fortnight, then across to London for the next leg. After that it's Dublin, before a week in Rome to finish the season. I'd been told that the food laid on for the media was supposed to be pretty good when you went to overseas test matches, so seeing an array of Twinkies and cookies in front of us is a serious let-down.

There's Nigel from Radio Sport, Ross and Blair from Newshub, Hannah from Getty Images, Gregor from the *New Zealand Herald*, among others who have taken the 14-hour flight up from New Zealand. Then there's me, on the tour on behalf of Radio New Zealand, Māori TV and basically anyone else who wants to pay me for whatever I can capture on an iPhone 7 Plus. All of us carting around tripods, equipment bags and sweat-soaked shirts in what is a surprisingly warm Japanese climate. We're all about to take our positions for the first test of the tour between the All Blacks and the Wallabies.

A mate who lived in Japan for the better part of a decade told me that Yokohama was 'the Lower Hutt of Tokyo'. While he's kind of right in that it's an outlying part of the greater Tokyo area, that's about where the similarities ended for me when I first got there. For a start, Lower Hutt doesn't have a 73,000-seat stadium that will host the Rugby World Cup final in just over a year's time. Yokohama Stadium sits out in the middle of the local highway system that cuts its way through the megalopolis that is Tokyo. Yokohama is actually another city entirely, but on our way down there is no distinction between the two. It's just a mass of buildings and civilisation the entire way.

We knew this place was big, but you really don't figure out just how overwhelming it is until you're dropped right in the middle of it and left to chase the All Blacks around. In fact, so far the whole thing has more or less been one continuous ride on the Tokyo metro system with stops every now and then to watch the All Blacks train. That and sitting in on a series of mind-numbingly dull press conferences. They're being padded out by local journalists asking the team and staff numerous variations on what they think of Japan, Tokyo and Japanese rugby, with a few questions about what they've been having to eat thrown in for good measure. This is not at all uncommon whenever the All Blacks travel.

We knew this place was big, but you really don't figure out just how overwhelming it is until you're dropped right in the middle of it and left to chase the All Blacks around.

At least this time they've got a translator, so the entire thing doesn't devolve completely into farce. When we were in Buenos Aires the year before, captain Kieran Read fielded one post-match question in Spanish that took about a minute for the local journo to spit out. After staring at him quizzically for a few seconds, the All Blacks captain simply replied 'Sí'.

Even though the tour is only a week old, already you can tell that the repetitive nature of dealing with the media is beginning to take a toll on the team. Every question that comes out of the translator's mouth about what the All Blacks most enjoy about Tokyo is greeted with a half sigh, then a stare into space as they try to recall the pre-taped answer in their head.

Like most things with the All Blacks, though, you don't really need to hear them talk specifics. In fact, you don't need to be a rugby expert to figure out what coach Steve Hansen is trying to do with this tour. To the best of his abilities, these five weeks will be a dry run for next year's World Cup: two to get the squad settled in to the base that they'll use, and then the matches against England and Ireland as consecutively tough assignments to mimic the business end of the tournament. There's already been some rumblings that the way it's been gone about has been a bit of overkill, but this hasn't been too much of an issue in the first week. That's because the first test is against the Wallabies, who are in a complete shambles. The All Blacks have already thrashed them twice this year. Beauden Barrett went so far as to score four tries against them in the last test they played at Eden Park.

If there's heat on anyone this week, it's Wallabies coach Michael Cheika. Right now, both coaches are out on the field, watching their teams warm up. While they couldn't be further apart in terms of where their sides are at, both men are looking up at the massive stands, no doubt thinking about whether they're going to be standing in the same spot in a year's time. This is the start of the build-up to something much bigger.

It's unlikely Cheika or Hansen see our grumpy faces as we emerge from the door that leads out to our seats. Mine changes pretty rapidly, though. While Yokohama Stadium is a reasonably utilitarian edifice from the outside—rising up out of the landscape like a gigantic concrete monster—the inside is impressive. There's an athletics track around the field, but behind it bank up two decks of stands that are already filling up with fans. Two huge replay screens at either end flash commercials, and above us the sky is the perfect blue of a Tokyo spring. I realise this will be the first time I'll be watching the All Blacks play live in the daytime since the last test match at Athletic Park 19 years ago.

We head towards our seats. Unlike most other stadiums in the world, the media enclosure isn't on halfway, but shunted down to the 22 because of a gigantic VIP area to our left. We peer over. It's full of immaculately dressed Japanese businessmen in full suits and shined shoes. However, every now and then there's a flash of colour among the black and pinstriped masses. A t-shirt or a hoodie, worn by someone wandering about with the unmistakable gait of a hungover New Zealander. One by one, every former All Black and every Kiwis coach plying their trade in the Japanese Top League competition stumbles their way into their seats by flip-flopping their jandals up to the leather armchairs that make up the partitioned-off area.

For most of them, it looks like the aftermath of a big night out. All we can do is look on, but a beer would be fuckin' great right now. As if on cue, a team of girls with kegs strapped to their backs walk in front of us waving cups that look as though they could hold a litre. All we can do is flag them away—getting on it now would mean a decent hike to the nearest toilet sometime during the first half. We watch John Plumtree and Tony Brown head that way; apparently Dan Carter is there somewhere too. Richie McCaw showed up midweek at the All Blacks' training venue. He's got a pretty sweet deal after his awkwardly prolonged retirement announcement back at the end of 2015—nowadays he gets shuttled around by Fonterra to make appearances and shake hands.

We're treated to a Japanese cover version of 'YMCA' over the PA, prompting a few jokes about what Israel Folau might think of it.

McCaw has probably gone home now. He doesn't need to watch the All Blacks beat the Wallabies again—he got an on-field view for the 29 times that happened when he was playing. There isn't much doubt about what will transpire this afternoon, but it hasn't stopped the Japanese rugby public from showing up to see how it will happen. By the time the two sides take the field, there's around 50,000 in attendance. Just before that, though, we're treated to a Japanese cover version of 'YMCA' over the PA, prompting a few jokes about what Israel Folau might think of it. (It's been eight months since the Wallaby wing/fullback's last homophobic transgression via social media, and, unbeknown to us, six months away from his next.)

It only takes the All Blacks 10 minutes to provide a pretty good indication of where the two sides are at. Sonny Bill Williams throws a slick pass to Liam Squire 25 metres out from the line and the big flanker jogs through a giant gap to score near the posts, which brings a big cheer from the crowd but a groan from the Australian media—not of frustration, more of resignation. That was far, far too easy. It doesn't get any better later in the half when Kieran Read picks the ball up from the back of the scrum and rumbles over the line, carrying Ned Hanigan with him as the Wallaby loose forward's tackle attempt is reduced to a mere piggyback ride on the All Blacks captain.

Star All Blacks first five Beauden Barrett is having a mixed day at the office. At the end of the first half, Wallaby wing Sefa Naivalu blows through a tackle of Barrett's to score a try against the run of play and keep his team within striking distance despite the clear disparity in territory and possession. However, in the second half Barrett latches on to a pass to run 40 metres to score in the corner. As far as Beauden Barrett tries go, even a long-range effort like that pales in comparison to some of the magic he's conjured up since his debut back in 2012. But it's not his outpacing of the Wallabies' cover defence that's the important part of this try. In the lead-up, there's a clever switch of play that sees winger Rieko Ioane get clear down the sideline and free the space up for Barrett to finish. Plenty of people watching admire the move, but there's one set of eyes half a world away that is crucially storing it away for future use.

As he runs it in, untouched, it's hard for the All Blacks in his wake not to smile. There are about six of them following behind, in comparison to the two Australians who get nowhere near Barrett.

This is turning out to be the perfect start to the tour, and after only 57 minutes they can more or less shut the game down and start thinking about the next test. (Folau might have been thinking about the Village People when he threw a shocking intercept to Ben Smith to run away and score with, icing the result completely.) Barrett has another chance to remind us all why he's won World Rugby Player of the Year twice, with a flick-pass between his legs to set up Ioane for one more try, and the game finishes in a highly predictable 37–20 win for the All Blacks.

It's always nice when a game pans out the way you thought it would, but it takes a little bit of the fun out of it when everybody predicted this exact scenario. Even the Australian media sit back content in the box, knowing that they can simply go ahead with the post-match report and line of questioning that would've been conjured up on one of the many train rides around Tokyo over the past week.

One thing is for sure, though: Michael Cheika, a man who has a habit of losing his temper faster than his team loses games, is not happy. In fact, we've had an 80-minute surround-sound rendition of his descent from frustration to full-blown rage. The Wallabies coaching staff are only about 10 metres away from where we are on the other side of the dark blue VIP partition walls. We can't see him, but we can see the wincing reaction of assistant coach Stephen Larkham every time Cheika decides to make his feelings known with a tirade at the referee, his own players, or just the game in general. It's kind of like listening to your parents fighting when you're a kid, so the only thing we can do is just try to ignore it, and hope he cheers up by the time we have to talk to him next. But even the biggest optimist in the group knows that hope is pretty futile.

THE PRESS CONFERENCE ROOM IN behind the stands at Yokohama Stadium is vast—far bigger than anything we're used to in New Zealand. But such is the press presence at the game that all the seats have been filled by locals by the time we venture in. The Kiwi contingent is perched up between a pillar and one of the walls. We're told that Cheika and Wallabies captain Michael Hooper will be in soon, and we're braced for a continuation of the sort of shit that was spewing out of the coach's mouth during the game.

It's hard not to feel sorry for him, though. Cheika is, away from all the bluster, a good guy. The season before, I found myself running late to the post-match presser at ANZ Stadium in Sydney, a game which the All Blacks won 54–34 and at one stage were leading 47–6. Hurrying out of the lift, I almost bumped into the back of the Wallabies coach, who was being consoled by his extremely well-dressed wife. It was a reminder that the guys who are running all of this are human too. A couple of minutes later, he strode into the room, heartily deflecting questions in a typically Australian no-nonsense manner.

This time is different, though. Maybe it's because his wife isn't there. Cheika and Hooper walk in, utterly deflated. Three times they've come at the All Blacks this year; three times they've been comfortably beaten. The looks on their faces show that it doesn't matter one bit that this one is the closest scoreline. Cheika slumps, offers half-answers, shrugs a lot and generally gives off the impression that he wants to be back out the door as soon as he can. Hooper is a little more upbeat—he's got one of those personalities that, no matter how refined and educated the Wallabies captain is, kind of reminds you of a golden retriever. Cheika lets him do most of the talking. Then John Campbell grabs the microphone.

Campbell's been with us all week, but isn't coming on the rest of the tour. He's been sent up by TVNZ to cover the game, and is the only non-sports journalist in the pack. He has, however, got some serious pedigree in rugby matters—back in 2015 he spearheaded a campaign to get the All Blacks to play a test in Sāmoa and is probably the most high-profile ride-or-die Hurricanes fan on Twitter. He knows his shit, but the experience has been interesting because it's been the first time the All Blacks have had someone in their press conferences who is actually as famous as they are. Beauden Barrett notably prefaces each answer with 'That's a great question, John', Sonny Bill Williams is more than happy to stride right past the rest of us to give him a hug, and even McCaw found time in his busy schedule to have a chat. If Campbell wasn't such a genuinely decent bloke, it'd be the most obvious journalistic flex ever—but it's been more humorous than anything else to see the All Blacks fan-girling out for once.

But Michael Cheika probably has no idea who John Campbell is.

Campbell begins his question with his typical, drawn-out saying of the subject's name, followed by a pause. 'Michael . . . You look devastated. Is that how you feel?'

There is a pause so pregnant that you can honestly hear everyone in the room's eyeballs shifting nervously from side to side. We're expecting Cheika to explode with rage, and he sits up, animated.

'Devastated: that's a big word. I care, mate, a lot. I care about my team, the players, I care about rugby in Australia—and there's one thing that comes with care is fight, too!'

He's breathing fire now. He leans forward and makes sure he's looking Campbell dead in the eye.

'And whatever is necessary, we'll make sure we get it done.'

'Devastated: that's a big word. I care, mate, a lot. I care about my team, the players, I care about rugby in Australia–and there's one thing that comes with care is fight, too!' Cheika says.

Even Hooper looks startled at his coach's defiant display of passion, one that won't go viral but will probably do more to raise the spirits of his side than any other post-match press conference he's ever given. Then, it's done. The Wallabies are out the door, not destined to figure in the All Blacks' orbit for another nine months.

After that, it seems like the All Blacks coaching staff and captain's turns on the podium will be something of a let-down in terms of quotable content. And we're right. If there's ever been a 'this was another day on the job' press conference by Steve Hansen, assistant coach Ian Foster and Kieran Read, this is it. All three plod through their analysis of the match, which was as good as over before half-time when Read scored his try.

It's all pretty dry until an Irish accent pipes up from the back. 'Steve, what do you make of Conor Murray's injury?'

Someone has flown all the way over from Ireland to ask the All Blacks about the build-up to the test match in three weeks' time in Dublin, which seems a little wasteful as they could've just asked one of the hundred or so journalists in attendance to ask it for them. Hansen responds by saying that he thinks the star Irish halfback's neck complaint might just be a ruse, and for some reason does so by putting on possibly the worst Irish accent ever. It's the only highlight of the whole presser, which again concludes with the All Blacks fielding about a dozen identical questions about what they think of Japan.

But that little, innocuous inquiry does very much bring home just what this tour is all about for the people the All Blacks are visiting. While the team itself is using it as a simulation for what's going to happen at the World Cup, Ireland and England only care about winning in front of their home crowds, and their press want to stir up as much shit along the way as possible.

02
WE HATE DISNEYWORLD

Maihama, 30 October 2018

WEEK TWO AND EVERYONE HAS, by now, got used to Japanese toilets and their preference for warm water spray instead of toilet paper. The food, however, is a different story. One night, three of us go out for dinner somewhere along the Tokyo metro green line and find ourselves in a restaurant where the waitress doesn't speak English, so we resort to simply pointing to items on the menu and hoping for the best. We end up with something called burdock, a green blob whose origins—animal or vegetable—are not immediately apparent.

The aftermath of the first test saw John Campbell take me and the Newshub boys out for dinner at a Yokohama restaurant near the stadium. The beers start going down quite nicely, and I mention to him that the train system in Tokyo is pretty entertaining if he ever runs out of story ideas. He leaves us and we carry on to a local Hub, which is a chain of British pub-themed bars that have obviously been set up specifically for foreigners. We get extremely drunk, and the next day wake up with gigantic hangovers and a whole bunch of pictures on our phones of us making friends with random people in the bar. I flick over to Facebook, and a story Campbell has shot that morning at the Yokohama station already has a thousand likes on the TVNZ page. It's essentially five minutes of him pointing at trains and saying 'marvellous'.

Things are about to get a bit stranger, though. The All Blacks have shifted from their hotel in the middle of the city out to Maihama, which is around the other side of Tokyo Bay. They are staying in the Hilton, a suitably plush hotel on the edge of a peninsula where they seem to have commandeered an entire floor to themselves. It's about an hour's journey by train from the city, but in order to reach the hotel you first need to circumnavigate the main attraction in Maihama—the Tokyo Disney Resort.

Once we get off the Japan Rail main line heading east, the only way to reach the Hilton is to jump on the circular Disney monorail from the main train station at the entrance of the park. This makes for a surreal experience, not least because the monorail is decked out with Mickey Mouse-shaped windows and has 'A Whole New World' on repeat for the entire 10-minute voyage. On every journey we're surrounded by young families toting prams and gift bags, and the odd gaijin (foreigner) there for the kitsch value—usually decked out in a full-on *Frozen* or *Little Mermaid* outfit. The attendants on the line wear cream 1930s cartoon-style uniforms, complete with hats and white gloves.

Then, not long after jumping off and walking across to the hotel via a wide avenue that's cooking from the early autumn temperatures, we stride into an air-conditioned press conference room to listen to the All Blacks coaching staff and players talk about test rugby. It's hard to concentrate on what they say— the song from the monorail is still stuck in my head and it's not going anywhere.

Out on the ground floor, puzzled families staying in the Hilton—because of its proximity to Disneyworld—stare at the massive men wandering around the corridors in shorts and jandals. A couple of tourists have asked me exactly who they are, because they probably weren't thinking they'd be sharing a hotel with 51 rugby players when they planned their Disney treat for the kids.

Puzzled families staying in the Hilton– because of its proximity to Disneyworld– stare at the massive men wandering around the corridors in shorts and jandals.

That's right, 51. By now the All Blacks squad has ballooned to its greatest size ever. Steve Hansen made the controversial call to expand the playing roster past the half-century mark so that the main body of players can now head on to London in a couple of days to start preparing for the big test against England. Meanwhile, what will be an All Blacks B side will play against Japan on Saturday across town at Tokyo Stadium. It will mean probably half a dozen new caps at least. It has also meant that ever since the tour party was named, back on 15 October in Wellington, we've had to do some serious study on a few guys who no one, not even their mothers, would have predicted would be in the All Blacks in 2018. Brett Cameron. Reuben O'Neill. Dalton Papalii. Tyrel Lomax. Gareth Evans.

The Japanese aren't worried about conceding points, as long as they score a few of their own, because they know that trying to hold the All Blacks by turning the game into a grind is a fool's errand.

Cameron and Papalii only arrive on the Monday, because they were both involved in the Mitre 10 Cup final at Eden Park between Auckland and Canterbury on the Saturday of the first test. It has made for an odd build-up, especially considering no one has anything to lose in this weekend's match. The Japanese aren't worried about conceding points, as long as they score a few of their own, because they know that trying to hold the All Blacks by turning the game into a grind is a fool's errand. Meanwhile, more or less everyone in a black jersey is trying to push their case to move up the depth chart and be involved in the squad for next year. This may well be the most fun test match we'll see in a while.

The reason the All Blacks are staying within the Tokyo Bay Hilton/Disney perimeter fence becomes clear when we travel out to their training venue, which is about six kilometres away from the hotel. Even though the Greater Tokyo area is home to

38 million people, the team has managed to find a place that seems like it's in the middle of nowhere, mainly because the Shining Arcs training facility isn't directly accessible by train. It's a car ride or long walk from the hotel or nearest main station, and sits in a suburban setting—which, in Tokyo terms, means surrounded by 30-storey apartment blocks.

It's a flash, modern set-up. The Shining Arcs are one of the two teams that represent the NTT Communications company in Japan's Top League competition, and have one of the comparatively less flamboyant names. They have a large gym, with one weights room and another for stretching. Outside in the sunshine, exercise bikes are set up for the All Blacks to warm up on—from there they can gaze out on the two full-sized pitches that will be their training base. The fields are surrounded by high fences that look like they're perfect for hanging black sheets of fabric up on this time next year—a typical All Blacks move to deter spies and media cameras. We have a brief chat about the fact that there's not much they can do about someone getting on one of the roofs of those buildings, though.

It quickly evolves into one about just how useful any footage of the All Blacks training would be to anyone if they did get their hands on it. Which then leads to one about paranoia in general, and then on to something about conspiracy theories. The All Blacks are keeping us waiting, as usual, for their interviews. So we stand around and kill time with rambling conversations that lead nowhere. Former Marlborough stalwart and owner of rugby's most broken nose, Rob Penney, stands up on the deck overlooking the scene. It's rumoured that the former number 8 is about to jump ship to coach in Wales, seemingly the latest in the principality's stocktake clearance-sale treatment of New Zealand players and coaches. It's hot, we're bored, and the only thing on offer for us today is some shots of the All Blacks doing weight training.

Afterwards, we have three hours before the next press conference, which will take place at the hotel rather than here at Shining Arcs. Nigel, Hannah and I decide to kill the time by walking back to the Hilton along the edge of the peninsula, discussing who will play in this upcoming game. The only sure bet is that Richie Mo'unga will be at first five, and no one is really sure who will be the captain. Dane Coles' name has been bandied about—he's the current skipper of the Hurricanes, and the Japan test will be his comeback match after spending all of 2018 out with a knee problem and concussion complaints. There were even strong suggestions he might well retire.

BACK AT THE HILTON, we gather in the upstairs conference room. The air conditioning isn't working, so we look out the window at the blue waters of Tokyo Bay and wonder just how nice it'd be to be on a beach somewhere. There are a dozen chairs set up, with a table at the front for the players to sit at and face the cameras. The All Blacks media man, Joe Locke, hovers near the door and ushers in the one guy we want to speak to.

Coles immediately shoots down any speculation that he'll be running out first for the All Blacks. In his typical rough-around-the-edges style, he drops a few unintentional shits and fucks into his press conference appearance, meaning that we have to redo several otherwise banal questions. Everyone is always pleased to see Coles striding through the door for one of these. He cuts straight to the point, and doesn't seem to have a script in his head to which he refers for each question. Even his body language suggests a fair degree of honesty, often throwing his arm behind his head and rocking back on his chair to look at the ceiling while he searches for the right words.

He's all smiles and confidence, and quickly turns something we thought might be a bit of a dirge into one of the best debut All Black pressers ever.

Next in is Dalton Papalii. The Auckland flanker has just turned 21, and for his birthday got a call-up to the All Blacks probably two years earlier than he would've thought. He's all smiles and confidence, and quickly turns something we thought might be a bit of a dirge into one of the best debut All Black pressers ever.

It's not so much what he says. It's the confidence with which he says it.

'My first goal was to try and make my way into Super Rugby, try to get a few games and maybe even make the bench. But things can change in a short amount of time—just look at my pathway this year.

'I never thought I was going to be in the All Blacks this year. My goal right now is just to make an impact in the black jersey and help this team go forward and be successful.

'I have to admit, I've made it pretty far now.'

Papalii's position is, while welcome, slightly fortunate. He is one of the few success stories of the Blues' miserable Super Rugby season, and even then his starting spot week after week was only due to an injury to Blake Gibson. Everything that he says dispels any notion that he doesn't deserve to be there, however. In fact, by the time he's said goodbye and left, the media pack are raising our eyebrows at each other and telling Locke that we wouldn't mind having Papalii speak more often in future.

03

INFLUENCERS

Tokyo waterfront, 31 October 2018

MIDWEEK SEES AN EVENT ON the Tokyo waterfront, not far from where the bullet trains emerge from their underground link to the central station and accelerate rapidly along an elevated track, heading south to Osaka, Nagoya and Nagasaki—all places that will be hotbeds of World Cup activity next year, but just travel destinations today for the folks enjoying another sunny morning in Tokyo. The bullet trains speed down the line, within a few minutes of leaving the tunnel reaching their cruising speed of 320 km/h. They're long and white, with sloping noses that gradually bank up to the driver's compartment, which gives presumably one of the best views in the world. One whooshes past us while we wait outside an event venue; we're not allowed in yet.

One of the perks of being on tour is that you get to see how the All Blacks are perceived overseas, which is often a real eye-opener. Today is the launch of the new All Blacks jersey by Adidas—something that is often treated like a bit of a joke by New

Zealanders given there's essentially nothing they can change other than switching the collar from white to black and back again.

Instead of the usual crusty local rugby journos and well-dressed TV presenters, the front few rows are taken up by social media influencers.

That is, more or less, what they will do today in Tokyo. But it's still a big deal. We finally get let in to walk through a display of all the renditions of the All Blacks jersey dating back to 1999, and enter a long room with a staircase at one end from which the players will emerge wearing the new kit. There are rows of chairs and about a dozen cameras set up behind them. One thing that is immediately noticeable is who is sitting in the chairs, because they certainly don't look like the usual people that we see at an All Blacks press event.

Instead of the usual crusty local rugby journos and well-dressed TV presenters, the front few rows are taken up by social media influencers. The oldest of them can't be more than 22, while all of them have dyed, highly stylised hair and wear the sort of Japanese haute couture that they effortlessly pull off but would look utterly ridiculous on any gaijin game enough to try to fit in. All of them are glued to their phones, and none show even the slightest bit of interest in being there. I can see in the reflection of a couple of pairs of designer sunglasses that they're mostly mainlining Instagram, which is what they've presumably been paid to post photos of this event on. Just like us, they're at work—except they've found a much easier and probably far more lucrative way to make money out of what's happening today.

We're there in case any of the All Blacks who will be modelling the new jersey want to talk to us, which makes the Insta kids' business plan way more efficient than ours, because they can just split after the photo-op session is done. Fuckin' good on them, I guess.

The presentation is slick. The people from Adidas know how to put on a show, and through the dry ice and lights come Kieran Read, Ryan Crotty, Rieko Ioane, Sonny Bill Williams, Beauden Barrett and Aaron Smith. We only ever get two of these guys at a time for our regular media opportunities, and it's never two absolutely key players at once. This has turned out to be a very useful outing.

But first, they have a little fashion show to put on for us. The jersey is, unsurprisingly, all black except for a new white collar. AIG still sits prominently on the chest, and at a glance it looks virtually the same as the last iteration. Up close, though, it does have some sort of pattern woven into the fabric and the players are extremely keen to talk about how light it is.

We get given one to play around with, and indeed they are fantastically lightweight. Maybe it's the light show and massive abundance of chocolate brownies on a side table to help ourselves to, but we're being won over by Adidas. Especially when they tell us that we can grab a training top off a rack at the back of the room to take home. What started out as a day grumbling about how we had to cover this on our day off has become a quick way to do some Christmas shopping that won't weigh down our checked-in luggage.

All the players chat away happily, and we get a good stint with each while the others take turns fielding questions from the local non-sports media about what they think of Japan. By now the white-haired bowl cuts and faux-grunge army jackets of the influencers have sashayed out the door, but their experience has been documented on Instagram as an emoji-filled afternoon of awesomeness.

> **By now the white-haired bowl cuts and faux-grunge army jackets of the influencers have sashayed out the door, but their experience has been documented on Instagram as an emoji-filled afternoon of awesomeness.**

None of the All Blacks on show will be taking part in the game this weekend. Tomorrow morning they'll be on a plane to London, to probably repeat this exercise for the European Adidas people. I ask Aaron Smith about which out of the Ireland or England tests the team is more focused on, and he gives a vintage dead-bat answer about all games being of equal importance for the All Blacks, blithely disregarding the fact that the Japan test clearly isn't, otherwise he would be playing in it.

Smith has a personality that runs at full speed, all the time, and he always seems to be extremely happy. The day before I was sitting in the lobby of the Hilton getting some work done and a group of the players, including Smith and Read, sat down at the next table to order a coffee. The halfback held court for the entire wait for the drinks, spinning some yarn that was impressing the younger members of the group but was clearly causing Read to roll his gigantic eyes either out of disbelief or because he'd probably heard it 900 times before.

I say goodbye to Smith, and the rest of them. The next time we'll cross paths will be in London.

04

HAIRY HANDS HYPNOTISM

Tokyo, 2 November 2018

TWO DAYS LATER AND WE'RE back at Shining Arcs. It's been a mad day—I tagged along with Newshub out to Tokyo Stadium to catch the Japanese team captain's run. It's our first real brush with Japanese bureaucracy as well.

We had requested an interview with Japanese captain Michael Leitch in English. Leitch was born in Christchurch but has lived in Japan since he was 15. He's 30 now, and the assembled horde of local media hang on his every fluent word in his adopted language. However, the Japan Rugby Football Union officials can't seem to organise between themselves how he can possibly do a follow-up interview in English. The first bloke advises us to set our cameras up away to the side; the next says the interview isn't possible because of time constraints. We ask to speak to his boss, and while they're away in a back room having a meeting about what to do about the gaijin who aren't following the rules, Leitch simply walks over and gives us the two minutes we need. In fact, he gives us the only real answer we need—that this Saturday is the best chance Japan have to beat the All Blacks and it's now or never.

He shakes our hands, and smiles warmly, showing off his perfect front dentures. Leitch has the face of a man who has smashed his way into a million rucks, with deep grooves in his flesh and a pair of beautifully mangled cauliflower ears. The local media refer to him by the Japanese pronunciation of his name: *Rīchi Maikeru*. To us it sounds like they're referring to Richie McCaw, which isn't too far off given his status within Japanese rugby. His words make us think, *Man, could this actually happen?* These guys did knock off the Boks at the last World Cup, and this is an All Blacks team in which some of the players have probably only just met each other this week. Maybe this one will be a bit more interesting than we first thought.

We know the team now. There are going to be eight debutants, including our new favourite guy Dalton Papalii. The side will be captained by Luke Whitelock, who will follow in his brother Samuel's footsteps and lead the All Blacks in a test. Because of the wait time for Leitch, we're now behind schedule to get back to Shining Arcs and the All Blacks captain's run media session.

A train ride isn't going to do it, so we flag down a cab and use Google Translate to tell the driver we're in a great hurry to travel across Tokyo city. The ride ends up costing $350. Uber isn't really a thing in Japan—they've regulated that and Airbnb pretty much out of the market by making them more expensive than the established taxi and hotel industries. Cab drivers are pretty sweet, though—they don't have a problem dealing with dumbass gaijin having to resort to using their phones to communicate with them.

Kieran Read knows exactly what needs to be said, whether it's in Wellington, Buenos Aires, Sydney or wherever. That's one of the reasons they made him captain, presumably.

Shining Arcs is bathed in late-afternoon sunshine for the captain's run. It's basically a way for the teams to give some footage to the media for their Friday bulletins and stories in the lead-up to the test, and the talking is reserved for the skippers. So far this year we've had Kieran Read for every Friday session, giving pretty much the same answers to pretty much the same questions. Respect for the opposition, sticking to game plans, core roles, et cetera. He knows exactly what needs to be said, whether it's in Wellington, Buenos Aires, Sydney or wherever. That's one of the reasons they made him captain, presumably.

If that is indeed one of the reasons he was given the top job, it becomes pretty clear it's a key factor in Luke Whitelock's ascension as well. For five minutes he does the best possible impression of Read, and of his brother as well. Samuel has an innate ability to stand there and rattle off answers that have absolutely no relation to the questions asked, and this is clearly what Luke has been briefed on, too. He even adopts his brother's way of standing with his hands in front of him with palms upturned, moving one on top of the other as he makes each point. I remember getting taught that technique in third-form English to help give class speeches.

It's almost mesmerising the way he does it. I find myself more and more transfixed by his rhythmic hand movements—is he trying to hypnotise me? I think he is, damn it—the press conference is over, and all I've done is stare at his huge hairy hands rolling over and over each other instead of asking any bloody questions. He walks off, back to his team. Quickly I listen to the audio of what just transpired. It's a jumble of non-answers and misinformation—he hasn't given us anything at all we didn't already know, and I don't think I was the only one transfixed by his sinister hand trick. Damn you, Whitelock, you win this round.

First stop is a baseball batting cage, and Marshy jumps straight in the first one and cranks the machine directly up to the fastest possible speed to show us who's boss.

Later that night we head out into the middle of the city. We're joined by some of the Sky TV crew, including commentator and former All Black Justin Marshall. First stop is a baseball batting cage, and Marshy jumps straight in the first one and cranks the machine directly up to the fastest possible speed to show us who's boss.

He proceeds to strike out 20 times in a row. I like Marshy, he's a good guy, but he certainly doesn't like me when he turns around after about the twelfth swing and a miss to see me cracking up. He holds this grudge against me for the rest of the tour—in fact, probably to this day.

Next we head over to the bar district, but the entire street seems to be running the same scam in which we have to pay an entry fee that doesn't get revealed until we call in the tab. After some aimless wandering, I call it a night and get ready for test day.

05
THE NEW BOYS

**Tokyo Stadium, 3 November 2018
(321 days to the Rugby World Cup)**

ALL BLACKS	**69**
JAPAN	**31**

WELL, WELL. LOOKS LIKE LEITCH'S claims that Japan will come out firing were a promise, rather than a threat. We're looking at the scarcely believable scoreline of Japan 7, All Blacks 3 after only five minutes of the game. The crowd, 50,000 strong, are thunderous. The vast majority have shown up wearing the beautiful red-and-white hooped national team's jerseys, meaning the double-decked stadium (which is again ringed by an athletics track) looks like a seething mass of people dressed as Where's Wally for Halloween. They're in hot form. Even though Tokyo Stadium, which is perched on the edge of what you'd call Tokyo city, is smaller than Yokohama Stadium, the noise is about three times as loud as last week.

The shock lead is courtesy of a charge-down by Samuela Anise, who brushed past the man who kicked the ball, Jordie Barrett, to touch down next to the posts. The youngest Barrett brother has been in the gun for the latter half of the year. After a highlight-filled Super Rugby season, his world came crashing down after a crucial error in the All Blacks' shock 36–34 loss to the Springboks in Wellington. In fact, that night was a bad one for both him and his brother Beauden, due to the superstar first five's sudden inability to kick goals.

This is Jordie's first start back in an All Blacks jersey since then, and his presence on the tour has been heavily scrutinised despite the fact that essentially every half-decent rugby player in the country is included in the squad. Jordie is quickly becoming a divisive selection, and this first-touch blooper hasn't helped his case either. He wasn't aided by the fact that the man supposed to be running a block play, Luke Whitelock, simply stood there and watched Barrett's low kick ricochet off Anise and sit up in the in-goal for the Japanese lock to fall on.

Another man who is in the gun is out on the right wing. Waisake Naholo hasn't been the same since the All Blacks beat the Pumas in Buenos Aires the previous month, and he needs a big game to reclaim a spot in the top XV. Naholo, who memorably fought his way back into the 2015 World Cup squad by overcoming a broken leg thanks to traditional Fijian treatment overseen by his uncle, had a torrid time underneath a barrage of high kicks to his wing by the Argentinians.

It's not a great time to be losing form if you're an All Black winger—as if there ever is, though. On the bench is George

Bridge, the Canterbury and Crusaders wing who never seems to do anything wrong. He's been earmarked for a call-up to the test side seemingly ever since he made his Super Rugby debut. Bridge sits alongside Mitch Drummond, Dillon Hunt, Lomax, Cameron and Evans. The other two debutants, Papalii and Matt Proctor, are in the starting XV. The reserves stay in the large plastic shelter pitch-side as the All Blacks gradually edge back in front with a couple of tries. With 170 test caps between them, a third of which belong to Dane Coles, this is the least-experienced All Blacks side in a long time.

It's already a fast, loose game. The Japanese score two more tries before the break, and even have the audacity to start a scrap after their second. Nothing comes of it—it's the usual little melee of collar-grabbing and staring down, but it shows they've come a long way from the side humbled 145–17 at the 1995 World Cup in South Africa. After all, their beating the Springboks in 2015 will likely be the greatest upset in rugby, if not all sport, forever. They are here to show that they're not going to be pushovers next year when the tournament is played on their home soil—and if they do lose, they'll go down fighting.

With 170 test caps between them, a third of which belong to Dane Coles, this is the least-experienced All Blacks side in a long time.

Bridge comes on to replace Nehe Milner-Skudder at half-time. He wastes little time perpetuating his reputation as rugby's Midas straight away, scoring with his first touch of the ball. By now the All Blacks have broken away from the Japanese, and the rest of the game is just a matter of how many tries each team is going to score. Bridge again stars when he sets up Proctor for his own try on debut, then gets another to complete the All Blacks' scoring. Japan grab two stunningly entertaining tries of their own in the second half, meaning that they've managed to score as many tries in one test as the Wallabies have in three against the All Blacks in 2018.

What was supposed to be nothing more than an interesting anomaly on the tour has thrown up a couple of serious talking points for the All Blacks. As well as Bridge announcing himself as a genuine contender for the wing spot next season, Ngani Laumape has also picked up a hat-trick and reminded everyone that he's not just a one-dimensional battering ram. Both of these men have started knocking on the door, and it's only going to get louder by the time the next Super Rugby season rolls around.

Japan grab two stunningly entertaining tries of their own in the second half, meaning that they've managed to score as many tries in one test as the Wallabies have in three against the All Blacks in 2018.

This is the latest chapter of the ongoing midfield saga of the All Blacks. It is the one area of the team that hasn't shown any sign of stability for the last season and a half—in fact, you can mark down the point where it all got a bit disjointed as the second test in 2017 against the British & Irish Lions. That night Sonny Bill Williams was sent off, and ever since the second five/centre combination has been a succession of changes. Laumape himself had to make his debut that evening, then got a start the next week in the dramatic drawn third test. Jack Goodhue and Ryan Crotty have been used this season, with Williams in and out of the side due to injury.

Right now, though, you'd have to give Laumape the award for the most consistent performer. He does benefit from a playing style that lends itself to getting more prominent touches of the ball—most notably, his undeniable ability to run it off his own goal line and give his team room to clear the ball upfield. Laumape also has a stunning turn of pace for a guy built like a brick shithouse and has been developing a strong kicking game. He was also the Hurricanes' player of the season, one of the shining lights in a season that saw the team finish in the top four. Even without this three-try effort today in Tokyo, there are plenty of people who think he should be in the top test XV anyway.

06
PUB TRIVIA

Tokyo Stadium, 3 November 2018

TOKYO STADIUM'S PRESS ROOM ISN'T anywhere near as big as Yokohama Stadium's, but it still manages to cram in around the same number of journalists. We listen to a very long press conference from Leitch and Japanese coach Jamie Joseph, conducted in Japanese of course. We're not sure why, but the local journos take an awfully long time to ask their questions—much more in-depth than the usual 'can we get your thoughts on that game please' fare that we shovel out after any match in New Zealand. It's pretty late by the time Steve Hansen, Ian Foster and Luke Whitelock come out to take our questions.

Hansen gives off the demeanour of a man just happy that it's done and he can move on to the next big fortnight against England and Ireland. The week at the Hilton and Shining Arcs has clearly been a success from a logistical point of view, and the All Blacks have ticked their boxes around the quality of the facilities and travel times to and fro.

The All Blacks coach does give a special lot of praise to the players who have effectively filled in this week, though. He knows full well that some of them are going to play a huge part next season, and acknowledges that Laumape and Bridge have had statement games.

Whitelock seems in a daze; he non-answers a few questions and doesn't even blink when Hansen jokingly (but not really) blames his inaction for the first Japanese try.

After that, we're hustled into the next room, where the day before we'd set up our ambush interview with Leitch. We get five All Blacks brought out to us—first Bridge, who is understandably all smiles after his perfect debut. Bridge is a true Canterbury rugby product—as in, he was born and raised somewhere else before being identified as a teenager and brought in to their outstanding development programme. After leaving school in Gisborne, Bridge moved south to Christchurch and made a name for himself as a dependable winger with a stunning turn of pace. This year with the Crusaders saw him score 15 tries. He's cut his hair since then, which had got so long he'd been forced to wear tape around his head to keep it out of his eyes. He still has a bit of a mop, though, and all he really needs is some chewing gum to complete the picture of effortlessness he shows us when talking about the game he's just had.

Bridge even opens up with an unwitting reference to one of the most famous All Blacks post-match speeches of all time—he admits he's 'buggered'. He's always on the verge of bursting out laughing at the realisation of how good he's got it. Bridge is the embodiment of having things always fall into place at the right time, and he knows it.

Next up, though, is a man giving off a very different vibe. Brett Cameron, also from Canterbury and a second-half replacement debutant, stands nervously in front of us. He looks uncomfortable in his All Blacks blazer and tie. Out of all the new All Blacks, he is the one who has gained the most attention—mainly because even we journalists had to do some feverish research on him. Like Bridge, he was brought in to Canterbury from elsewhere—in his case, Whanganui, where he was handy enough with a cricket bat to be selected for the New Zealand Under-17 side. However, it's a tough assignment getting into the Canterbury and Crusaders' first five position. Ahead of him stand Richie Mo'unga and Mitch Hunt, meaning that Cameron has only played one game of Super Rugby so far. A few weeks ago he probably would've been thinking about his break between now and when pre-season training starts, but here he is in Tokyo, an All Black.

Cameron isn't a big player, around five foot eight and 80 kilos. He shuffles in nervously with his hands in his pockets. The common theory is that Hansen sees him as a running first five, and the eight or so minutes he played at the end gave us at least one opportunity to see him do that after he found himself in a bit of space out wide.

'It's definitely a dream come true,' he tells us, before quickly pivoting to, 'but it may be a little while before I get to taste it again. It's given me goals for the future.'

Cameron leaves and none of us, including him, are in any doubt that we probably won't see him at another All Blacks post-match press conference for a while. It's a strange and somewhat sad little exchange—it's not his fault he got picked out of nowhere and played a minimal part in one test match while the media had to figure out who he was. While bolters used to be part and parcel of All Blacks touring squads in the old days, at least they'd have a bunch of midweek games to tell their kids and grandkids about, as well as a decent trip overseas. Cameron has been in Tokyo for less than a week, and played in less than a tenth of what might be his only ever match for the All Blacks. While he has achieved what every rugby player in New Zealand supposedly dreams about and would probably give their right arm for, the feeling about Brett Cameron's All Blacks experience is that it's an oddity rather than an achievement. He is, for now, a pub trivia question.

The match at Tokyo Stadium has served a perfect purpose, though. The All Blacks served up an exciting display that engaged the local fans, but the Japanese team went one better by recording their highest-ever score in a test against the world's best team. It's been a stunning advertisement for the World Cup in a year's time, and demonstrated that the Japanese will not be pushovers in their group, due to the vociferous yet extremely good-natured support they enjoy.

From the All Blacks' perspective, however, it's given absolutely nothing away about their plans for the next few weeks.

07
LONDON'S DRIPPING

London, 5 November 2018
(319 days to the Rugby World Cup)

THE OLD COUNTRY GREETS US with greasy autumn weather. Everything is wet and grey, double-decker buses hurtle down the streets, and I'm still bowing to everybody as I leave a shop or walk past anyone dressed like they're in a position of authority. Tokyo habits are hard to break, even if you've only been there for a fortnight. One thing being in Japan has shown me is just how dirty Westerners are. In comparison, most of London seems like a bunch of old statues overlooking a slowly dissolving rubbish pile. But we're here, walking into work on a Monday morning and saying hello to one another as if we haven't all just taken 14-hour plane rides across two continents to get there.

The All Blacks are based in The Lensbury in Teddington—the same place they were for the 2015 World Cup. It's a complex specifically set up to house travelling sporting squads. On the walls there are framed jerseys of teams that have passed through. Most of them are rugby teams. The Lensbury is only a few miles down the road from Twickenham in the south-west of London. It's a quiet suburban area. Yoga-pants-clad mums bounce over to the tennis courts across the road from the hotel's stately entrance to take advantage of what the Brits would call a break in the weather.

The truth is, it's already very dark in the afternoons in the UK. By the time the first press conference finishes—a predictable session in which the All Blacks are happy to be settling in, blah blah blah—the level of light suggests it's time to go to the pub. However, the next day the most predictable of narratives rears its head in the English media. It's hard to really empathise with them about why they seem to want to talk about the haka so much. Headlines abound about the appropriateness of the famous pre-match All Blacks challenge, which are pointless at best and subtly racist at worst, and no one in the travelling media wants to have to discuss it.

If we're giving our English counterparts the benefit of the doubt, it's probably because of some decades-old edict by their editors that this subject has to be broached at every possible opportunity. Luckily though, the New Zealand media are afforded embargoed sessions a day in advance so that our stuff will be ready to go by the morning back home, but we know there's going to be at least one haka-related moment between now and when the team actually performs it.

The Lensbury has a training facility and gym on-site, so the

All Blacks never have to leave its leafy surrounds. Their field is cordoned off by a corrugated-iron fence, and the players don't even have to bother removing their boots when they head back to their rooms. They're at home here. You get the feeling that they like the fact that they're in a place that has all the comforts of home (minus the weather), and knowing that most of the pressure this weekend will be on the opposition.

Hansen versus Fast Eddie was looking like the number-one coaching duel of the end of the decade. England's stars excelled on the British & Irish Lions tour, and showed New Zealand that they were very much for real.

This test match was supposed to be the heavyweight championship of the rugby world. Problem is, it was announced two years ago, when the All Blacks had just come off a 16-test-win streak and the English were embarking on a 17-test run of their own. After their Six Nations triumph in 2017, England looked like they would be lining up the All Blacks for another big win like they'd achieved in 2012. Coach Eddie Jones was being hailed as some sort of genius— after all, he was the same man who'd masterminded Japan's shock win over the Springboks at the last World Cup. Hansen versus Fast Eddie was looking like the number-one coaching duel of the end of the decade. England's stars excelled on the British & Irish Lions tour, and showed New Zealand that they were very much for real.

This test match couldn't come fast enough.

Then 2018 happened. England lost, then lost again, and then again. They crashed to their lowest finish in the Six Nations for 30 years. The English press, who have never been noted for their patience (unless it's to do with seeing if they can get an answer to the same old questions about the haka), started circling Jones: England were too one-dimensional to have a sustained period on top. Everyone had worked them out.

Some, with long memories, were not surprised. The Australian Jones' track record at the teams he'd coached before followed a suspiciously similar pattern: success for a couple of seasons, then the sometimes too-honest-for-his-own-good Jones would piss someone off and be forced to move on after a couple of years. The only exception so far was his stint with Japan, because he signed a short-term deal and then was quickly snapped up by the Stormers to coach them in Super Rugby. He never made it to Cape Town— England came knocking with a deal that was presumably too good to turn down.

So now the showdown at Twickenham looks more like a last chance to dance for Fast Eddie. If the All Blacks crush the English, he may well find himself out of a job again. It'll give them just under a year to rebuild under someone else, and—unlike New Zealand, Ireland, Australia and South Africa—they won't get much help from their domestic set-up in terms of managing player workloads. Clubs in England are privately owned; their players are contracted to them, not the RFU. Instead they're loaned out and receive whopping match payments in the realm of $40,000, which became widely publicised the season before when it was revealed that it was almost 50 times the amount that their Sāmoan opponents were getting for their fixture at Twickenham. However, the big story around English rugby this year is about a player of theirs who has spent his entire career, indeed life, in New Zealand.

Brad Shields is due to play a role in this weekend's test match—it'll be his fourth English cap after debuting on their mid-year tour to South Africa. He had to get a special dispensation from his Super Rugby team, the Hurricanes, and the RFU to play. It was an unprecedented move by Jones to effectively scout out a foreign-born player not even playing in the Premiership. It turned into even more of an issue because it was made to look like a seriously desperate move after England's dramatic loss in form during the Six Nations, with Jones frantically trying to find some way of getting them back to their winning ways. The situation was massively compounded in New Zealand by the media somewhat rightfully pondering why England had to go shopping for a guy like Shields when they had a perfectly good pro competition of their own.

The truth, of course, was a little more complicated than that. Shields had been keen for a shift to England long before their slump, with the writing seemingly on the wall regarding his chances of an All Blacks call-up. The former NZ Under-20s rep and Wellington and Hurricanes stalwart on the blindside flank was once within reaching distance of playing test rugby, but by 2017 those days were gone. His place on the depth chart had dropped below Liam Squire and Vaea Fifita, and by 2018 it was obvious that Shannon

Frizell would've been above him too. Rumours of his departure started to circulate during the 2017 season, and they made sense— Shields was a regional stalwart, a dependable, hard-working player. Some other time in history he might have played 50 tests for the All Blacks and never once looked out of place, but, like so many others, he had the misfortune of pursuing a career at the same time as a few guys who offered just a little bit more.

The Baabaas game at Twickenham was essentially an All Blacks trial game using someone else's ground and money to make it happen.

So when it came time for Shields to finally announce he'd be going to English club Wasps, no one was surprised. Then things got interesting when Jones wanted him in an England jersey before he'd ever set foot on English soil. But the shit really hit the fan when Steve Hansen said that he'd wished Shields had stayed, because he might have called him up for an All Blacks jersey. It confirmed a rumour that had been swirling around since the tour the year before to France, Scotland and Wales. New Zealand Rugby had contrived to make it so that every top player in the country was in Europe at the same time—the All Blacks had a 38-man squad overall, the Māori All Blacks had 25, and a bunch of others had been selected in the Barbarians side to face the All Blacks in their first game. This meant that the Baabaas game at Twickenham was essentially an All Blacks trial game using someone else's ground and money to make it happen. It also meant that they could call on anyone they wanted at short notice if an injury crisis somehow eventuated.

Shields had been in the Baabaas set-up, and it was widely believed that Hansen had then approached him to jump on the bench for the All Blacks in their non-test midweek game against a French XV in Lyon a week and a half later. If that's true then Shields, knowing full well that if he said yes then his impending English test career would be toast, refused. That would put him among a rare set of players who have said no to an All Blacks jersey—except in this instance his reasoning would have made perfect sense. Being the honest, loyal grafter that he is, Shields also possessed enough popularity to know that if it was in fact true that Hansen was trying to use an otherwise meaningless All Blacks performance to deprive England of a selection, and therefore the player himself a massive pay day every time he turned out in a white jersey, the public opinion would be overwhelmingly with him.

So, in the lead-up to this test match, Shields is part of the storylines. But he's not the only Kiwi who's going to be wearing enemy colours this week.

08
MITCH'S JOURNEY

Pennyhill Park, London, 7 November 2018

EDDIE JONES' CO-COACH FOR THE English side is none other than John Mitchell. Despite being a former All Black who then moved on to be a relatively successful coach of the national side, his reputation among New Zealand rugby fans is one of bewilderment rather than respect. To understand how 'Mitch' came to be viewed in this light, you need to go back to a very different global rugby landscape to the one that exists today.

After the 1999 World Cup, the Wallabies were rightful champions and enjoyed regular victories both at home and away against the All Blacks. John Hart, the architect of the All Blacks' only series win on South African soil, fell victim to the new professional era by getting sacked in the fallout from that World Cup. He was replaced by Wayne Smith, the former All Blacks first five of the early '80s, whose tenure always seemed like that of a caretaker (although he was in charge of the team when the All Blacks and the Wallabies met in what is generally regarded as the greatest test ever played, the 39–35 Bledisloe Cup test win in front of a record crowd at Sydney's Olympic Park in 2000). After a disappointing couple of years in which the Bledisloe Cup still couldn't be regained (the Wallabies had held it since 1998), the drums were beating for a new coach. Such high turnover in the head coaching role was a new experience for All Blacks fans.

Meanwhile, former Waikato and six-game All Black Mitchell had been coaching ever since he had retired in 1995. His coaching career was almost entirely based in the northern hemisphere, rising up to assistant England coach under Clive Woodward. He was appointed coach of the Chiefs Super Rugby team in 2001 and, despite guiding them to an unspectacular sixth place that season, he was then handed the All Blacks coaching job later that year.

Mitchell came in with a perceived persona of a 'no-nonsense straight shooter'; an All Black himself who knew what it took to wear the jersey. However, he began making some questionable decisions, most notably selecting an under-strength side on the 2002 end-of-year tour. They fell to England at Twickenham and drew with France in Paris, making it the All Blacks' worst return from a northern tour in almost 20 years. The New Zealand public had got used to England being our whipping boys ever since Jonah Lomu had danced all over them in 1995, so that loss was a little hard to take, especially as it contained some less-than-legendary selections (Keith Lowen, Danny Lee, etc.).

That year did, however, lead to another Tri Nations (now known as The Rugby Championship) title, but the Bledisloe Cup was lost in a tight Sydney test, and questions were starting to be asked about the team's seeming inability to close out important games. Given that the World Cup was only a year away, it was becoming increasingly clear that Mitchell's job and ultimate legacy would most probably depend on the team's fortunes at the tournament.

The New Zealand public had got used to England being our whipping boys ever since Jonah Lomu had danced all over them in 1995, so that loss was a little hard to take.

It was around this time that Mitchell's unusual persona started to raise the hackles of pretty much every rugby correspondent in New Zealand. Questions were always responded to with an air of ambivalence and arrogance, and often with downright baffling answers. Mitchell's constant, mystical insistence on claiming that the All Blacks were 'on a journey' contrasted harshly with his hard-man reputation and led to ridicule from the general public. In addition, his selection of assistant coaches could be rather cynically seen as a jobs-for-the-boys arrangement. Former teammates Ross Nesdale and Darryl Halligan were given cushy roles in the All Blacks set-up, but it was the appointment of Andrew Martin as manager that sticks in the memory the most. The former military man was given the nickname 'Colonel Cuddles', due to his overenthusiastic embrace of All Blacks returning to the bench during test matches.

However, the results of the 2003 Tri Nations blew a lot of those perceptions out of the water. Record victories over the Springboks and Wallabies in successive weeks (in Pretoria and Sydney, no less) eased the national collective psyche leading into the World Cup. No need to worry about close results when we can put 50 on the Wallabies on their home ground, right?

The early games in the tournament certainly seemed to support that view, although it's not like the All Blacks were in a particularly challenging pool. They did haemorrhage 37 points against a very game Wales side—easily a record for the men in red—however, the clinical dispatching of the Springboks in the quarter-final led most to believe that a victory in the final was a foregone conclusion. Ten minutes into the semi-final against the Wallabies, Stirling Mortlock had other ideas. The big Aussie centre picked off an errant Carlos Spencer pass and galloped 80 metres to score under the posts, setting up an unassailable Wallabies lead and an early flight home for the All Blacks. It also gave the New Zealand Rugby Union a valid reason not to renew Mitchell's contract post the World Cup. He left the country after a couple of NPC seasons in charge of Waikato, banished to coaching in Australia and South Africa before landing a job as the US national coach.

Given Mitchell's overall win percentage of 82, the NZRU's decision to punt him into touch actually looks pretty harsh. Considering the strength of the Wallabies at the time, the three losses suffered at their hands isn't anything to cry yourself to sleep over, either. In fact, that record puts him well inside the top five All Blacks coaches of all time. So was it his performance off the field that cost him his job? Pretty much, yes.

Mitchell got himself offside with the New Zealand media early and often, mostly by creating a closed-shop environment around the team. Mark ('Cowboy') Shaw, another one of Mitchell's mates who was an assistant coach, went on record describing the media as 'fleas'. Add to that a strained relationship with some senior players—most notably former captain Anton Oliver, who in his autobiography states that Mitchell allowed, encouraged and participated in a serious drinking culture, to the point where the team's travel plans had to be held up while the coaching staff could recover from their excesses.

Mitchell had the benefit of some very, very good players while he was in charge of the All Blacks, but couldn't always pick the best XV when needed. The most infamous example of this deficiency was dropping Christian Cullen (arguably the greatest fullback to ever pull on an All Blacks jersey) for the 2003 Rugby World Cup, for no other reason than to include the hardly amazing Leon MacDonald in the team.

Mitchell's subsequent record in Super Rugby in charge of the Western Force and Lions from 2006 to 2012 was hardly anything to write home about—most tellingly, he was given the boot from the South African team after complaints from players about the way he'd treated them. Add in a mysterious departure from Sale after only a few weeks and it was no wonder he ended up being relegated to coaching a South African university side. If you're a cynic his original fast-track appointment to the All Blacks' top job could be seen as an unfortunate consequence of the NZRU desperately trying to put a former player in charge at any cost after the public's backlash against John Hart. The high-handedness with which Mitchell went about surrounding himself with his mates and backtracking the All Blacks' public relations to 1981-like levels couldn't have been lost on his masters.

But now, in his latest incarnation, he's back in All Blacks discussions for this week, anyway. Mitchell has mellowed out a bit, at least in public, because the New Zealand media would crawl over broken glass to elicit some sort of inflammatory comment from him. He's off-limits to us when we go and visit the English training facility at Pennyhill Park down the south-west motorway from Teddington. Jones brought him on board to be England's defence coach earlier in the season, and it seems as though he wants the players' tackling ability to do the talking for him.

09
HAKA HEADLINES

The Lensbury, London, 9 November 2018

SATURDAY AFTERNOON'S TEST MATCH WILL be played on 10 November, one day before the hundredth anniversary of the end of World War I. At least that's what everyone has been told—the war didn't actually officially finish until 28 June 1919, when the Treaty of Versailles was signed. But poppies are out in full force this week in London. So is talk of the main issue of the day, and it's not the All Blacks.

Brexit has thrown the entire UK into a state of limbo, where no one can start or finish a conversation without bringing it up. It's been inflicted on us ever since we got off the plane. British journos joke about asking the All Blacks what they think of it during one of their press conferences—we warn them not to bother because the answer they'll get will be far less hilarious than the one they're imagining in their heads.

Instead, we get news that one of the All Blacks has suffered a pretty disturbing injury. Joe Moody, for reasons we're still trying to figure out, has had half his eyelid torn open due to some freak accident at training. Our best guess is that someone's hand slipped through while they were lifting each other in a lineout drill, with a finger going straight into the big prop's eye. His tour is done.

The jersey for the weekend is dramatically revealed to us–until we realise it's just the same one but with a poppy on the sleeve to commemorate the cessation of hostilities 100 years ago.

We head outside, along a wet track to the training field where the All Blacks are doing their drills. The jersey for the weekend is dramatically revealed to us—until we realise it's just the same one but with a poppy on the sleeve to commemorate the cessation of hostilities 100 years ago. Kieran Read comes over to talk to us.

Normal shit. Big challenge, can't underestimate them, blah blah. He does let slip one bit of All Blacks inner-sanctum knowledge into the public magisterium, though: England are the team that the All Blacks hate losing to the most. It's about the only time you'll ever hear an All Black differentiate anything about their opponent in a negative way (unless you count descriptions of the French as 'unpredictable', which are pretty far-fetched these days because France are quite easily the most useless Tier 1 rugby nation there is, given the amount of resources they have at their disposal). The All Blacks want you to know they hate losing to the English—because in the world of sport, that's okay.

Everyone playing the Poms at anything hates losing to them. In Argentina they just hate them full stop.

The haka's a shop window into Māori culture for the entire world, jealously guarded and protected. Something New Zealanders, even the ones who wouldn't usually care about matters cultural, take very seriously.

And then, as if we didn't need any more evidence, we get it from a local journo who asks about the haka. It's the same question they got asked last time they were here, and it's the same one as before that, going all the way back to the 1888–89 New Zealand Natives tour when Victorian-era Brits would've first seen the challenge.

'Do you think it still has a place in the game today?'

Yeah mate, because the All Blacks will stop doing the haka. It's only the most iconic tradition in the entire sport and the one thing that anyone who even has the faintest idea of what rugby is will know. The haka's a shop window into Māori culture for the entire world, jealously guarded and protected. Something New Zealanders, even the ones who wouldn't usually care about matters cultural, take very seriously.

So it's no surprise when eyes collectively roll to the backs of our heads.

Except Read's. He gives a sigh, then a diplomatic answer

about tradition, when it's obvious he just wants to stare down incredulously the guy who's asked the question. Thankfully, one of the Kiwi reporters says what we're all thinking, and asks Read if he gets sick of having to deal with these sorts of questions about the haka. Every. Single. Time.

Read doesn't flat-out admit it, but the look on his face says it all. The look on the local journalist's does too—instant regret. Now that the issue is dealt with, we can move on and look forward to the actual game.

10
RUGBY'S CATHEDRAL

**Twickenham, London, 10 November 2018
(314 days to the Rugby World Cup)**

ALL BLACKS	**16**
ENGLAND	**15**

'HEADQUARTERS', AS THE ENGLISH CALL IT, lies a couple of train stops down the line from Teddington. The carriages are crammed full of fans, all rugged up and with looks on their faces that belie a serious amount of unease about this test. England are currently on their knees, rugby-wise. A decent blow from the All Blacks, say a 25- to 30-point win, will send them into a spiral that they probably won't have time to pull out of by the World Cup—let alone the upcoming Six Nations.

The All Blacks' last two matches at Twickenham have been essentially benefit events to showcase their own dominance.

The last time was in 2017, when they beat a Barbarians side made up of New Zealand fringe players. The time before that was the World Cup final, in which they comfortably beat the Wallabies. If any team walking out onto the perfectly manicured turf this afternoon will be feeling like they own the joint, it's them. Nevertheless, it doesn't stop a fair bit of bravado and the inevitable Brexit talk wafting around the packed-in punters, infiltrating through the eiderdowns and beanies insulating us against the November weather. Outside the train, it's getting darker and greyer. It hasn't started raining yet, but it will. It has every day this week.

If any team walking out onto the perfectly manicured turf this afternoon will be feeling like they own the joint, it's them.

It's spitting by the time I get to the main gate at midday. Kick-off is another three hours away, but the crowd is already building up nicely in the outside bars. Twickenham holds 82,000, and it will be full, but a glance at the day's sports pages is a healthy reminder of the enormity of the city and the sporting culture we're in. Tomorrow, just a few stops back up the train line, Chelsea are going to be playing Everton in front of a packed Stamford Bridge. Up north, Manchester City will play Manchester United, and the touring Kiwis are playing the Wayne Bennett-coached England at Elland Road in Leeds. Barely anyone attending those games will have the slightest bit of interest in what's about to transpire at

Twickenham this afternoon. Most probably wouldn't even know the test is on.

Twickenham is the only ground I've been to so far that has separate working areas for the broadcast and written press. The newspapermen have their own room on one side, complete with an honours board for the annual rugby writer of the year. There are waiting staff to serve us up dinner, and hearty handshakes and slaps on the back as the local press make their way in.

I know a few of them from the Lions tour in 2017. Now I'm on their turf, and it's pretty intimidating to be sitting among the writers whose prose will be splashing across the UK's broadsheets tomorrow. Nearby is Stephen Jones, the man who has made a living off annoying New Zealanders with blatantly agitating pieces antagonising the All Blacks. When he's not doing that, which is admittedly the vast majority of the time, he's an incredibly astute pundit—not that anyone back home will admit it. Not far away from him is David Walsh, who everyone knows is not just a rugby writer. He was also the only journalist with the balls to question why Lance Armstrong got so good at winning the Tour de France all of a sudden, and got a movie made about what ended up being arguably the biggest sporting story of the century. Tokyo, even with its gigantic pool of journalists and press conferences, was nothing compared with this. This is the big time, but that feeling is amplified by about a thousand when we take our seats.

Twickenham is an incredible stadium. Its three decks bank steeply upwards, rows of dark green seats getting steadily filled by the expectant masses. The field is immaculate despite the persistent rain throughout the week, and even though it's only 2.30pm, the lights are starting to take effect due to the precipitation arriving back just in time for kick-off. The moody conditions and ceiling of dark grey sky above lend the stadium a Gothic atmosphere that makes it feel like the absolute cathedral of rugby, suffusing it with a chilling sense of foreboding.

This isn't some jacked-up new stadium fitted out with mod cons to keep neophytes coming back. Twickenham is assured of its place at the top of the heap—it doesn't need any further assistance apart from reputation and reverence. Overhead, a passenger jet makes its surprisingly low approach to the nearby Heathrow Airport. I'm reliably informed that once the game kicks off, you won't be able to hear any other flights over the crowd noise.

The moody conditions and ceiling of dark grey sky above lend the stadium a Gothic atmosphere that makes it feel like the absolute cathedral of rugby, suffusing it with a chilling sense of foreboding.

By the time the All Blacks and the English march onto the field, it's awash with now-heavy rain. Those in the open rows of seating below us are getting soaked, as are the squads of soldiers on the pitch who have brought out giant flags and a poppy to commemorate the armistice centenary. Prince Harry and his new wife Meghan Markle are in attendance, and the red-headed royal lays down a wreath. The crowd sings 'God Save the Queen'—the most perfect national anthem in the world because of its brevity and the fact that it's a song all about wanting an old lady to be happy.

To a thunderous reception of 'Swing Low, Sweet Chariot', the All Blacks perform the haka. The English have been singing this increasingly problematic Southern American plantation slave song since the late 1980s, as a tribute to black winger Chris Oti. The irony of spending a week discussing the suitability of the haka instead is probably lost on the crowd. A quick glance around behind where we are positioned, bang on halfway on the third deck, shows just why Brexit is happening. An English rugby crowd is overwhelmingly made up of the sort of people who believe Great Britain is indeed still great, and that if things went back to the way they were and all the upstart colonials did what they were told the world would be a much better place.

Then the game starts, and it seems like all their middle-aged, leather-elbow-patched dreams are going to come true. The English tear into the All Blacks, and drive deep into their 22 after only a minute and a half. Halfback Ben Youngs spots that Rieko Ioane has made a terrible defensive read, and floats a perfect pass out wide to Chris Ashton to dive over in the corner. The Brexiteers around us erupt, pumping up the volume even further than their response to the haka.

Just a shaky start? There's 78 minutes to go, we remind ourselves. But over the opening quarter it becomes apparent that something is clearly amiss with the All Blacks, as the English rip into them and dominate possession and territory. People are starting to wonder if the teams have swapped jerseys before kick-off, because this is going completely against everything predicted during the build-up. Things get decidedly serious when the English take a lineout 10 metres out from the All Blacks' line, and put together a textbook drive to score.

It's not immediately clear what the worst part about it is: the fact that they made it look so damn effortless, or that the ball was grounded by Dylan Hartley, the turncoat hooker from Rotorua who has made it his life's goal to be a thorn in the side of the team he presumably wanted to play for when he was a kid.

Owen Farrell has tacked on a dropped goal in between tries, so after 25 minutes the score stands at 15–0 in favour of the home side. The rain keeps tumbling down, illuminated by the lights atop the vast cauldron that is now bursting with belief. *This is it!* England, so maligned for the entirety of the season, are back in business. Eddie Jones is sitting directly opposite us, around 100 metres away, but I swear I can see his Cheshire grin from here.

For the All Blacks, though, the scoreline is an ominous one. Six years ago at Twickenham, they were down 15–0 at half-time in a test they'd go on to lose 38–22. It stands as their heaviest defeat by England, and one of the highest scores they've ever conceded in test matches. It was a brutal reality check for the recently crowned world champions, and one that was played out under a similar pre-test presumption of dominance by the New Zealand public and media. So, while a three-score deficit with an hour to play is something that the All Blacks have mowed down easily in the past, unease is definitely in the ascendant right now.

However, an unlucky break for Sonny Bill Williams inadvertently changes the flow of the game. The big, dual-code, sometime boxing champ is forced from the field with a knee injury. This ushers in Ryan Crotty, a man who hasn't exactly been setting the world on fire this season, but who will come to play a pivotal role in what happens next.

Crotty fires like he's been shot out of a cannon straight in between Farrell and openside flanker Sam Underhill, before he's hauled down five metres short.

Williams' offloading and distribution just hasn't worked at all so far in the game. Crotty, a far more direct player who takes the ball into contact and sets up go-forward on the deck, is exactly what the All Blacks need right now. Almost as soon as he comes on, the tide of possession completely changes as Read marshals the forwards into playing the ball close to the ruck, and instructs Beauden Barrett to start kicking far more than usual. After 37 minutes they hang on to the ball for around two dozen phases before winning a kickable penalty in the English 22.

Read needs to make a statement before half-time, though. Instead of calling for the kicking tee, he opts for a scrum. Crotty fires like he's been shot out of a cannon straight in between Farrell and openside flanker Sam Underhill, before he's hauled down five metres short. One phase later and Barrett turns the ball back inside to Damian McKenzie to slide in next to the left-hand post. They're not done, though, squeezing in one last first-half assault that draws a penalty straight out in front of the sticks that Barrett calmly knocks through to make the score 15–10 at half-time.

The reaction from the crowd after the try was a massive gasp, and there's a slow groan as the sodden teams leave the park. England's lead has been cut to less than a converted try, and they more or less haven't touched the ball since their last score. The game has been completely flipped on its head, and it seems like the All Blacks will put the hammer down and walk out of Twickenham with the comfortable win that everyone expected.

Except, over the next 40 minutes, that's not what transpires. The game settles back down into the sort of wet-weather slugfest the 82,000 onlookers are more accustomed to. Both packs bash away at each other, and the opening score of the second half is a dropped goal from Barrett—the first of his career. Now the All Blacks are within one score of the lead. Fifty-eight minutes go by and French referee Jérôme Garcès raises his arm once again for England being offside in their own 22. Barrett sends the ball tumbling through the posts and, just like that, the All Blacks have the lead.

There's still 20 minutes to play, though. While England haven't looked like scoring at all since their last try, all it will take is a penalty anywhere along the halfway line, because they have a long-range kicking option in winger Elliot Daly. The All Blacks know all about him already—last season on the British & Irish Lions tour he sent over a howitzer from his own half at Eden Park to help seal a dramatic draw in the series decider. Right now, we realise that what we are seeing is exactly what Hansen had sought to engineer on this All Blacks tour, because this test has become one where the result hangs on a knife-edge. It will come down to one big play, and the crowd is now roaring for it to be England's.

With 75 minutes gone, they appear to have got their wish in spectacular fashion. TJ Perenara, on for Aaron Smith, goes to box kick the ball deep into English territory from the All Blacks' 10-metre line, but only succeeds in getting it as far as the massive tattooed arms of Courtney Lawes. The English lock commands a fair bit of respect among the New Zealand media due to his abrasive and expansive play, and the ramifications of his charge-down look like giving his team the win. The ball bounces into Underhill's hands, and the big flanker rumbles down into the 22 with only Barrett to beat for the tryline.

Convention says Underhill will try to use his weight advantage to plough over the top of Barrett. If he does, he may well find himself tackled, but the English can set up camp in the All Blacks' 22 and play for a penalty or a dropped goal. Instead, he deftly turns inside and out, leaving Barrett with his back turned and giving himself a free run to the line. He dives in, sliding along the wet turf and sending the crowd into a frenzy. It's the only time since their last try that the English have really pressured the All Blacks' line, but the long-suffering fans don't care. They're about to witness one of the biggest upsets since the last time they toppled the All Blacks here in 2012.

There's a sharp blast on the whistle, though. High up in the Twickenham stands, surrounded by TV monitors, television match official Marius Jonker has seen something and wants Jérôme Garcès to have a look. Everyone's eyes are locked on the big screens that shine through the gloom. It appears that Lawes was ever so slightly offside, and the longer the ref looks at it, the more likely it becomes that Underhill's try will get rubbed out.

The RFU has provided us with radio links to what the ref and his assistants are saying, so we can hear the decision before it's announced to the crowd. In his heavily accented voice, Garcès utters the fatal words: 'So ze decision ees no try?' Jonker's deep Afrikaaner tone gravely booms back: 'Yes, that's right.'

> **This has gone beyond parochialism, or even the good old British superiority complex. It's out-and-out hatred, and it's heaving down as hard as the rain that's now flowing in sheets off the players.**

Garcès blasts his whistle again, signalling to the English, who have walked back to halfway save for Farrell, who is waiting to tee up the conversion. His arms swing below his waist—no try. The crowd is apoplectic. An unremitting howl of derision, much louder than anything that has come before, replaces the roar that had been willing their team on. This has gone beyond parochialism, or even the good old British superiority complex. It's out-and-out hatred, and it's heaving down as hard as the rain that's now flowing in sheets off the players.

The final four minutes see the All Blacks grind out the game, to a cacophony of boos. TJ hammers the ball into touch, and the game is done.

11
EVERYONE'S
A WINNER

Twickenham, London, 10 November 2018

POST MATCH SEES US DOWN in the bowels of Twickenham, packed into a media room and awaiting the arrival of the coaches. Hansen, Foster and Read come in, get asked several different ways about the Lawes offside call and give the same answer, which is unsurprisingly in complete agreement with the ref. The All Blacks coach does stop short of addressing the one elephant that has lumbered its way into the room as well—that had it not been for a temper tantrum Eddie Jones threw in England's Six Nations win over Italy the year before, the rule around offside would not have been amended to consider Lawes to be in an offside position. The Italians, knowing they had very little chance of winning, had taken the piss by not committing anyone to the rucks, running into England's attack line and therefore not being offside while they waited for the ball to be played.

No one asks Jones about it, either, when he comes in. It would be a bit of a shame to spoil the mood, because while the All Blacks are relieved and happy to get that win under their belt, the one-point loss has basically saved Jones' job. Finally, after a year of getting dismantled both on and off the field, England have shown that they have the backbone to recapture the form that saw them win 18 tests in a row. The World Cup now looks a lot less like a pipe-dream—and man, doesn't Jones know it. He holds court with the local journos, most of whom are in the palm of his hand.

However, it doesn't disguise the fact that the All Blacks have made an exceptionally powerful statement of their own. After a season in which they've scored 452 points at an average of 41 per test, they suddenly flicked a switch and took on England at their own game. But this wasn't some preconceived move all along to trick their opponents into a trench fight—the All Blacks had to abandon plan A after finding themselves down 15–0 after 20 minutes. The introduction of Crotty gave them a hard-carrying ball-runner, and he responded by having possibly his best game in the black jersey. The set piece was solid and the ball was looked after well. When it was kicked away, it found land rather than hand.

The man who did the majority of the kicking, Beauden Barrett, comes out to meet us resplendent in a crisp All Blacks suit. He's flanked by his brother Scott, who had another useful shift off the bench. First question to the All Blacks first five is about that dropped goal, though. It's extremely noteworthy given that it is the first in his 71-test career, but even more so because he's spent the last month and a half copping an inordinate amount of heat for not breaking his duck in the 36–34 loss to the Springboks in Wellington—the same test that saw his other brother, Jordie, fall down the depth chart.

It's said that Barrett will grin uncontrollably when asked a question he's uncomfortable answering. Which makes it difficult to know if he's genuinely happy about slotting the 30-metre strike, as well as the clutch penalty that put the All Blacks into a one-point lead that was never relinquished. He's got his hands in his pockets and lets out an audible breath when he talks about it.

'I've been working on it for . . . years, ha ha. Oh, it was a no-brainer.'

Barrett was probably feeling pretty good about it, though, and the grin was there from start to finish in the stand-up press conference. It's pretty obvious by the end that it'd be hard not to feel good given the discussion around his kicking boots and decision not to take one in the only loss in 2018 to date.

It was nothing, really. Nothing at all for a guy of his talent. Barrett has just played his seventy-first test in his sixth season with the All Blacks—a player who had the ultimate torch-passing moment in the last World Cup final, scoring the last try after the incredible final performance in a black jersey by Dan Carter. Ever since then, it's just been presumed that Barrett will simply carry on from that moment, a perfect replacement for what we all thought was an irreplaceable player.

Barrett has probably suffered the highest amount of criticism in his career so far this year, which is somewhat perplexing given that he's not too far removed from being the two-time World Rugby Player of the Year. His Hurricanes side, stacked with talent, posed little threat to the eventual champion Crusaders in Super Rugby. Richie Mo'unga was highly touted as taking over from him, despite never having played a test. When the Springboks got over them in Wellington, it seemed like the biggest chink in Barrett's armour had been found—when his goal kicking is off, it stays off. That's what it means when you're the All Blacks, and even more so when you're the All Blacks first five. Scrutiny, scrutiny, and a bit more scrutiny.

All the talk of the All Blacks not having a plan B when a team gets on top of them has seemingly been put to rest, mainly because of the most un-All Black of game plans.

But he stands in front of us, still grinning, and with the giant presence of his younger brother looming close by. Questions have been answered. All the talk of the All Blacks not having a plan B when a team gets on top of them has seemingly been put to rest, mainly because of the most un-All Black of game plans. The English rose to the occasion, and were ground down in a dramatic display of how the All Blacks can beat a team at their own game.

Now, though, they have seven days before they have to do it all again.

12
DUBLIN'S CALLING

Dublin, 12 November 2018

O'CONNELL STREET, 9PM. I WALK past the statue of James Joyce balancing himself on his walking stick, trying to picture Leopold Bloom wandering the wide, tram-tracked byways. It's greasy and wet like London, but that's about where the similarity ends. The River Liffey stretches out horizontally in front of me as I walk south to cross the O'Connell Bridge. It's busy; people are still either heading out or heading into the city, with the main bus and tram stops on the wide street that's dominated by the famous post office and spire.

There's a rumbling behind me, and an angry, heavily accented voice.

'I keep fookin' tellin' ya, I'm on me way home!'

It's a man, aged in his mid-fifties, wearing a soft cap and pulling a wheeled suitcase. He's talking on a flip-phone, and doesn't seem to care at all that everyone can hear what is obviously a heated conversation.

'I've left the fookin' pub, fook ya!'

He rolls up next to me. We're standing at the lights, waiting for the traffic to stop and let us cross. By now it's obvious that he's talking to his wife, and she's not happy. I've been in this guy's shoes before. I look across at him and offer a sympathetic smile, a 'don't worry mate, she'll calm down when you get home' sort of look. His eyes lock on mine and I can see his Guinness-fuelled brain formulate a plan.

'Ya don't believe me? Here, I'll prove it to ya—'

He thrusts the phone into my hand.

'Tell me wife I'm comin' home and we're not at the fookin' pub.'

'What?'

'Just tell her.'

I put the phone to my ear and feel the wrath of some woman in the suburbs of Dublin who has had to put up with this guy's antics for far too long.

'Hello?' I say.

'Who da fook are you?' is spat with vitriol by the furious voice on the other end of the line.

I umm, ahh, and hand the phone back. There is nothing I can do for this guy. I walk across the bridge, take one look around and immediately realise I've booked my hotel on the rough side of the river. But North Dublin is my home for the week, and I'm wondering how many more phone calls I'm going to be taking on behalf of inebriated local husbands.

THE NEXT DAY I'M WANDERING back through the city from the bus stop. It must be because I'm carrying a tripod, as a man stops and asks if I've taken any pictures of the local artworks. No, I say, not yet. But I do like the Dublin Spire that towers 120 metres over O'Connell Street.

'Oh that,' he says. 'We call that the Stiletto in the Ghetto.'

I refrain from telling him I'm staying across the street from said stiletto, which makes me an inhabitant of said ghetto. He tells me about the Floozie in the Jacuzzi, some mermaid water feature across town.

'And that James Joyce fella, he's the Prick with the Stick.'

Whereas the game against England last weekend was a pitched battle that had its rules of engagement hashed out in a civil manner in the press, this upcoming fixture at Aviva Stadium feels like an ambush, guerrilla warfare with no quarter.

It's all fun and games with the locals in Dublin—they're a friendly lot. But as I'm walking past the O'Connell Street General Post Office, now a museum to the 1916 Easter Rising, it becomes clear that the reason we're in Dublin is a deadly serious one for the All Blacks. It stands as a monument to Irish nationalism, pockmarked with the bullet holes inflicted over a century before as the British army took aim at the rebellious fighters inside. The General Post Office is the unsmiling flex of stoicism next to the Dublin Spire, or

'Stiletto in the Ghetto'. Even that has a violent backstory—before the Spire was built, it was home to a replica of Nelson's Column. In 1966, 50 years after the original uprisers tried and failed to blow it up, their descendants returned and finished the job. A large quantity of explosives took off the top of the monument to the famous English admiral, and local police were noticeably less than enthusiastic in their pursuit of the perpetrators. Those responsible were never caught, and the decapitated monument was eventually replaced by the Spire in 2003.

For all the jokes, it shows that there's a very serious side to the Irish. Whereas the game against England last weekend was a pitched battle that had its rules of engagement hashed out in a civil manner in the press, this upcoming fixture at Aviva Stadium feels like an ambush, guerrilla warfare with no quarter.

13
UNSMILING GIANTS

Dublin, 15 November 2018

THE TEST AGAINST IRELAND WILL mark a couple of milestones for the All Blacks. Aaron Smith will play his eighty-second test, which makes him the all-time most capped halfback for the side. His form since the first Rugby Championship test in Sydney has been impeccable. After a slightly quiet Super Rugby campaign, Smith has completely regained the number 9 jersey from TJ Perenara.

The other is that Brodie Retallick and Samuel Whitelock will pack down together in their fiftieth test match, also a record for a locking duo. Whitelock played his hundredth test overall in the aforementioned encounter in Sydney, which means he has now played around 1300 more hours of test rugby than his brothers Luke and George. Retallick scored a try in the Sydney test as well— dummying and running 40 metres to score untouched—which is being widely regarded as the highlight of the season. Both of them are sitting in front of us at the All Blacks' hotel in Blanchardstown, a suburb north-west of Dublin that has sprung up around a giant mall built back in the 1990s.

The conference room is packed with local journalists again, as well as the New Zealand media touring party. Steve Hansen has come and gone, taking a barrage of conjecture from the press about what he thinks of Irish coach Joe Schmidt. Unsurprisingly, he gave little away, if there was anything to give away in any case. If anyone was hoping for a scoop, they're at the wrong press conference speaking to the wrong guy. They're probably covering the wrong sport. It didn't stop the Irish from flying someone all the way to Tokyo to ask Hansen about Conor Murray's injury, mind you.

This should be a fun, light-hearted session— except neither man seems to be in the mood to joke around. Especially when they're asked if they enjoy cuddling one another so often.

Retallick and Whitelock are both huge men, with the latter sporting an impressive beard and shaggy mop, and the former making a valiant attempt to grow a mullet. The hairstyle has become a topic of conversation for the All Blacks because a few of them have apparently formed a 'Mullet Movement'. So far, Jack Goodhue, the young Northland centre, has made the most progress. This should be a fun, light-hearted session—except neither man seems to be in the mood to joke around. Especially when they're asked if they enjoy cuddling one another so often.

It would've made a decent sound bite if either had actually bitten, but instead there's just a few embarrassed snorts and a short denial of anything even vaguely homoerotic. Then they're asked if they know each other well enough to read one another's minds. Again, this draws blank stares and a brush-off.

Retallick and Whitelock are proving exceptionally tough nuts to crack today, even for All Blacks. Usually some sort of joke will elicit a bit of dry humour, but not this time. Perhaps it's the tension in the air about the test. Ireland have been lying patiently in wait. Even though they've won the Six Nations and are currently enjoying the best run of their entire history, there is still a feeling among All Blacks fans that they're an aberration. So, we gain nothing of interest out of the session—an outcome that is probably exactly what Retallick and Whitelock intended.

THE NEXT DAY WE TROOP out to see Whitelock again, this time in front of a large statue that has been erected at St Stephen's Green in the middle of the city. It's called the Haunting Soldier, a five-metre-high figure made from old engine parts and horseshoes, dedicated to the Irishmen who fell in the Great War. The ground on which it stands is an immediate talking point, because St Stephen's Green was another key battle site in the Easter Rising. You can even still see the bullet holes in the stone archway entrance where a British machine gun fired upon rebels from a nearby rooftop. Whitelock is there to lay a wreath on behalf of the All Blacks, along with a representative of the local Dublin Gaelic football club. It's probably no coincidence that both organisations are sponsored by AIG.

Despite the fascinating juxtaposition of a memorial to the sacrifices of locals in an army that was trying to put down a rebellion against their own homeland, the big lock is in no mood to discuss any sort of history other than the one that the All Blacks have carefully cultivated towards their connection to both world wars. Whitelock's grandfather was on active service during the second one and he repeats the stat that 13 All Blacks died in the first, including 1905 Originals captain Dave Gallaher, who was born in Donegal in Northern Ireland. Again, this could've been something quite interesting, but we're fed the party line that pretty much all official business to do with World War I has been over the past four years: that it was a great sacrifice and we should honour everyone who died (on our side, that is), and not actually discuss the nuances of why it actually happened.

We leave feeling a little bit deflated– this very much felt like a box-ticking exercise, an unnecessary conflation of sport and war that is particularly out of place given the complexities of the Irish experience during that time period.

Whitelock, Nepo Laulala and Liam Squire lay their wreath, then get taken on a walk around the Green, which has information boards every 50 metres or so detailing the fight against the British sent to put down the rebellion in 1916. We leave feeling a little bit deflated—this very much felt like a box-ticking exercise, an unnecessary conflation of sport and war that is particularly out of place given the complexities of the Irish experience during that time period. It's a reminder that New Zealand's own experience of World War I may well be very different to the one that's being taught to us, and that there's probably a lot more to it than that heroic and valiant version the All Blacks are playing their part in perpetuating.

A week later, after we are all gone, someone goes into St Stephen's Green with a bucket of red paint. It's tossed all over the Haunting Soldier and the wreath the All Blacks laid.

14

EYES OF ICE

Aviva Stadium, Dublin, 15 November 2018

THE TEST, OF COURSE, IS the latest in the burgeoning rivalry between the two coaches. On one side, Steve Hansen, who has guided the All Blacks to a World Cup and a win record of 89 per cent. On the other, another New Zealander; but unlike John Mitchell, Joe Schmidt is now held in probably the highest regard of any expat plying their trade overseas—player or otherwise.

Schmidt is, like so many other coaches, a former school teacher. He taught and coached at some of the powerhouse colleges in the country: Palmerston North Boys' High, Napier Boys' High and Tauranga Boys' College. He moved on to coach Bay of Plenty, and won them the Ranfurly Shield in 2004. After that he was picked up by the Blues. Things should've been on an upward curve from there. This was back when the Blues were coming off a Super Rugby title (as of 2019, their last), and the safe presumption was that while the Auckland franchise were destined to have a bad year here and there, they'd remain one of the perennial contenders forever. You know, because of population and stuff.

Except they weren't. Schmidt's arrival coincided with a downturn in fortunes that the Blues have never really been able to recover from, and after three frustrating years he was shown the door and made his way to the airport. After landing a gig at Clermont Auvergne, where his nickname was 'Les yeux de glaces'—eyes of ice—things started to pick up. Following a few years in France, he was offered the top job at Leinster, taking over from our old friend Michael Cheika. But things really got going for Schmidt when Leinster won the Heineken Cup in 2012, and Ireland, for so long the also-rans in UK rugby affairs, appointed him head coach. One of his first assignments was against the All Blacks in Dublin at the end of 2013.

If there were any question marks back home over just who Schmidt was and whether the Blues had (like they often do) made a mistake by letting him go, they were answered that day. Ireland were up 19–0 at half-time, and it took perhaps the calmest and most composed last play in the history of test rugby by the All Blacks to deny them a famous win. The next time the teams met, in Chicago in 2016, Schmidt completely thrust his name into the consciousness of everyone back home when the Irish managed to go one better and win their first-ever test against the All Blacks by 40–29. That, in itself, was enough for plenty of people to start asking why this particular New Zealander was coaching Ireland and not New Zealand. Failing that, why he wasn't being lined up for the job of next All Blacks coach. This, despite everything Hansen and Schmidt have said otherwise, is the big storyline of the week, if not the entire tour.

However, not everything Schmidt has done has endeared him to the Irish rugby media. He is a notoriously guarded coach, and keeps any contact with the team to an absolute minimum. In fairness, it was probably one of the reasons behind the Chicago result—while the All Blacks were out being paraded around to promote rugby and their naming-rights sponsors AIG, the Irish quietly tucked themselves away and plotted the downfall of the team that had been bullying them into defeat after defeat for 111 years.

But now we are to get first-hand experience of what it's like to deal with a team that doesn't want anything to do with the media, by the coach's own edict. Trainings are scheduled at the exact same time as the All Blacks. Their media liaison thinks nothing of cutting journalists off halfway through a question and imposing pointless embargoes midway through a press conference.

While the All Blacks were out being paraded around to promote rugby and their naming-rights sponsors AIG, the Irish quietly tucked themselves away and plotted the downfall of the team that had been bullying them into defeat after defeat for 111 years.

The most bizarrely paranoid move comes when it is revealed (under embargo, of course) that Irish flanker Dan Levy will miss the test through injury. It's a big loss, given that Levy himself is playing in the place of Seán O'Brien, who had impressed on the

Lions tour the year before. We're told there is no injury specified, which is completely absurd. When pressed further, the liaison concedes that Levy is suffering from 'general body soreness', a woeful attempt at spin-doctoring that simply increases the frustration among the locals and causes us to really understand why they have been making jokes about what sort of nonsense we'd hear at this press conference.

The presser is held underneath the main stand at the Aviva Stadium, in a large room that probably doubles as a lecture theatre the rest of the week. We file out, shaking our heads. Levy's mysterious injury is of no real concern to us, though, because after the England win we're pretty confident the All Blacks will take this test. By now, it has been revealed that Conor Murray is indeed out, so this latest bit of injury news merely confirms our belief.

Not one British, let alone Irish, player is mentioned during the little All Blacks love-in we have. To make matters worse, we're laughing arrogantly the whole way through it.

As we wait for our emails of audio to make their way via the stadium WiFi back to New Zealand, a very loaded conversation is started up among the Kiwi journalists. Someone wonders aloud: 'Who out of all the other test players in the world would you pick for the All Blacks?' We're sitting within earshot of a TV crew from Belfast. Making sure all of them can hear us, we start spitting out names—Siya Kolisi, Malcolm Marx from the Springboks. Michael

Hooper, even. I chip in with a name that gets a fair few nods: Israel Folau.

It's not who we *say*, though. We all know full well it's who we *don't*. Not one British, let alone Irish, player is mentioned during the little All Blacks love-in we have. To make matters worse, we're laughing arrogantly the whole way through it.

15

OUT-PASSIONED

Aviva Stadium, Dublin, 17 November 2018
(307 days to the Rugby World Cup)

ALL BLACKS   9
IRELAND   16

THERE'S THIS SICKENING FEELING YOU get after you've watched a fair few All Blacks tests. It happens when you realise they're not going to win, and it's sort of like your brain telling you to get your affairs in order for more or less every conversation you're going to have for the next week or so, then intermittently for the rest of your life. That's because while people like to talk about All Blacks wins, it's far more of a Kiwi pastime to pick apart All Blacks losses. Usually that feeling starts happening deep into the second half of a test, when it becomes clear that there's not enough time left to score a couple of tries or whatever it is they need. Suffice to say, it doesn't happen very often.

But it's happening tonight—and far earlier than usual.

101

Something is wrong with the All Blacks. No one is playing well, at all. Schmidt's Ireland seems to have a plan for everything they do—it's as if they've read Hansen's mind before the game. The adage for the past decade or so, for at least those in the know, was that you had to score around 30-odd points to beat the All Blacks. There was no point trying to tackle them out of the game, because they'd just find a way to get through. You couldn't kick it all day, because they'd just run it back. Even when the weather was bad, they'd churn you up and beat you at your own game— as England found out the previous weekend. But the weather is perfect tonight, and so is the Irish defensive line.

We're high up on the second deck of the Aviva Stadium, formerly known as Lansdowne Road. It's an oddly configured park. The stands are in almost a horseshoe shape, with the southern end rising high above the surrounding neighbourhood, and the northern end just one little stand backed by a massive windowed wall that looks through to the nearby River Dodder, which runs off the Liffey. Our seats are on the absolute edge of the broadcast area, which comprises about 10 very steep rows going back up the stand. There's very little to separate us from the actual crowd, a couple of whom have realised we are New Zealanders and have decided to give us a few words of advice for the commentary. Before the game, it's all very friendly, if a little tense.

The place is absolutely crammed. Tickets for this game have been nigh on impossible to get ever since they went on sale. In fact, when Hansen needed to get some he ended up asking Schmidt for his help. Schmidt procured the tickets, and we watched during pre-kick-off as 'Shag' handed him an envelope containing €700.

Right now, though, halfway through the first half, Hansen's probably wishing he'd never forked over the cash. Passes are getting dropped, lineouts are being lost, and the All Blacks are generally getting bullied. But still, the score is only 9–6 at half-time and Beauden Barrett has decided to make sure there's absolutely no doubt over his ability to kick dropped goals by slotting his second in two weeks.

If the try looks familiar, it's because it was the same play that saw Beauden Barrett score in the second half of the third Bledisloe Cup test in Yokohama.

But eight minutes after half-time, the killer play comes. Ireland win a lineout on halfway and reverse the play back to the blindside. Winger Jacob Stockdale is on hand to kick ahead, regather and score. If the try looks familiar, it's because it was the same play that saw Beauden Barrett score in the second half of the third Bledisloe Cup test in Yokohama. The switch of play created a gap down the blindside, which the winger burst through. Barrett came looming up in support of Rieko Ioane against the Wallabies, while Stockdale did it himself with a well-timed chip and chase.

It makes the score 16–6, an ominous omen for the All Blacks. That was the final result for the only match they have lost at Lansdowne Road, back in the 1991 World Cup semi-final. It ended more than a few All Blacks careers—both coaching and on the field. Right now, it looks like it'll end the dream of marching through this tour unbeaten.

While the All Blacks held their nerve to punch and counter-punch their way through the English the previous weekend, they have nothing in response to the Irish this week. They never even look like scoring a try. That's why, when the final whistle comes, it's such a hard loss to take. This is the lowest score the All Blacks have managed in a defeat since 1999. It's also their lowest score in a game since the 2011 World Cup final. It's the second game in two years where they haven't scored a try (after the second-test loss to the British & Irish Lions in which they lost a player to a red card). It's their first loss in Europe in six years.

I head to the lift that will take us back down to the press conference theatre. Just as the doors are closing, in jumps the TV crew we subjected to our conversation about which foreign players would make the All Blacks. The female presenter grabs my arms and gives me the biggest smile I've seen since I landed in Dublin.

'What are you lot going to do now?' she says. I'm not sure whether she's talking about going to the pub or whether the All Blacks can win the World Cup.

What are we going to do now, indeed?

16
FAVOURITISM

Aviva Stadium, Dublin, 17 November 2018

ONE BY ONE, THE NEW ZEALAND media slip into the lecture theatre. A couple of days before, we'd been rolling our eyes at the handling of Levy's injury; now we're just raising our eyebrows at each other. An All Blacks loss is a double-edged sword: on the one hand, it means that more than the usual number of people will be reading our stories and watching the bulletins back home. On the other, it means we have to spend all bloody night on them because now we have to do about three times as much work. First things first: get what we need out of Hansen, Foster and Read—they're up first.

As per usual with Read, there's this relieved kind of look on his face. I sometimes wonder if it's because with every All Blacks winning streak the complacency of the New Zealand fans doesn't take long to set in, and now that the team has lost they can command the public's attention once more. Or maybe he's just happy to have got through the game in one piece.

He almost didn't, though. Stockdale's try came about because

Read was lying flat on his back, having been dropped out of the lineout. Had he been on his feet, the Irish winger would've been an easy tackle and the outcome of the game might well have been a lot different. The blow to his back will be scrutinised in depth over the next 24 hours, but not as much as his captaincy. This will be the most serious examination Read is subjected to since he took over from Richie McCaw. He probably knows that full well, too, but he's not letting it show. Steve Hansen is pretty diplomatic about the whole thing.

'They took their one, and we didn't take ours,' he says of the opportunities that were presented to both teams—even though implying that the All Blacks had any is a bit of a stretch. He talks about courage, heart and effort. He talks about lack of accuracy. He talks about how the envelope exchange at the start of the match—which someone is desperately trying to make a story out of—was simply him paying Schmidt for tickets. Then, just to show everyone that he's still the boss, he dryly picks on another local journo who makes the mistake of asking a question that has already been thoroughly covered previously, patronisingly goading him into asking another that 'will be a good question this time'.

But then, after that uncomfortably comical interlude, he drops the big one: 'I said this at the beginning of the week: you had the two best sides in the world playing each other. So, as of now, they're the number-one team in the world.'

Hansen hasn't won on the field, but he's just played the only card he's got left that may well turn this into a long-term victory after all. He's just put the Irish somewhere that they've never been before, and now it's up to them to see whether they belong there or not. The All Blacks can go home and watch on as the northern season moves towards the Six Nations.

> **Hansen hasn't won on the field, but he's just played the only card he's got left that may well turn this into a long-term victory after all. He's just put the Irish somewhere that they've never been before, and now it's up to them to see whether they belong there or not.**

Not that the All Blacks would ever admit it, but there are at least some legitimate reasons for the loss. It is the end of another long season for the All Blacks. Ireland are a genuinely good team with a very astute coach, who would've gone in with confidence given that it wasn't that long ago that they had won a test match between the two sides for the first time. Most tellingly, all of the All Blacks' key players had their quietest games of the year. So, putting aside the New Zealand public's expectation that the All Blacks should win every single match they play, this loss at least made a little bit of sense.

It's just the way it happened that is a bit hard to take. Usually they go down while at least inflicting a few gashes on their opponents. Chicago saw the Irish concede 29 points; the loss to the Boks in Wellington was a six-try-to-four affair, in which the All Blacks got more.

It's evident that Schmidt is fully aware of that significant fact when he, defence coach Andy Farrell and captain Rory Best come in to take a seat. The New Zealander, who has just coached a side to beat the team we're all thinking he wants to coach next, is all smiles. He happily concedes that he probably copied the move that saw Stockdale score from the All Blacks, and even says that he pilfers moves from every competition, even the Mitre 10 Cup.

Rory Best, meanwhile, is coming to terms with the fact that he's now led his country to victory over the All Blacks at home for the first time ever. He's asked how it compares to their win in Chicago.

'Well it's different,' he says, his vocal intonations giving even the most untrained ear the obvious clue as to his Northern Irish roots, 'but it certainly doesn't feel any worse.'

17
OFF THE RECORD

Rome, 19 November 2018

'OKAY, IS EVERYONE HERE? Let's turn the cameras off.'

It's been 48 hours and 2500 kilometres since the loss to Ireland. We're in the All Blacks' hotel in Rome, just outside the ancient city walls. This week was supposed to be a little holiday for us, but now on the back of the unexpected loss we've been slammed with the need for opinion pieces and explanations. What should have been a quiet post match in Dublin ending in a few Guinnesses turned into an all-nighter then a dash to the airport.

Hansen is the one member of the All Blacks we've heard the most from on this tour—in fact, all season. And yet there's a weariness about him that is hard to really figure out: on the one hand, it seems as though he doesn't enjoy dealing with the media, but on the other he knows full well that his carefully chosen words will shape every headline from now until the next game. He is in control of this room, no matter where it is in the world.

Well, almost. Earlier in the season at Eden Park, Hansen let his political leanings get the better of him when Prime Minister Jacinda Ardern attended the Bledisloe Cup match, gruffly noting she was wearing a Black Ferns jersey rather than an All Blacks one, and launching into a surprisingly prolonged rant about how the government should be providing funds to keep key players in New Zealand. The comfortable All Blacks victory that night played second fiddle to a week of Hansen ending up in the wrong news sections, mostly questioning why he had never raised this issue with one of Ardern's predecessors, John Key—a regular visitor to the All Blacks' changing rooms.

Now, the heat is on for answers. There's been enough time to ruminate on the Ireland result, but the All Blacks coach has an interesting request for this press conference. No one is allowed to record what is said for the first part of the session. This will be Hansen off the record, for the first time on the tour.

For a moment, no one really knows what to say. Then it dawns on the room that if we just ask what we were going to anyway, we'll probably get a far more honest answer.

That's not to say Hansen isn't honest. He's just got that way of talking around questions and being so imposing that it's hard to pluck up enough courage to actually ask what you think people want to hear.

Hansen doesn't have that much to tell us that we couldn't have figured out for ourselves, really. It's just mildly amusing to hear him swear quite a bit throughout the session. However, it soon becomes apparent why he asked for the cameras to be switched off. Opinion pieces from back home have slammed the All Blacks for the loss, and have leapt to a few pretty extreme conclusions. He looks us all in the eye and praises us for being the 'touring media', and in doing so invites us into the conspiracy. We're the ones who have access to write 'what's really going on'. He even blankly states that he's telling us all this so we 'can write better stories'.

After 40 minutes of this carry-on, we turn the cameras back on, ask all the same questions and get a whole bunch of far more sanitised answers. It's a weird, long time in the room with Hansen, who doesn't even touch on the fact that the All Blacks have one more match on the tour—with Italy this weekend.

> He looks us all in the eye and praises us for being the 'touring media', and in doing so invites us into the conspiracy. We're the ones who have access to write 'what's really going on'. He even blankly states that he's telling us all this so we 'can write better stories'.

There is, of course, one big matter to address that everyone in New Zealand is particularly interested in. As well as being dropped on his back out of a lineout, the All Blacks skipper drew attention in the test loss to Ireland for another bad reason. It has quickly become regarded as the worst game he's played in the black jersey, and questions are being raised as to whether Kieran Read is the right man to lead the All Blacks going into the World

Cup. Hansen is forthright in his assessment.

'Some of those articles are ridiculous, written by people who have never been in our environment, who have never seen him at a rugby game.'

Just a nice little reminder of the point of the previous off-the-record bit.

'Is it frustrating when you read some of the stuff from people who should know better?'

'Yes, it is. They've also got a job to do—usually it's to sell a newspaper or to get somebody to click on their stories. Once you understand that part of it as well, it doesn't bother you too much. A good thing people could do is not click on it, then they wouldn't have a job; it'd be great.'

It's probably the biggest swing at the media Hansen's ever had, and it won't be the last time that his loyalty to Read will be on show on the tour.

There's a lot to see and do in Rome. Most of the ancient ruins are within walking distance of where we're staying in the city. The drab British weather has unfortunately followed us south—by now it's almost the end of November and winter has completely set in. It's hard to fathom that Italy is on the same longitude as Japan, where we were gallivanting about in shorts just a few weeks ago. Still, the pasta is delicious and everyone dresses a damn sight better than anywhere else we've been.

18
REGULATION HIDING

Stadio Olimpico, Rome, 24 November 2018
(300 days to the Rugby World Cup)

ALL BLACKS	**66**
ITALY	**3**

IF STEVE HANSEN'S WORDS DURING the week about Kieran Read weren't enough to reinforce the team's commitment to their captain, the All Blacks spring an even more symbolic gesture after the anthems are done prior to kick-off in their final match of the year.

The team forms a pyramid shape on their 10-metre line to perform the haka. However, instead of TJ Perenara or Aaron Smith leading it, Read is the one lurking behind the third row. He stalks back and forth, then settles into 'Ka Mate'. Even though we've all seen the haka hundreds of times, it's clear this one has a fair amount of effort thrown into it.

They finish with the familiar stomp and 'HI!' High up in the media enclosure, the Italian press turn around and pick out the New Zealanders, asking in broken English what the deal is. For them, the haka is always led by a Māori player. All we can answer is that we don't quite know, and that it'll be best to ask Read himself in the post-match press conference.

What follows is 80 minutes of what happens when the All Blacks come off a loss. To be fair, this is probably what would've happened to the Italians anyway—their record against the All Blacks is about as compelling as their country's military history post the fifth century AD, and, despite a ropey opening quarter, one-way traffic starts to run at a high pace. The star of the show today will be a man who has had the microscope on him for a couple of months now. Jordie Barrett picks the right time of the season to have his best game yet for the All Blacks.

After his patchy display against Japan and the massive blunder against the Springboks earlier in the year, there've been questions over whether he even has a future in New Zealand rugby. His brother Beauden scored four tries against the Wallabies at Eden Park back in August. Now Jordie is on his way to matching that tally, with his first finishing off a break started by Dane Coles. His second is off a cross-kick from Beauden's boot that would look right at home in the NRL. The third is off another kick, but this time from an unlikely provider in reserve hooker Nathan Harris, who sends the ball across the deck for Jordie to run onto and score. The last comes on the stroke of full-time, when Richie Mo'unga pops him a pass to finish off. In all, Jordie hasn't even been touched running in his four tries. He and Beauden now stand as the only brothers to each score four tries in a test match, let alone the only ones to do it in one season. His main rival for a spot in the All Blacks' top 23, Damian McKenzie, also cashes in with a hat-trick.

It is comforting to see the All Blacks put on a show in a place that holds so much symbolism for New Zealand sport. Ringing the Stadio Olimpico field is the track where Murray Halberg and Peter Snell won gold medals within an hour of each other at the 1960 Olympics, and the stadium itself is another magnificent venue, although we are reminded just how differently football fans are treated here with the massive safety-glass screens separating the Curva Nord and Sud stands. That's where away fans are segregated during matches involving the two local clubs, Roma and Lazio. It was handy to find out that Lazio have rather strong links to the local Fascist political scene, in time to stop me from buying one of their shirts.

> **It is comforting to see the All Blacks put on a show in a place that holds so much symbolism for New Zealand sport. Ringing the Stadio Olimpico field is the track where Murray Halberg and Peter Snell won gold medals within an hour of each other at the 1960 Olympics.**

There are only 57,000 in for the game. While that might seem a lot, it's well short of the 71,000 that Stadio Olimpico can hold and has regularly drawn for previous All Blacks fixtures. That says more about the way the Italian team has been faring, though. Despite an upset win over the Springboks the season before, confidence in the side has fallen dramatically a year out from the World Cup after yet another wooden spoon in the Six Nations. The fans are not that enamoured with witnessing another hiding, and nor are the local press. Most of them smoke constantly throughout the game, chomping through cigarettes and cigars, with one guy even lighting up a pipe while tapping away on his laptop. It fits with the theme of Rome—while it is a beautiful, historic place, it also reeks like a gigantic ashtray.

STADIO OLIMPICO'S ENORMOUS PRESS CONFERENCE room looks like it could seat about 500. There are only a few dozen in attendance for the post-match talks, which is less than half of those who actually watched the game. Come to think of it, there were even fewer in the stands than for the sumptuous pre-match banquet put on for us by the Federazione Italiana Rugby, which means a good number of local journalists only came for the free feed.

For the last time (at least we think it's the last time) in 2018, Steve Hansen sits in front of us. He's at a giant desk on a stage, and we're handed a microphone by a member of the stadium staff. In true Italian fashion, they are all good-looking women decked out in black power suits and high heels.

The first question is about the haka, and is answered with a yarn I'm not entirely believing about the All Blacks preparing for more than a year for Read to lead it. The response seems to me to be made up on the spot, considering that if they were going to switch up and make a Pākehā the kaea (leader), it should have been launched on a much grander scale than this: an easy win that kicked off at 3am New Zealand time. Any insinuation that the move was in direct response to the criticism that Read copped during the week is quickly shot down. But whether the All Blacks are telling the truth or not, it doesn't really matter. It's shown that any lingering doubts over whether Read will be leading the team next season have been put to rest. This would not have happened otherwise.

Hansen seems tired, and clearly wants to get this over with. He inadvertently lets slip that the All Blacks have a test match scheduled against Tonga in 2019, which has not been officially announced. For us, it's more of an annoyance than a breaking story, because it means we have to haul ourselves out of bed the next day to talk to NZ Rugby boss Steve Tew about it in a hastily called interview.

> **Whether the All Blacks are telling the truth or not, it doesn't really matter. It's shown that any lingering doubts over whether Read will be leading the team next season have been put to rest. This would not have happened otherwise.**

We get to talk to the two players who between them scored over half of the All Blacks' points. Jordie Barrett acknowledges that it was 'nice to be on the end of the chain', while Damian McKenzie reiterates what we've all been feeling all along on this tour.

'It's going to be exciting coming into next year, when we can really get stuck into our Super seasons . . .' he says, which makes us all realise that it isn't even that far away.

'. . . and obviously the main goal being the Rugby World Cup.'

And that's not far away either: there are fewer than 10 months now until the All Blacks will step back out onto Yokohama Stadium.

Plenty will happen between now and then.

19
HANSEN'S ANNOUNCEMENT

The Heritage Auckland, 14 December 2018 (280 days to the Rugby World Cup)

A FEW WEEKS LATER, WE'RE gathered in the conference room of the Heritage Auckland. It already seems like a while since the tour was over. The sun is out and I've been to the beach for the first few times of what will be a scorching summer. At the Basin Reserve, the Black Caps are getting ready for their first home test of the season. But, as we like to joke often, rugby never sleeps. All the folks from the tour are here, along with an awful lot more media. John Campbell is back, shaking hands and looking sharp. We've been called in by NZ Rugby for a special announcement.

You can tell straight away what Steve Hansen is going to say to the throng. He strides into the room wearing a plain, long-sleeved shirt. It's the first time I can remember in the past two seasons that he's fronted the cameras without an All Blacks branded suit or tracksuit jacket. It's jarring. He doesn't look like the man some of us had been following around New Zealand and the rest of the rugby world for the previous six months. Hansen is a constant fixture at every major announcement to do with the team, whether it's naming the match-day 23 or breaking injury news. Now, though, he's sitting in front of us having shed the skin of his role as one of the most powerful people in the country, appearing just like any other middle-aged New Zealand bloke.

Hansen doesn't look like the man some of us had been following around New Zealand and the rest of the rugby world for the previous six months.

He cuts right to the chase: 2019 will be his last season in charge of the All Blacks, and the World Cup will be his swansong. He then spends 20 or so minutes dead-batting any questions about what everyone really wants to know—what will happen next. In a rare glimpse into his life outside of rugby, he says that the decision was heavily influenced by his desire to spend more time with his family. In years gone by, an All Blacks player or coach saying that he consulted with his 'big boss' would be seen as a punchline. However, it's touchingly clear that he wants to pay tribute to his wife, Tash, in an honest and meaningful way.

Hansen is flanked by NZ Rugby CEO Steve Tew and Chairman Brent Impey. The trio then combine to give absolutely nothing away about their preferred candidate for the job as rugby enters its new dawn in 2020. There's plenty of speculation that it will simply be a shift of seats for assistant Ian Foster, and that Hansen will stay on in a 'Director of Rugby' type role that will essentially still give him control of the All Blacks from afar.

For now, though, Hansen is going to have to play the hand he's dealt himself. Like it or not, his legacy will ultimately be judged on what happens back in Japan.

PART TWO
THE LEAD-UP

20
BIGGER THAN RUGBY

**State Highway 1, 15 March 2019
(189 days to the Rugby World Cup)**

IT'S BEEN THREE MONTHS SINCE Hansen's announcement in the Heritage. The weather is stinking hot, and three of us have piled into a car I've borrowed to head off on the hour-and-a-half journey south from Auckland to Hamilton, where the Chiefs are hosting the Hurricanes. Due to the abominable nature of traffic getting out of the city, we've left well in advance of the 7.35pm kick-off time.

Super Rugby has been going for a month now, but already it looks like the Crusaders are going to win it again, and the Chiefs still haven't managed to win a game. Chris from the *New Zealand Herald* and Ben from live-streaming platform *RugbyPass* are with me. We're talking about the big topics of the moment: a proposed realignment of the test season by World Rugby and what it'll mean for the All Blacks. It's grabbed everyone's attention, mainly because it's clear that the plan will pretty much shut out the Pacific Island teams from ever making any money.

But it's still summer. The season has been pushed forward to accommodate the World Cup, hence we're all wearing shorts and t-shirts for this away trip. We're making good time as we cruise down the Southern Motorway, over the Bombay Hills and into the Waikato. There's a cricket test about to begin in Christchurch between the Black Caps and Bangladesh, and I turn on the radio.

We're under the thick power lines coming out of the Huntly Power Station, still about half an hour down the bank of the river that runs next to us, when the voice of a newsreader crackles: 'Reports of a serious situation in Christchurch . . . armed offenders unit called out . . .'

'Are you guys hearing this?' I ask. I've cut Ben off mid-tirade about the foolishness of the World Rugby plan, and Chris mumbles something about how the cricket's been delayed. Apparently, whatever is going on is happening close to Hagley Oval. The static grows louder as we pass under the lines, and I turn the radio off. We re-engage in a passionate debate about the state of the game, and what it means for the World Cup—through Huntly and past the classic Deka sign, through Taupiri and its roundabout that deposits us on the Waikato Expressway.

The city is bathed in sunshine when we drive in. I haven't turned the radio back on, but everything seems quite subdued—even for

Hamilton. I feel my phone vibrate in my pocket as I park the car a couple of streets away from FMG Stadium Waikato. It's Amanda, the Chiefs' media liaison. She wants us all to inform her when we arrive, before we go into the grandstand to set up for work. We're not sure why—usually we can just flash our accreditation and roll in whenever we like. Then we see the police cars.

Slowly, the gears in our heads start turning. Because they've been in overdrive about the state of the game, it's taken us this long to figure out that something way bigger is going on. Amanda comes to meet us at the gate, and it's then we realise that today is going to be way bigger than rugby. I get another text—this time it's my boss at Radio NZ saying that coverage of tonight's game has been cancelled.

Slowly, the gears in our heads start turning. Because they've been in overdrive about the state of the game, it's taken us this long to figure out that something way bigger is going on.

This Chiefs versus Hurricanes match-up, even before the season began, has been pegged as one of the highlights of the season. Both teams would have a full complement of All Blacks on deck, it'd be played in conditions that would probably yield a lot of points, and the home side would mark the occasion by wearing replica jerseys of the ones worn in their first-ever season. A decent crowd is expected. There's another huge New Zealand Conference derby tomorrow night as well—in Dunedin, between the Highlanders and the Crusaders. Last year that game sold out Forsyth Barr Stadium, and was the highest-attended Super Rugby match in the country in 2018.

Amanda explains that because of the situation in Christchurch, the game might not go ahead. A police car cruises by, with both pairs of eyes inside on high alert. A gunman, or gunmen, are on a rampage down there, and people are dead. I see Marcus, the director from Sky Sport. He's scratching his head and wondering what to do.

'What the hell's going on?' I ask.

'Bro, there's like 20 or something people dead.'

The others' phones start buzzing too. They're off the job for tonight as well. It's around 3pm by now. If they're going to call the game off, they'll have to do it soon.

21
THE HARDEST POST MATCH

FMG Stadium Waikato, Hamilton, 15 March 2019

IT'S 9.30PM. WE'RE STANDING IN the midst of the unmistakable smell of a rugby changing room, beneath the grandstand—sweat mingles with the plastic matting beneath our feet. This is where we wait for the players and coaching staff post match. The previous hour and a half has been like nothing any of us have ever experienced before, and the actual gravity of the situation still hasn't really dawned on us.

Needless to say, the game kicked off on time. Both teams went to the middle of the field, shouldered arms and stood for a minute's silence. The crowd, who had indeed showed up in numbers, fell silent with them. You could have heard a pin drop during that first official acknowledgement of what will become known as the Christchurch mosque attacks.

'Thirty.'

'Jesus...'

By the time it started, we'd been joined by Aaron from Stuff and Ross from Newshub. No one was working, but none of us were particularly interested in the game, either. We had our laptops open, religiously refreshing Twitter for updates. Every time the death toll grew higher, someone would announce the number, to a sharp exhalation and profanity from the rest of us.

'Forty.'

'Are you fucking serious?'

So now we're in the changing rooms, about to conduct the only New Zealand media event of 15 March that won't involve talking about the ethnically motivated murder of dozens of people. Amanda tells us we're not to mention it. But Ross is having none of that, and asks for the one player we all know can be counted on to say the right thing, right now.

After coaches Colin Cooper and John Plumtree come and go, muttering the boilerplate reactions you'd expect from a game that ended in a 23-all draw, TJ Perenara makes his way in. He's still in his uniform, and his boots tap softly on the ground as he steps in front of the camera and microphones. Aaron's looking at his phone, and mutters softly under his breath.

'Forty-nine.'

Perenara has often been referred to as the conscience of New Zealand rugby. The Porirua-born halfback came out guns blazing on social media after Israel Folau's homophobic nonsense in late 2017. He made a beeline for Prime Minister Jacinda Ardern after the Bledisloe Cup test at Eden Park in 2018, and together with

Ardie Savea blithely ignored any regard for perceived political bias by giving her a warm embrace on the field after she'd handed over the silverware. He is a thoughtful, smart guy. Tonight there is a terrible sadness in his eyes as he speaks.

Perenara is the first high-profile New Zealander, outside of the government, to make a televised statement about the attacks. The general consensus among those of us left in the room is that he was the perfect man to do it, rugby or otherwise.

'Today was bigger than rugby. Not only for us, but for the Chiefs and for the rest of New Zealand. Regardless of what happened, the game wasn't the most important part of my day, and I don't think anyone in this circle and in New Zealand would say that.

'My mind was on the game while I was in the game, but today was bigger than rugby.'

He walks out, head bowed.

Perenara is the first high-profile New Zealander, outside of the government, to make a televised statement about the attacks. The general consensus among those of us left in the room is that he was the perfect man to do it, rugby or otherwise.

It's almost crazy to now realise that the game went ahead at all, but by the time anyone had really fathomed the extent of what this day will mean for the country, the ball was already in play. Dozens of police patrolled around the ground for its duration.

It was an ultimately meaningless game, given that it ended in a draw, but it provided some in a shell-shocked nation a brief respite from what's going to be a long, long period of soul-searching. The game between the Crusaders and the Highlanders the next night is called off. On Sunday, when the facts are established that the alleged killer was an anti-Islamic white supremacist, the debate starts to rage about whether the Crusaders should change their name.

In all, 51 lives were taken.

22
RESHUFFLING THE NORTHERN DECK

Europe, February/March 2019

THE CHIEFS AND HURRICANES' TRIBUTE to the victims of the terror attacks is replicated by all the teams in Super Rugby. On the other side of the world, back where the All Blacks had played their last campaign, the tributes flow too. Twickenham, Aviva Stadium and Stadio Olimpico are all in use right now, and just as busy as when the tour swept through them in November. The Six Nations is in full swing, and the way the World Cup challengers from the northern hemisphere are stacked up is about to change quite dramatically.

Like John Mitchell and Joe Schmidt, there's another expatriate coach lurking in the British Isles and plotting World Cup success. He knows it will probably involve beating the All Blacks, which is something he managed to do in 2017. Warren Gatland, the former Waikato prop and owner of rugby's most consistent buzzcut since the mid-1980s, has been in charge of Wales for the past nine years. His most recent brush with the All Blacks was leading the Lions on a tour to New Zealand, where the unheralded team (at least in the eyes of the Kiwi media) pulled off a remarkable and dramatic drawn series.

Warren Gatland, the former Waikato prop and owner of rugby's most consistent buzzcut since the mid-1980s, has been in charge of Wales for the past nine years.

Gatland loved every minute of the final press conference at Eden Park, walking into the packed room with a red nose on as a pointed reminder of an ill-judged cartoon of him dressed as a clown that ran in the *New Zealand Herald* before the tour. The general consensus up until then was that Gatland had a cushy ride at Wales, able to take advantage of the frequent seismic shifts in Six Nations rugby and the comparatively low expectations of the Welsh public about their chances against southern hemisphere teams. But something is different in 2019. The weekend of the attacks in Christchurch, Wales are within touching distance of a Grand Slam. All that stands between them and the prize is the last team that beat the All Blacks: Schmidt's Ireland.

Since that historic home win against the All Blacks in November, things haven't gone according to plan for the Irish. They were soundly defeated in their first game, outscored 32–20 in a very flattering scoreline in Dublin. Worse still, the team to beat them was England, who had clearly used what they'd learned from their game against the All Blacks to hone a plan for the run-in to the World Cup. They've ambushed the Irish, and by mid-March it's starting to look like a blow that's done far more damage than at first thought. Since then, Ireland haven't looked anywhere near the world-beaters they were just a few months earlier, as they've struggled to victory against Scotland, Italy and France.

Gatland is the only coach in the world to have a style of rugby named after him—and 'Warrenball' brutally strangles the English over 80 minutes of torrid tackling in the middle of the park.

However, Jones' England veers off-script too. After being hailed as geniuses for concocting and executing a plan that exposed and fed off Ireland's frailties (something that Steve Hansen couldn't—or maybe just didn't—do), they are tipped over in Cardiff by Wales. Now the mantle of genius is bestowed on Gatland. As far as wins go, Wales earn every bit of it in the 21–13 result. Gatland is the only coach in the world to have a style of rugby named after him—and 'Warrenball' brutally strangles the English over 80 minutes of torrid tackling in the middle of the park. The English, so effective against the Irish, have their flowing attack reduced to a trickle as the Welsh smash into them in a series of close rucks.

It's impressive, but not as much as the contributions that two other Kiwis are making to Welsh rugby. Cast-offs Gareth

Anscombe and Hadleigh Parkes are having stunning seasons in the red jersey, which is making a few people scratch their heads back in New Zealand. That is literally a few: Six Nations rugby, while enormously big news in the UK to the point of being the highest-attended international sporting event in the world, is barely worth raising an eyebrow about in these parts. After all, it's still the cricket season, and most New Zealanders are far more concerned with going to the beach than staying up into the small hours watching a game of what's perceived to be inferior northern hemisphere rugby.

Anscombe and Parkes' integral roles actually go some way to confirming that belief. Anscombe was supposed to be the long-term first five for the Blues as a 20-year-old back in 2012, but his career hit the skids as the seemingly cursed franchise plummeted to the bottom of the newly formatted New Zealand Conference (a position they've held ever since). After a move south to the Chiefs, Anscombe became the model overseas signing by having a blinder of a 2013 season in two positions, then cashing in on his newfound market value and heading to Welsh club Scarlets.

Meanwhile, Parkes has quickly become a bit of a folk hero in Wales. His long rugby journey has taken him from Palmerston North to Auckland to Wellington to Port Elizabeth and now to Cardiff, where he's played over 100 games for Scarlets. Known mostly as a bit-part player off the bench in Super Rugby, with a name that sounds like a law firm, Parkes is now an integral part of what's going to be a famous Six Nations campaign for the Welsh.

In front of 74,000 at Principality Stadium, both men play their part to comprehensively beat Ireland 25–7. The only Irish points come on the last play of the game. The northern hemisphere deck, much like it was the year before, has been shuffled around again to relegate the Irish back a couple of places and the English to at least having a question mark hanging over their heads.

There is now a serious amount of belief that Wales can keep the momentum going and win the World Cup. If that happens, Gatland could probably mount a decent case for being considered the best New Zealand coach of the decade, despite never having coached the All Blacks. But the World Cup is still six months away, and that amount of time could see the deck reshuffled yet again—after all, that's the amount of time between now and when the All Blacks ran into trouble against the teams that Wales have just beaten.

But then, a few months later, Gatland ups the stakes. He wants to come back to New Zealand in 2020 to coach the Chiefs, and one day presumably the All Blacks. Like Hansen, the 2019 World Cup will be the end of an era for him—but to beat the man whose job he ultimately wants could be the dramatic dawn of a new one.

23

THE UNLUCKIEST BREAK

**Hamilton, 13 April 2019
(160 days to the Rugby World Cup)**

THE TEAM WARREN GATLAND WILL eventually take charge of, the Chiefs, are having quite a time of it in Super Rugby before that announcement gets made. It's fair to say that by the middle of April their season has been testing the patience of even their most loyal fans. Starting the year without an entire team's worth of players due to various injuries, they made the worst start to a season in the franchise's history, losing their first four games. In fact, the first game they didn't lose was the massively overshadowed draw with the Hurricanes.

The team slunk out of New Zealand on a road trip to Pretoria and Buenos Aires to face the Bulls and Jaguares, and somehow managed to win both fixtures. Things are looking up by mid-April, and the team are drawn to face the Blues in Hamilton.

We're back up in the media room that we all sat in so numbly through the 15 March game. To call it a 'box' is pretty generous—Waikato Stadium does have a proper media working area down the other end of the main stand's top level, but the powers-that-be have converted it into a makeshift corporate space to squeeze a few more dollars out of their home games. It means we're crammed into a tiny room adjacent to the 22, with anyone not sitting directly up against the window not actually able to see much of the field.

Brad Weber reads fellow one-test All Black James Parsons like a Friday-night booty-call text and picks off his attempted pass.

The Blues have been having a very interesting start to the season, too. Under new coach Leon MacDonald, they would have beaten the Crusaders in the first game had it not been for a couple of missed shots at goal. Since then, they've embarked on a four-game winning streak, and beaten the Highlanders—their first win against another New Zealand team in 21 games. People are starting to believe that this may be the year the ill-fated franchise finally starts to get its act together.

However, it doesn't start well for the Blues. Brad Weber reads fellow one-test All Black James Parsons like a Friday-night booty-call text and picks off his attempted pass. Sixty metres later and Weber is dotting down under the sticks and firmly in the conversation about making the test squad. Damian McKenzie is having a blinder, too, mainly because he's been thrown the keys to the entire Chiefs attacking vehicle after their poor start to the season. His skill sets up their second try to Lachlan Boshier, before the Blues hit back just before half-time.

The game is firmly in the balance as the teams trot back out for the second half, but this will be the last time McKenzie steps onto a rugby field for the year. Shortly after the resumption of play, he goes down just on the Blues' side of halfway. Up in the box, we don't notice straight away because the furious pace of the game quickly carries the ball away across the field. When the whistle blows, though, it's obvious something is badly wrong.

The guys in the back row can't actually see that McKenzie is down in a heap, because their view of that part of the field is completely obscured. They squeeze forward and peer over our shoulders at the unmistakably blond shock of hair shaking back and forth below. McKenzie was the last All Black we talked to last year, saying that 2019 was all about the World Cup, and it's fair to say that he would've been a pretty key part of it, too. The look on his face as he hobbles off the field tells us that's all over now. It's confirmed shortly after: he's blown out his knee. Season over. Holy shit.

It sends the New Zealand sporting public into a tailspin. Who will back up Beauden Barrett and Richie Mo'unga now? It's almost insane that this is the issue that's gripping the All Blacks—any other test nation would be happy to have a 12-year-old as their third-choice first five if it meant you could have those two players in front of him. But McKenzie's misfortune will mean a rethink of the All Blacks backline entirely—up until the injury, he was also the starting fullback. Someone will have to slot in and fill that gap.

After McKenzie hobbles off the field, the Blues take the game to the Chiefs. One of their tries is scored in brutal fashion by the most talked-about man in their team, 36-year-old Ma'a Nonu. He crashes into the line off a short ball from a five-metre scrum and smashes through three tackles to plant it down. He's part of a burgeoning selection dilemma of a different kind outside of where Barrett and Mo'unga will be, because right now Nonu is the form midfielder of the competition despite only being there due to a desire to be closer to his family after a four-season stint in France.

Nonu has played 104 times for the All Blacks, pocketed two Rugby World Cup gold medals, and has a career stretching all the way back to 2003. It's astounding he's even out there at all, let alone leading the pack for those chasing a 12 or 13 jersey at this stage of the season. But the Blues have desperately needed someone like him for years and he's completely repaying the faith they've placed in him. Nonu was only supposed to be playing every second week, but an injury to Sonny Bill Williams has meant that he's shouldered far more work than anyone, including probably himself, expected. He's provided a perfect link between the Blues' inexperienced inside backs and lethal but still raw back three.

THE MIDFIELD HAS BEEN SOMETHING that Steve Hansen hasn't quite locked down ever since Nonu and long-time partner Conrad

Smith moved on. It's quite obvious that he views Williams as the key man in that area—more or less all of the All Blacks' set-piece moves run through the former rugby league player, utilising his ability to offload and free up the likes of Beauden Barrett who can loop around to take advantage of the instantaneous overlap he creates. Now Hansen has Nonu and Ngani Laumape pressing their cases in Williams' absence.

After that, Nonu never appears anywhere near the media. According to the Blues, he's so deeply offended at being misquoted that he has no time for us at all anymore.

Nonu is quickly becoming the people's choice, and not just because it'd make a good story for a man of his age to be playing test rugby again. This is despite a very strained relationship with the media, which has been a talking point ever since it was announced he would be coming to the Blues in September of 2018. The franchise decided against making him available for interviews for the entire summer, which raised the ire of a press corps already acquainted with Nonu's deep-seated suspicion of the printed word. That doesn't stop us, because when he does finally front, after his strong start to the Blues' season, he's confronted with an entire warehouse-worth's-full of microphones.

After giving a few non-answers and regulation quotes about doing his best for the team, some sub-editor at the *New Zealand Herald* somehow turns his words into a headline about his 'desire to wear the All Blacks jersey again'.

After that, Nonu never appears anywhere near the media. According to the Blues, he's so deeply offended at being misquoted that he has no time for us at all anymore. That, or he's just using it as an excuse to not have to do something he clearly doesn't relish.

It all adds to the enigma of Ma'a Nonu. Around Wellington's eastern suburbs, where he was raised and played all his college and club rugby, he is revered as the absolute favourite son of an increasingly gentrified area. He is fiercely loyal to his Oriental Rongotai club, emblematic of the fact that he burst onto the rep scene through the old-school channel of grassroots rugby. Nonu's break-out game that first put him on the radar was against the man that many would readily compare him to: Tana Umaga. The still-teenaged Nonu comprehensively outplayed the then-current All Blacks centre and future captain that day on a club ground in Petone, which set him on a course to eventually emulate and arguably overtake Umaga's deeds in the black jersey.

Nonu was a casualty of the clean-out of the Hurricanes enacted by coach Mark Hammett in 2012, at which point Nonu left for his first stint with the Blues. He ended up back in the Canes by 2015, making it all the way to the team's second-ever grand-final appearance. After the 2015 World Cup he said what was apparently a well-earned goodbye, along with Tony Woodcock, Keven Mealamu, Dan Carter and Richie McCaw.

And now he's back, with a healthy dose of professionalism and inspiration for a young Blues side that's at long last bringing a bit of interest back to Eden Park. It's also helping that across town the Warriors are having a very patchy start to the year. However, despite their good form, the Blues hit a roadblock at Waikato Stadium. McKenzie's injury notwithstanding, the Chiefs hang on to win a pulsating game 29–23, which resurrects their season for a second time.

And now he's back, with a healthy dose of professionalism and inspiration for a young Blues side that's at long last bringing a bit of interest back to Eden Park. It's also helping that across town the Warriors are having a very patchy start to the year.

This performance, though, ensures that from now on Nonu's name is never far from all serious discussions for the All Blacks in 2019.

24
A TALE OF TWO HALFBACKS

Waikato University Ruakura training field, 15 May 2019
(128 days to the Rugby World Cup)

THE CHIEFS, MINUS MCKENZIE, TURN OUT to be the story of the Super Rugby season. After a 0–4 start and a loss to the Sunwolves, by the start of June they're looking like they are contenders for the finals. That form is shown to its full potential when they travel to Suva and play the Crusaders in front of a capacity crowd at ANZ National Stadium. On a stinking-hot night, the Chiefs find themselves down 20–0, only to come back and win 40–27 in what will go down as the game of the season. It also goes down as yet more evidence that a Pacific Island presence in the competition is probably a pretty good idea.

But as early as mid-May I'm compelled to talk to one of the men who is playing a starring role in the season, because he's making a very, very strong case to overturn what seems to be a cast-iron selection for the upcoming All Blacks season. Brad Weber is now 28. Colin Cooper has promoted him to captain this season and Weber has revelled in the role, and right now is the form halfback, if not player, in Super Rugby. He has played one test for the All Blacks, back in 2015 against Sāmoa in Apia, in a line-up that didn't include any players from the Highlanders and the Hurricanes. It seems unlikely he will be adding to that tally, though.

Last season, Te Toiroa Tahuriorangi was the designated third halfback in the All Blacks behind Aaron Smith and TJ Perenara, coming off the bench once during the Rugby Championship and starting the test against Japan in Tokyo. He had a job that presumably involved a lot of watching, running opposition at training, and learning. Tahuriorangi would be the first to admit that, and he knows full well that he's in line to get roughly the same amount of game time this test season. However, it looks like he's barely going to have much rugby leading up to it, either; Cooper sees the bench as the most suitable place for him at the Chiefs, because Weber is proving absolutely unstoppable when he gets on the field.

Weber is also a straight-up guy to interview, which is a nice change from the usually humble, shy, or just plain pre-recorded responses you get from a lot of players. Before leaving for Suva, he acknowledged he is in the form of his life. Earlier in the season, he stopped short of using the word 'hatred' to describe the relationship between the Chiefs and Blues, but did admit that former loose forward Liam Messam sent them a video message during the week that detailed his feelings for the team from up the road. From the look of Weber's tightly contorted face when asked about the specifics of the message, it's obvious that it was extremely not safe for work. But now he's just talking about himself and the responsibility that being the main man in the team has meant.

'The consistency is what I'm most happy with. In the past I'd have one good game but now I'm going week in, week out. Running a game is something that's come on a lot, and that comes with experience.'

Down the years, plenty of guys have played out of their skins and not even turned the heads of the All Blacks selectors. But this would have to be the first time in a long, long time that the player in question was starting ahead of the very man the selectors will pick.

While he talks about his role as captain and the way the team has been performing at length, he has only two words when it comes to whether he's had any correspondence from the All Blacks on his big season: 'Nah, nothing.'

On the surface, that's not that unheard of. Down the years, plenty of guys have played out of their skins and not even turned the heads of the All Blacks selectors. But this would have to be the first time in a long, long time that the player in question was starting ahead of the very man the selectors will pick. Not just starting, but finishing too: Weber has put in several rare 80-minute shifts in a position that is religiously substituted in the professional era. It also shows that perhaps Steve Hansen doesn't have quite the sway over Super Rugby coaches that everyone presumes he does. Cooper's plan for the Chiefs is rightfully revolving around Weber, now that McKenzie (a player who seemed to be getting shifted between positions at Hansen's behest) is out for the rest of the season.

While he has a year left on his contract with the Chiefs, Weber can opt out and cash up overseas. Tahuriorangi re-signing with the team through to 2022 is a pretty clear indication that this may well turn out to be the case. It would end a unique New Zealand rugby career for the dynamic Chiefs and Hawke's Bay halfback; except the future has other plans in store.

25

SUPER RUGBY OUT OF THE WAY

New Zealand, June/July 2019

IN THE END, THE CHIEFS do squeeze into the finals. The Hurricanes have a typically Hurricanes-like season, in which they blow a golden chance to finish in the all-important top spot by losing a crucial round-robin game at home to the Jaguares, who will now be the Chiefs' opponents in the play-offs. It also means the Crusaders finish top, so once again it looks as though the showpiece match of the supposed best domestic competition in the world will likely be played at Christchurch Stadium—a pitiful, stopgap contraption of scaffolding that has somehow seen almost a decade of use after the earthquake that destroyed Lancaster Park and much of the rest of the city. It's a nightmare of a look for the SANZAAR bosses—or at least it would be if any of them gave a damn about such things. Super Rugby seems to have little strategy or direction right now, so having the final potentially played at a ramshackle pile of poles and plastic in the middle of an industrial wasteland is just one of a list of many, many things they should be concerned about.

True to form, the Blues bomb out and finish bottom of the New Zealand Super Rugby Conference. Coach Leon MacDonald finds out the hard way just how difficult it is to come up with new ways to describe losses, exactly like his predecessor Tana Umaga the year before. There is a wee bit to get excited about other than Nonu's sudden re-injection into the national consciousness, though. Young flanker Tom Robinson, out of Kerikeri, has emerged as a serious contender for what is now an open try-out at blindside flanker.

That's because down south at the Highlanders, Liam Squire has barely been seen at all this season. A hip injury sidelined him for the opening month, and just as he was back into full training he tore the medial ligament in his knee. Squire returned to the Highlanders in time for the play-offs, putting in a superb performance in their play-off-clinching win over the Waratahs, but was then yellow-carded in their eventual quarter-final loss to the Crusaders. That will be his last act in a Highlanders jersey, as he's signed a deal with Japanese club NTT Docomo Red Hurricanes for next season. However, it's the non-injury-related absences that have caused people to wonder whether the six-foot-five-inch Squire will even be in the frame for the All Blacks.

He withdrew from the Highlanders' clash against the Jaguares in May only hours before the game, then the team's resulting tour of South Africa, with what coach Aaron Mauger described as 'personal family issues'. For us, that's code for concussion. Squire seems to be following the same path as Dane Coles did in 2018, when the hooker injured his knee and then took an exceptionally long time to recover. Coles played no part in the Hurricanes' season, fuelling speculation that he might well retire, before making his comeback in Japan on the end-of-year tour.

As well as Squire's absence, Ben Smith prompts a collective gasp in the Highlanders' pulsating 31-all draw with the Chiefs in Dunedin, leaving the field with a hamstring injury. It's serious enough to make Steve Hansen, who has travelled down for the match, get out of his seat and walk down to the bench to check on his veteran wing/fullback. While Smith will be okay for the test season, this act underlines just how much Hansen is concerned with the welfare of his players with the test season looming.

IF IT WERE UP TO Hansen, though, the All Blacks probably wouldn't be playing at all. The players had a never-publicly-confirmed limit on the game time allowed this season. The closest we got to confirmation was Aaron Smith blurting out what he thought it was earlier in the year, possibly by mistake. From what we can surmise, the top players were limited to 180 minutes of action through the opening three rounds of Super Rugby, and must observe two stand-down weeks during the season in addition to their team's bye weeks. Smith also made it clear that when they were on their stand-down weeks they must leave the team and its training schedule entirely—something he admitted was actually more detrimental than helpful. Players were also limited in how many matches they were allowed to play in a row. There's confusion over whether it is five or six, but Hurricanes coach John Plumtree's persistent selection of Ardie Savea and then keeping him on the field for 78 minutes of each game means that it's clear there are different rules for everyone.

If it were up to Hansen, the All Blacks probably wouldn't be playing at all. The players had a never-publicly-confirmed limit on the game time allowed this season.

It's hard not to sympathise with the Super Rugby coaches. A number of them are fighting for their jobs in an incredibly competitive market, so for MacDonald his aim is to stay off the bottom of the table, not dutifully send his best players off for an unwanted holiday. Plumtree has to contend with the fact that his side is a completely different, far shittier one without Beauden Barrett. Most importantly, the level of interest in Super Rugby is affected. The number of empty seats in New Zealand stadiums is high (and shockingly higher in South Africa, whose issues with its domestic game could fill a decent-sized book of its own), and there are constant question marks over the future of the competition.

The Crusaders, meanwhile, have just kept doing what they've done for the past two seasons under coach Scott Robertson, which is consistently winning. They were everyone's pick to take out their third Super Rugby title in a row before the season even started, and thanks to the Hurricanes' ineptitude, their home-ground advantage indeed leads them to host a quarter, a semi, and eventually the final. It's against the Jaguares, and the Argentinian team making the final will have some far-reaching consequences thanks to the two flights across the Pacific Ocean they have had to make. It's a dull, ugly game befitting of the dull, ugly ground it gets played in. The Crusaders win 19–6, and the only memorable thing that happens is another Robertson break-dance at the end.

Despite the national aversion to the Crusaders, the entertaining 45-year-old is an awful lot of people's pick to replace Hansen after the World Cup. A break-dancing All Blacks coach? Unheard of. The only real argument against him is that he hasn't had any experience coaching a team that hasn't dominated like Canterbury and the Crusaders. Logically, though, that makes him a suitable candidate, given that the All Blacks are the most dominant sports team in the entire world.

But at least he knows he's done all he can to press his case now. Three Super Rugby titles in a row isn't a bad stat to have on your CV when applying for the job sometime early in the new year, so Robertson can put his feet up and watch the man who will probably be his main rival try to impress NZ Rugby. At this stage, it looks like it's coming down to a choice between him and Ian Foster, and the incumbent All Blacks assistant coach has just helped name the first squad of the year to play in the Rugby Championship.

26
THE FIRST NAMING

Auckland, 2 July 2019
(80 days to the Rugby World Cup)

THE FAMOUS PONSONBY RUGBY CLUB has been in the news a bit recently. In order to get a bit of game time after his injuries and the Blues' inevitable lack of participation in the finals, Sonny Bill Williams turns out for their premier side against Grammar TEC a couple of weeks before the first All Blacks squad of the year is announced. Ponsonby is the powerhouse club of the Auckland competition, winning the Gallaher Shield 11 times so far this century, and 46 times overall. Williams is just another addition to the extremely long list of All Blacks on their books. By a twist of fate, my own lower-grade team is playing on the field next to him at Ōrākei Domain, where around 3000 people have gathered to watch. I look up from one ruck and survey the line of the backs of people's heads, and wonder how Williams is getting on only a matter of metres away.

He gets through it with a solid, if unspectacular, performance. His presence on the field for Ponsonby raises a few eyebrows, given that he isn't even contracted to play for Auckland so should therefore be ineligible to play for one of their clubs. However, while they lose the game, Grammar TEC aren't complaining. Their clubrooms are completely packed afterwards, and the entire scene is reminiscent of when this used to be the norm in New Zealand rugby.

The next reason Ponsonby comes up is because that's where the first All Blacks squad of the year is to be named—which is more than a little ironic given how far down the priority list club rugby has fallen for the game's governing body. Nevertheless, we gather at the clubrooms in Western Springs as Steve Hansen, Ian Foster and selector Grant Fox (who would've spent a fair few after-match functions here when he played for University against Ponsonby) enter into the blaze of lights and intrigue.

While they lose the game, Grammar TEC aren't complaining. Their clubrooms are completely packed afterwards, and the entire scene is reminiscent of when this used to be the norm in New Zealand rugby.

The squad gets read out by Chairman Brent Impey, and it's a big one: 39 names. It means that by late August eight of them will not be going to Japan. Like it or not, the next four tests are trial matches.

At first glance, there will be a few easy culls before the World

The first All Blacks squad of 2019	
Hookers	Asafo Aumua, Dane Coles, Liam Coltman, Codie Taylor
Props	Owen Franks, Nepo Laulala, Joe Moody, Atu Moli, Angus Ta'avao, Karl Tu'inukuafe, Ofa Tu'ungafasi
Locks	Brodie Retallick, Patrick Tuipulotu, Samuel Whitelock
Utility forward	Jackson Hemopo
Loose forwards	Sam Cane, Vaea Fifita, Shannon Frizell, Luke Jacobson, Dalton Papalii, Kieran Read, Ardie Savea, Matt Todd
Halfbacks	TJ Perenara, Aaron Smith, Brad Weber
First five-eighths	Beauden Barrett, Josh Ioane, Richie Mo'unga
Midfielders	Jack Goodhue, Ngani Laumape, Anton Lienert-Brown, Sonny Bill Williams
Utility backs	Braydon Ennor, Jordie Barrett
Outside backs	George Bridge, Rieko Ioane, Sevu Reece, Ben Smith

Cup. Aumua's inclusion is presumably to keep him interested in staying in New Zealand. One of Fifita, Frizell and Jacobson has to be cut, and it's likely that it will be the young Chiefs flanker, who is probably as surprised as everyone else at being named. Papalii is again a future project, and Josh Ioane can only get in if Beauden

Barrett or Richie Mo'unga get injured. One who is in for the duration, though, is Brad Weber. In an absolute exemplification of being too good to ignore, Hansen has had his hand forced into including Weber at the expense of Te Toiroa Tahuriorangi. Weber can now pretty much start planning what he's going to get up to in Japan, because there is no logical way he can be shifted from the third halfback spot unless he somehow injures himself at training.

Squire is indeed ruled out, at his own behest; Hansen telling us that 'Liam has made himself unavailable. He doesn't think he's ready to play international rugby yet, which I think is a heck of a brave decision and a good decision for him to make.' The unanimous feeling in the room is that it's just a matter of time before Squire makes his return.

The tightest battlegrounds are the midfield and the outside backs, though. On form, any of the players selected would be accepted as part of the top XV, except maybe Jordie Barrett. Even then, his status as the only viable long-range goal kicker makes him part of any selection discussion. One man who has probably relied on his reputation more than any other is Rieko Ioane; he's had the misfortune of being on the end of a Blues backline that fell to bits by the end of Super Rugby. He obviously still has the height that Steve Hansen likes in at least one of his wingers, but has to listen to his All Blacks coach surprisingly let rip on his older brother, Akira. The big number 8 was in good form throughout the season, and benefited from at least getting a lot of touches of the ball for the Blues. Akira Ioane was being talked up as back-up for Kieran Read, until Hansen brutally shoots down that suggestion like it's the first day of duck-hunting season.

'It's the same problem he's always had,' Hansen snaps, paying scant regard to the fact that he's sitting in the Ioane brothers' own club, where their former Black Fern mother Sandra is rugby development officer.

Akira Ioane was being talked up as back-up for Kieran Read, until Hansen brutally shoots down that suggestion like it's the first day of duck-hunting season.

'He came into the season probably not as fit as he could've been, and played every game for the Blues at the same time as trying to get fit. He's a tired athlete. Did we see the best of him? I don't think we did in Super Rugby, and other people played particularly well and put themselves in front of him.'

Ouch. Sounds like Akira—who had been tagged as a fantastic World Cup story for the past few years, given that he was born in Tokyo and has the same name as one of the most iconic Japanese animated movies ever—will have to wait for Hansen to retire if he ever wants to play test rugby.

27

THE BLACK CAPS GRAB THE LIMELIGHT

Somewhere over the Pacific Ocean, 14–15 July 2019 (67 days to the Rugby World Cup)

SOMETHING UNUSUAL HAPPENS ON the way to the first test match of the season. The day before the squad leaves, the Black Caps win a thrilling Cricket World Cup semi-final over India, which puts them into the final against England at Lord's. The CWC has been a slow burner over the past few weeks due to all the matches being televised during the early hours of New Zealand mornings, but has now burst into the wider consciousness as there is a real chance the Black Caps can win.

While it's good news for most of the population, it's not for Steve Hansen and myself. Our 11-hour flight to Buenos Aires is scheduled for the night of the final and, in a cruel little twist of fate, is slightly delayed for boarding, making the take-off around about when the first ball is bowled in London. Air New Zealand has said it'll provide WiFi for the plane ride, but it doesn't work. One by one, we all fall asleep hoping to wake up to some good news.

All of a sudden the All Blacks, who had been in their familiar role of being the only news in town at this time of year, are completely forgotten as the crazy finish to the cricket dominates the news cycle for the entire week.

Of course, that final turns out to be perhaps the most dramatic sporting event in recent memory. About an hour before landing, we get an update across the screen on the back of our seats that condenses the result into a telegram: final was tied, super over was tied, England win because they scored more boundaries. It ignites a firestorm of controversy. This has suddenly become New Zealand's biggest grievance since 'The Underarm'. Social media is dominated by people venting their frustration, column inches and click rates skyrocket, and people who aren't even sportswriters suddenly have forthright opinions on a sport that has happily existed in its summer window and overlapped with Super Rugby without complaint for the past 23 years. All of a sudden the All Blacks, who had been in their familiar role of being the only news in town at this time of year, are completely forgotten as the crazy finish to the cricket dominates the news cycle for the entire week.

The importance of the test against Argentina is diminished even further due to the fact that there are only two travelling media personnel in-country: me and Nigel Yalden from Radio Sport. Between us, we ask all the press conference questions—which for the Monday session, at least, consist mostly of asking the All Blacks what they thought about the cricket. Somehow they'd been able to watch it despite being in South America (Hansen didn't arrive until two days after the squad).

Going in to work on a Monday morning knowing that the All Blacks have won over the weekend signals a return to normality.

Dane Coles is back on deck for the day's press conference and gives a typically forthright analysis of the cricket loss, managing to hold his language just on the right side of broadcastable. It becomes clear that the All Blacks are once again in the familiar position they've found themselves in across their history—the correcting force of New Zealand equilibrium. A test win goes a long way towards restoring the country's balance, and not just from sporting turmoil, either. Going in to work on a Monday morning knowing that the All Blacks have won over the weekend signals a return to normality.

Coles also gives an honest appraisal of the new scrum laws that World Rugby has rushed in. Honest as in he doesn't seem at all sure how they'll work until he's experienced them in a game, which says a great deal about the governing body's regard for this series of test matches. They're intended to make scrums safer, reducing the load that a hooker will have on the top of his head from the opposing pack by widening the gap before the engagement—so all of a sudden we're seeing a reversal in the direction scrummaging was taking. For a while there it looked as though it was headed towards inevitable depowerment, but this seems to signal that it is indeed going back to the old days of a decent hit when the two packs come together.

Which seems fine, in theory. But it's also a wee bit ludicrous that such a major change, with the ability to turn an entire test match (the consequence of transgression is a penalty, and scrum penalties are often haphazard at best anyway), has been rushed in the week before what will be a stern test for the All Blacks.

At least it means we can actually complete the Argentina leg of this year by getting back to asking questions about scrums and not feeling like total hacks in doing so. We've all been doing the other part of the Argy-double, eating steak, so it feels like we've done things the traditional way here to start the week off.

28
A DAY AT THE MUSEUM

Buenos Aires, 18 July 2019
(64 days to the Rugby World Cup)

WEDNESDAY IS THE TEAM'S DAY OFF, so apart from an embargoed team naming in the evening, it's our day off too. I want to get away from rugby and the All Blacks for a while, because all I've really seen of Buenos Aires so far is the one-kilometre stretch that I've been walking between the team's plush hotel and the extremely not-plush one I'm staying in.

Central Buenos Aires is a beautiful and grand sight. We're right next to the gigantic Avenida 9 de Julio (9 July Avenue), named for the date in 1816 when Argentina obtained its independence from Spain. It's the largest city avenue in the world, stretching 14 lanes wide, and often takes me several minutes to cross. The buildings that flank it are a mixture of modern and classical, but it's a fair call to say that everything there probably needs a lick of paint.

The same could be said about Argentinian rugby. It is, in keeping with the tradition of the English upper classes that brought the sport here, a rich and elitist pursuit. The Unión Argentina de Rugby was the last major holdout against professionalism, and the Jaguares project probably should've got off the ground about a decade before it actually did. If it had, there's a very good chance that Argentina wouldn't be going into this weekend's match still searching for their elusive first win over the All Blacks.

Clubs here, like San Isidro where the All Blacks are training this week, are large multi-sport complexes that will house a hockey turf and tennis courts as well. Crowds are predominantly older and male, and the game itself does seem to be somewhat rooted in its old-school past, with one glaring example being that Argentina is the only Tier 1 nation without a women's test side and virtually no female rugby to speak of at all.

The last time we were here, we were pelted with cans and abuse thrown from the freeway by passing football fans.

Speaking to various cab drivers in broken Spanish reveals a healthy disdain for rugby from the working-class population, which is hooked on not only the intense local rivalry between football clubs River Plate and Boca Juniors, but also the four other Primera División clubs in Buenos Aires alone. Indeed, the last time we were here, we were pelted with cans and abuse thrown from the freeway by passing football fans from the nearby San Lorenzo club (ironically best known for being the Pope's favourite team), who were incensed by the massed crowd of their rugby counterparts making their way to the game.

It's extremely unlikely that this section of the population will ever be won over by the oval ball code. Especially since, as in England, the people running the game probably don't want them to be anyway. However, rugby does have a loyal following that turns up in droves for test matches. Given that Los Pumas are facing an All Blacks side shorn of some of its key components and with five debutants, they will be coming into Estadio José Amalfitani this Saturday with expectations that this test will not follow the same script as the previous three Buenos Aires encounters. It's a pretty well-worn script, too: 2016 saw the All Blacks win 36–17; 2017 was 36–10; and 2019 was 35–17. Not only that, but they've followed exactly the same pattern: the All Blacks shoot out to a fast start, kill off the enthusiasm of the crowd, then go flat. The Pumas score a try, someone gets yellow-carded, and the game disintegrates into a mess. If you're a gambler, it is the most predictable All Blacks fixture going.

But right now I'm not thinking about that. After negotiating my way across the vast Avenida, I've made it to a cramped train that's speeding me away to a place where I can put my mind on something else for the day: the Memorial Museum to victims of Argentina's 'Dirty War' of the 1970s and early '80s. It's on the site of the former naval academy grounds, a group of grand but decrepit buildings. Leopoldo Galtieri, the former president and architect of Argentina's attempt to claim the Falkland Islands in

1982, once walked these grounds as a student. His death squads also used the academy buildings to secretly torture and murder opponents of the military *junta*, and as soon as I step through the gate after my long train ride it feels like a place where evil things happened.

As I approach the entrance to the museum, I spot a group of large men wearing shorts. It's the middle of winter, so I can only assume they are New Zealanders (I am also wearing shorts).

There's a large parade ground in the middle of the complex of low-rise buildings. That's where they used to force their kidnapped victims on to helicopters, then fly them out to the Río de la Plata and drop them to their deaths. Around the grounds there are large pictures of the faces of the people who disappeared and a statue of the mothers who gathered in the Plaza de Mayo to grieve them and demand answers for over three decades.

Then, as I approach the entrance to the museum, I spot a group of large men wearing shorts. It's the middle of winter, so I can only assume they are New Zealanders (I am also wearing shorts). One of them is stopped by a local and poses for a photo. Shit, it's the All Blacks. They've come to the same bloody museum as I have on their day off. They turn towards me and I panic. I don't want them to think I'm following them, and quite frankly I don't want to have to awkwardly share a museum with them either, so I do the most logical thing that occurs to me and duck behind the nearest tree as they lumber past.

Instead, I go to the nearby Museum of the Malvinas, where I try to learn about the other side of the Falklands War story through exhibits with Spanish captions and cartoons. Turns out the Argentinians have a pretty different view on the way that all went down, which I already knew through having a very passionate conversation with a 50-something-year-old taxi driver the last time I was here. He was as surly as hell until I explained, 'No soy inglés' ('I'm not English'), then wanted to be my best mate after I told him New Zealanders weren't too keen on the Poms either.

29
PUBLIC RELATIONS

Buenos Aires, 19 July 2019
(63 days to the Rugby World Cup)

STEVE HANSEN SIGHS HEAVILY. It's one of those sighs that makes you feel bad straight away, like something your dad does when he knows you've just lied to him about dinging the car. I've just asked him about Sevu Reece, one of the five new All Blacks named for the weekend's test and the only one in the starting line-up. He was also arrested and charged with assaulting his girlfriend in 2018.

Hansen hates having to talk about it. He's tried to flick the issue off his pads by dropping Reece into his earlier answers, but I know every headline in the country about the team naming will be about the Fijian-born winger, so we need a definitive quote. The All Blacks coach eyes me warily, and says that they are delighted with his progression as a player and a person throughout the season. He's not going to discuss domestic violence anymore, because only two weeks ago he told Jim Kayes on Radio Sport that it 'wasn't a gender issue', sparking outrage back in New Zealand and serving as a reminder to the All Blacks that their coach's words carry an awful lot of weight. It's a reminder they definitely shouldn't have needed, given the indignation at Hansen's remarks about government funding the previous season.

This issue has brought out the worst in every keyboard lawyer. Reece's charge was dropped, ostensibly so it wouldn't affect his playing career and ability to travel overseas. If it had stood, there might well have been a chance he would've been deported back to Fiji. However, despite the judge's intention, Reece did very much find himself on the outer with Waikato and the Super Rugby team he was most likely to play for, the Chiefs. They could ill afford any bad PR around a female-related issue given that they were still trying to claw back a decent chunk of their reputation after allegedly mistreating a stripper at their 2016 end-of-season party.

While the matter was being sorted out in the courts, Reece signed with Irish club Connacht. It was a pretty obvious play by the IRFU to eventually have him playing in a green test jumper after a three-year stand-down period. Meanwhile, Irish rugby was having a PR crisis of its own: earlier in the year three contracted players were found not guilty of rape in a Belfast court, yet the subsequent release of WhatsApp messages between the players in which they laughed off the events as being 'like a merry-go-round at a carnival' led to swift public condemnation. Two of the trio, Paddy Jackson and Stuart Olding, were banished from Irish rugby.

Connacht had clearly been taking notice, and withdrew Reece's contract. His career looked finished before it had really started, but in December 2018 he was thrown a lifeline by the Crusaders. It didn't really cause much of a ripple—the champion side already had All Black George Bridge, the highly rated Braydon Ennor, Manasa Mataele and even veteran Israel Dagg on their books.

There is confusion over whether he is even eligible for the All Blacks, but NZ Rugby do their paperwork when Hansen says he wants to give the 22-year-old a taste of test rugby.

Fast-forward six months. Reece has taken advantage of an injury to Mataele and become a mainstay in the Crusaders' starting team. He scores 14 tries in their charge to a third consecutive championship. There is confusion over whether he is even eligible for the All Blacks, but NZ Rugby do their paperwork when Hansen says he wants to give the 22-year-old a taste of test rugby.

Now he's in. It's 4pm in Buenos Aires and 6am in New Zealand, so there's still a bit of time before everyone wakes up to find that all the headlines about the team naming contain Reece (and probably the word 'controversial'). This is, without a doubt, a very timely reminder to NZ Rugby, the All Blacks and Hansen that it doesn't matter how far away they are and how long ago things happened, there's going to be a blow-up if the media can find one. Hansen has given his last word on the matter for now, though. Reece can only go out and play this Saturday, and his performance is what will fill up the columns back home.

But it's fair to say that it won't be the last we hear of it, because these things have a habit of popping up no matter how far you run from them. Just one month before, Paddy Jackson had emerged from playing at French club Perpignan after his departure from Ireland and signed with London Irish. This brought the rape case firmly back into the spotlight, causing principal sponsor Guinness to break a 40-year relationship with the club over fears about its image. If nothing else, it should be a massive wake-up call to players behaving badly in this day and age, and a warning that they can expect the full scrutiny of the media, and of a massive percentage of the public who normally wouldn't give a shit about rugby any other day of the week.

THE FACT THAT THE SIDE in Buenos Aires has no Crusaders in it means that it requires a stand-in captain for Kieran Read. Sam Cane is given the job for the third time, and is striding confidently down the crushed brick path of the San Isidro sports club towards the waiting media. We're about 20 minutes' drive from the middle of the city, there are several hundred fans waiting outside to come in and take pictures of the team as they run through their final preparations for the game, and I've only just managed to make it in time for the session because of a cab driver who tried to guess his way here and failed miserably until I handed him a map on my phone.

Cane has been in a similar predicament this season regarding timeliness. So far he's played only a handful of games in 2019. This is his second visit to Argentina's capital in only three weeks, after the Chiefs were knocked out in the Super Rugby quarters by the Jaguares, but Cane is raring to go—for a lot of us, his return to the field is one of the better stories of the season.

Last year in Pretoria, there had been every chance that the 27-year-old was going to be spending an awful lot longer than six months on the sideline after being stretchered off 36 minutes into what had been a lacklustre All Blacks performance. He connected awkwardly with Francois Louw in a tackle, staying down long enough for anyone watching to grow extremely concerned for his welfare. The prognosis was the two words that send a chill through any rugby player, no matter how tough they consider themselves: broken neck. From an on-field point of view, it wasn't a great time for Cane to have an injury, either. Ardie Savea came on to replace him and, as well as having an outstanding game, eventually scored the winning try. Savea's form through the end-of-year tour was impressive, too, widening the debate outside of just his native Wellington that the loose forward should be rated higher than Cane anyway.

The prognosis was the two words that send a chill through any rugby player, no matter how tough they consider themselves: broken neck.

After the All Blacks departed South Africa following their dramatic 32–30 win, Cane remained in a Pretoria hospital for two weeks until he could safely walk again. Crucially, he hadn't suffered any nerve damage to his spinal cord, and was expected to make a full recovery. A week before his birthday in January, Cane could finally take off the neck brace he'd been wearing since he was sprawled out on the Loftus Versfeld turf in October.

He then had to look on while the Chiefs struggled through their early season, before announcing he'd return for their game against the Blues in May. We spoke to him at the team's training venue, where it was obvious that he was a little bit nervous about stepping out on a rugby field again. This was, after all, a return from an injury that could've ended his career and dramatically altered his entire quality of life. But Cane was determined to find the form that had seen him play 60 tests for the All Blacks.

Maybe it was that the break did him some good. Maybe it was the challenge that Savea posed. Whatever the reason, Cane's return was nothing short of sensational, as he quickly re-established himself as one of the most effective tacklers in the world. There is little actual coincidence in the fact that his return to a Chiefs jersey coincided with their run in to the play-offs—something that had seemed impossible after their four-loss start to the season.

Maybe it was that the break did him some good. Maybe it was the challenge that Savea posed. Whatever the reason, Cane's return was nothing short of sensational.

He stands before us—myself representing the entirety of the New Zealand media contingent alongside about a dozen local journalists. I get first crack at the line of questioning, and ask if the All Blacks could possibly make this game a little easier on the nerves than the week's sporting results so far (the Cricket World Cup final, the Silver Ferns' one-goal loss to Australia the day before, and two consecutive Warriors games going to golden point). Cane is an affable, friendly, but massive guy—the sort who would be the older brother to the happy-go-lucky George Bridge and be called upon to give him a hiding every now and then. He remembers his media training, and puts his hands behind his back as he laughs and says they'll do their best to make the game as stress-free as possible.

However, that's unlikely and we all know it. The truth is that this game is probably the Pumas' best chance at beating the All Blacks since their 21-all draw in 1985. The Jaguares season has been so successful that there've been some (typically loaded) comments out of Australia that it's unfair having what is essentially the Argentinian national team playing in Super Rugby. They are seemingly timing their run in to the World Cup with perfection, and it's worth remembering that they went within one game of making the final in 2015. Argentinian rugby should now be a consistent force on the world stage.

Cane fields some inevitable but pertinent questions about the similarities between the Jaguares and the Pumas, and gives textbook dead-bat answers about respecting both sides for what they are. I have one more for him, though: does he feel like he's got any unfinished business out on the Estadio José Amalfitani turf after the Chiefs' recent loss?

He smiles and says no. I don't believe him at all.

We pack up and go to leave. In a move that does not shock me at all, the cab driver who I'd paid to stay outside and wait has decided he has better things to do, driving off with my crisp 500-peso note. I'm actually kind of relieved, because I'd heard a story from one of the Sky TV crew that they'd made a similar deal, only to return and find the cabbie stretched out on the back seat watching Pornhub on his phone. One of the AFP journalists is finishing a cigarette nearby and offers me a ride in her taxi, which has thankfully stuck around. I explain my situation to her in my woeful Spanish, only for her to exhale powerfully and reply in perfect English: 'Welcome to Argentina.'

30
FIRST TEST
OF THE YEAR

Estadio José Amalfitani, 21 July 2019
(61 days to the Rugby World Cup)

ALL BLACKS	**20**
PUMAS	**16**

I DECIDE NOT TO TAKE my chances with another taxi and ask the Sky TV guys if I can hitch a ride with them on game day. So at midday I'm sitting in the lobby of the vast Emperador Hotel with Jeff Wilson, Justin Marshall and Grant Nisbett. All three of them are impeccably dressed, so when the car arrives and they get up to put on their suit jackets, I can't help but quip 'Let's go to work', like the start of *Reservoir Dogs*. As soon as the words pass my lips I realise how lame this sounds, so I keep quiet for the rest of what turns into a long journey out to the stadium where the game will be played.

We cruise down Avenida 9 de Julio, then straight into a cloyingly interminable traffic jam on the highway. The others are sweating into their shirtsleeves. Finally we pull up outside the utilitarian edifice that is Estadio José Amalfitani, named for the long-time president of the Vélez Sarsfield football club who got the stadium built back in 1943. It was the same year a military coup took place in the country that led to the dictatorship of Juan Perón, but all we can see is that very little has been done to the stadium since then. The area behind the goalposts is still just concrete steps, and the main grandstands bank steeply upwards like the old Millard Stand at Athletic Park. Around the touchlines are 10-metre-high fences topped with barbed wire, and a dry moat below to deter anyone getting on the field. If anybody somehow did, they'd have to contend with the shotgun-wielding police that have been shadowing the All Blacks everywhere.

They stay deathly silent during the TJ Perenara-led haka, and it's rather eerie being able to hear the players perform it without the aid of microphones.

I take my seat down one end of the stadium. I'm the only English-speaking journalist in the media box, and it's filling up fast. In fact, I'm starting to notice that a lot of the people filing in don't even seem to have any work gear, which reminds me of the Italian food scramble back in November. When the teams hit the field in what's turned into an overcast but otherwise pleasant afternoon, the crowd—knowing full well that they could be watching history as an undermanned All Blacks side is taking on a very much full-strength and in-form Pumas team—belts out an extra-long version of the national anthem. They stay deathly silent during the TJ Perenara-led haka, though, and it's rather eerie being able to hear the players perform it without the aid of microphones.

By now, the media box is so full there are people sitting in the aisles and standing up the back. The game kicks off and it's a sloppy start, but most of the local journalists are cheering on the Pumas, which is something that would be viewed as career-ending back home. I realise this may be my only chance to actually watch a game like a fan for a change, and let out a few audible 'fuck's when the ball is dropped.

This means I swear a lot, because the first half is a bit of a mess. Ngani Laumape burrows over for the first try of the All Blacks season, then Brodie Retallick reads an Argentinian short-side raid like a book. He picks off a pass from Nicolás Sánchez and runs 50 metres to score next to the posts. It's 20–9, and it seems like this game is going to go exactly the same way as the previous three at this venue. However, this outing has one key difference that will have a serious impact on the rest of the season: while the All Blacks are concentrating on their defensive systems, they show enough of their hand on attack to give us a clue as to their intent with ball in hand.

Sevu Reece has spent the half being as busy as possible, touching the ball early and often. Aaron Smith and Beauden Barrett marshal their pack around the field. With the defensive line speed of Ireland so fresh in their minds, which neutralised their forward runners off the ruck, Hansen's new structure moves the ball away from the pressure spot usually brought by the third- and fourth-rush defenders. It targets the disconnection that develops a little wider, where the defence is not bringing tacklers forward quite as swiftly. This new system gives Barrett and others filling in at first receiver more time and space. However, the key man in the entire equation is Aaron Smith. His game-reading ability is crucial to this tactic working as effectively as possible, and for the first half it looks like it has. It also looks like Hansen has surmised that the tests this year are going to be low-scoring and defence-heavy, so has tweaked things ever so slightly to give the All Blacks an edge.

Cane calls the team in. He tells them that now this understrength team needs to put in one big last shift to avoid making history in Argentina for the wrong reasons.

But the second half turns into a tackling competition rather than any more glimpses of what is to come. The game is mostly played between the 22-metre lines, aside from a try out of the blue to Emiliano Boffelli for the home side. The Pumas have pulled the score back to 20–16 and, with 10 minutes to go, the crowd starts to believe again. All the Pumas need to do is have one last crack with the ball inside the 22, and the All Blacks give them one after a massive scrum effort by the home side turns into a penalty.

Cane calls the team in. He tells them that now this understrength team needs to put in one big last shift to avoid making history in Argentina for the wrong reasons. The crowd, including most of the dubiously accredited journalists surrounding me, are on their feet and roaring.

The Pumas set up a lineout about eight metres away from the All Blacks' line. The ball comes in and they set a drive, which splutters to a halt almost immediately. The referee blows time, and the game is over. Everyone stares at each other in disbelief.

31
BAG BOYS

Ezeiza International Airport, 21 July 2019

POST MATCH IS A BLUR. Air New Zealand has put on a special flight for the All Blacks, so we need to get our shit done quick otherwise we'll all miss our ride home at midnight. Everyone involved in the game from a New Zealand point of view—players, coaches, media and supporters—is on the direct flight to Auckland. It'll land, then we jump on the next flight to Wellington. At least that's the plan.

Because there's only Nigel and me to conduct post-match interviews, All Blacks management has offered to give us a ride back to the city, then to the airport. We talk to Sevu Reece, Luke Jacobson and Braydon Ennor, all excited about their first taste of an All Blacks jersey. Atu Moli also made his debut after a lengthy comeback from injury. However, first five Josh Ioane notably did not take the field, and that's not the last time we'll be hearing about that. We wait on the concrete steps of the ageing stadium, in a wide passage near where the bus is parked. We watch as one by one the All Blacks emerge from the darkness of the changing room, clad in their suits. The last three men out are Steve Hansen, Beauden Barrett and NZ Rugby CEO Steve Tew, who are all lugging the team's laundry.

Several of the cops, who are two to each bike, brandish shotguns and wave them at passing motorists as we speed down the highway and back onto the crowded streets of Avenida 9 de Julio.

We get our call to jump into the team's support vehicle, and before we know it we're rocketing out of the stadium and into a police escort. Twelve motorbikes flash blue lights and scream sirens as we take the exact same route home in about a tenth of the time. Several of the cops, who are two to each bike, brandish shotguns and wave them at passing motorists as we speed down the highway and back onto the crowded streets of Avenida 9 de Julio. It's a crowded, busy night in the capital, with all of the faces moving up and down the world's widest street illuminated by the cops' blue lights.

Nigel and I are feeling pretty grateful for this bit of assistance from the team, especially when we're told to chuck our bags into a large rented truck that will shift the All Blacks' luggage down to the airport. Ours are the first bags on, and we take our seats in a minivan with the support staff and the players who didn't take the field in the test match. Once again, we hit the highway and cruise through the *barrios* and advertising hoardings that stretch as far as the eye can see in this sprawling megacity. Naturally, when we get there we're so eager to show our appreciation that we volunteer to help unload the baggage truck, which seems like a fun little idea until the doors open and reveal around 300 bags. All of which are *very* heavy.

Sonny Bill Williams, wearing dress pants, dress shoes and a white Real Madrid shirt, leaps into the truck and starts handing down the bags to the rest of us. After about five minutes, his veins have swollen up to be almost popping out of his already fucking massive arms. After about 20 minutes, I'm soaked in sweat when he finally tosses down my suitcase. The poor bastard sitting next to me on the plane ride home is going to have to smell the fallout from this surprisingly intense burst of exercise, but at least I'm not wearing a light blue shirt like the rest of the players who did the unloading. Asafo Aumua and George Bridge are still hard at work pushing baggage carts into the check-in, and their armpits are forming very noticeable sweat patches. Now I realise why the veteran Williams had swapped shirts—so there's a lesson for the young players to be learned today.

There are two other passengers boarding the flight home just behind us in the passport queue. It's Josh Ioane's mum and dad, who have travelled all the way here to watch their son sit on the bench and be a spectator, like the 50,000 other people in the stadium. Right now, it seems unlikely he'll be getting another chance given the standard of opposition coming up. He may end up sharing an unwanted statistic—being an All Black who dressed for a game in Buenos Aires and never got on the field—with Jason

Spice, who managed to achieve that feat back in 2001. Obviously we didn't get a chance to speak with Ioane, but if we had it would probably have been something similar to the Brett Cameron experience back in Tokyo.

The plane jets out of Buenos Aires, over the Andes and out into the massive inky blackness of the Pacific Ocean towards New Zealand. Up front, the All Blacks recline in their business-class seats before drifting off to sleep. Steve Hansen probably isn't as relaxed as usual, though. He knows full well that this is just the first step on a long campaign. Plus, there's a very capable old foe waiting for them in Wellington.

32

THE OLD ENEMY

Wellington, 22 July 2019
(60 days to the Rugby World Cup)

THE SPRINGBOKS HAVE TREATED THE start of the 2019 season in the same pragmatic fashion as the All Blacks. Faced with tests in Johannesburg and Wellington, they've split their squad and sent an advance party to New Zealand. So far, it's worked pretty well— just before the All Blacks pipped the Pumas, the Boks recorded a comfortable win over the Wallabies at Ellis Park. It sets up the next edition of this fixture quite nicely—a little boost that it admittedly didn't even need anyway. The last three tests between the All Blacks and the Springboks have been possibly the three most entertaining encounters of the entire decade between any two nations, and have reaffirmed their rivalry as the premier heavyweight clash of the sport.

It all goes back to one of the darkest days in South African rugby history. In 2017 they travelled to Auckland to play the All Blacks. Not at Eden Park, mind you. Instead, the game that used to attract the sort of crowds that would queue up for days beforehand on the footpath had been shifted out to a place known as 'the stadium of echoes' due to its lack of usage. After the North Harbour Stadium test finished 57–0 in the All Blacks' favour, 'Albany' became a byword for disaster among South Africans, their Little Bighorn.

The defeat was so bad that even All Blacks fans were hoping the ref would call it off early and save the Springboks any further embarrassment. By the end of the season, despite rallying his side to come within one point of the All Blacks in their next encounter in Cape Town, coach Allister Coetzee had lost his job and was replaced by former Springboks flanker Rassie Erasmus.

The defeat was so bad that even All Blacks fans were hoping the ref would call it off early and save the Springboks any further embarrassment.

Erasmus is a big man, retaining the same physique that won him 36 caps in the late '90s. He was part of the most dominant period of Springboks history, when they won 17 tests in a row between 1997 and 1998. That, of course, included two victories in succession over the All Blacks. Erasmus exhibits the typically unfailing South African air of extreme politeness when he talks in English, and we can only presume he's doing the same when he seamlessly breaks into Afrikaans for the benefit of their media.

The sheer number of travelling journalists is the first sign that this test is being taken very seriously by the South Africans—the past couple of years there have been only two, while this year there are about a dozen. There's also a guy from L'Équipe, sent down from France to have a look at the southern hemisphere preparations for the World Cup. So far, though, the most interesting story about the build-up is how the All Blacks and Springboks were forced to share a plane to Wellington together, after fog in the capital delayed everyone's arrival. It meant that our trip back from Buenos Aires turned into an almost 30-hour ordeal, and Steve Hansen's Monday press conference had to be rescheduled to 7pm, during which I had to try not to fall asleep.

The sheer number of travelling journalists is the first sign that this test is being taken very seriously by the South Africans–the past couple of years there have been only two, while this year there are about a dozen.

Like Hansen, Erasmus has indicated he will step down after the World Cup. He has taken the Springboks coaching gig for only two seasons, as opposed to the All Blacks coach's eight. But as far as Springboks fans are concerned right now, he can keep the job for as long as he likes. Last season he brought his side to Wellington and pulled off one of the most memorable results in South African rugby. Under new skipper Siya Kolisi, the Boks weren't overawed by a fast start by the All Blacks, and sprinted to the finish to win

36–34 in a pulsating encounter. While the All Blacks pulled back the next test in Pretoria by the slimmest of margins, the belief in South Africa is that Erasmus has this side on its way to peak at the exact right moment to potentially win their third World Cup. They still have a vast number of issues, but probably the biggest talking point of their re-admission to international rugby has been well and truly proven to be a positive thing.

Without their controversial quota system, Kolisi would never have been captain. The tall, athletic loose forward is a true symbol of the progress made by South African rugby, because having black and coloured players isn't seen as an anomaly now, it's expected. The environment it has created has meant that the 28-year-old has been elevated to the top spot entirely on merit, and he is proving to be a popular and charismatic choice.

However, he is not here this week. After damaging his knee during Super Rugby, the skipper's being kept on ice until the World Cup. The man to lead them out this weekend is Duane Vermeulen, the monstrous number 8 who has spent the past four years playing in France and Japan. Vermeulen has fond memories of Wellington. When he played there in 2014, he put in a body of defensive work so brutal that it almost bruised the eyes of anyone watching. The Springboks lost that game, though. Both Erasmus and his stand-in skipper are determined to not let that happen again.

BY NOW, WE'RE WELL ENTRENCHED in the All Blacks media cycle. Every Monday we have two players to give their thoughts on the game just gone. On Tuesday we have Ian Foster and two more players. Wednesday is supposed to be a day off (most of the time it's just time to do more work). Thursday is the big one: we get the team for the weekend and Hansen explains his selections in the afternoon, then two backs and two forwards appear from the starting line-up. Friday is the captain's run, in which Kieran Read once again regurgitates the same weekly rhetoric regardless of what the questions are.

Because we're back home in New Zealand against a team that the All Blacks have a long and storied history with, every question being fired at the players and coaches has a serious amount of thought behind it. There is nothing about the haka, or any open-ended ponderance about what the All Blacks think of the city/stadium/country/team/local food/whatever. It's a reminder of how the lens definitely changes focus when the All Blacks play at home. On Thursday, that lens is on one of the most-talked-about men to ever pull on a black jersey.

Sonny Bill Williams is named to start at second five inside Jack Goodhue. The code-swapping superstar has had a disrupted season so far, but has seemingly been given enough time to recover from a string of injuries received playing for the Blues to be able to make his return. The last time he played for the All Blacks was at Twickenham, where his injury there ushered in an inspired performance from Ryan Crotty.

Williams has long been an object of both fascination and conjecture for the New Zealand public. In fact, his first time getting near the limelight was one of great controversy. As a 19-year-old member of the Canterbury-Bankstown Bulldogs, the first time anyone would've really seen him on TV was when the team was in the gun for a sex scandal during a training camp in Coffs Harbour. No one knew who he was back then in the 2004 preseason, but that would change dramatically by the end of the year. The Bulldogs went on to win the NRL Premiership and Williams was catapulted to stardom. He did a vanishing act from rugby league halfway through the 2008 season, going to France to play for Toulon's big money, which seemingly cemented the thought in many people's minds that this was his primary motivation for playing.

Williams has long been an object of both fascination and conjecture for the New Zealand public. In fact, his first time getting near the limelight was one of great controversy.

Yet he harboured a strong desire to play for the All Blacks. Despite the fact that doing so would mean taking quite a hefty pay cut, he was still seen as a mercenary when he arrived back in New Zealand in 2010 to attempt to reach his goal. He became part of a Crusaders side that went within one game of winning a Super Rugby title in 2011, in spite of not being able to play any home games after the Christchurch earthquakes. He won a World Cup with the All Blacks later that year, then moved to the Chiefs and won a Super Rugby title. In 2013, Williams returned to the

NRL and won a premiership with the Sydney Roosters. After two seasons in rugby league, he again came back to the All Blacks, and eventually replaced Conrad Smith in the 2015 World Cup final, setting up Ma'a Nonu's game-sealing try. By this time it was not too much of a stretch to say that he was one of the most prolifically successful dual-code athletes ever. But the criticism kept coming.

Why does Williams cop so much flak? Unless you're a very, very bitter Bulldogs supporter, there really is no reason to get annoyed by the fact that he's doing what anyone else who is highly qualified does in the workplace—obtaining employment from organisations that are eager to have him. That's especially so when another former All Black/rugby league convert, Brad Thorn, doesn't get any grief at all—in fact, nothing but universal admiration and respect. Teammates at the Crusaders and All Blacks, Thorn and Williams have careers that mirror each other an awful lot: NRL players, switching to union, back to representative league, and then a final switch to win a World Cup with the All Blacks. That image gets a lot clearer when you add in the fact that Thorn also walked out on a team at one time, as well as playing for an entirely different country.

The double standards displayed in reactions to Williams and Thorn could be because of Sonny's slightly dodgy boxing career, in which he became the second All Black after Kevin Skinner to become the New Zealand heavyweight boxing champion. Or maybe, just maybe, some of the New Zealand sporting public struggle to accept a handsome, confident and proudly Polynesian man as a role model or hero. There is still a certain demographic of

All Blacks fans that very much have a line for just how brown and proud it's acceptable to be, and it's quite clear that Williams burst over that line a long time ago.

But, admittedly, times are changing. Williams' embrace of social media has helped a lot, with his wholesome, family-orientated content coupled with thoughtful social commentary winning over many people ambivalent towards what he does on the field. His commitment to helping those recovering from the Christchurch mosque attacks was prominent in the media, as he is most definitely the country's highest-profile Muslim, having converted to the faith in 2009.

Williams is seemingly everything that the new Aotearoa sees itself as. However, there is the inescapable fact that he is now 33 years old, and there are some seriously legitimate options in the All Blacks midfield besides himself. Anton Lienert-Brown, Ngani Laumape and Crotty can all fill that gap, as well as the looming spectre of veteran Ma'a Nonu. Williams' advantage is that Hansen sees him as the primary weapon to unlocking space around the outside for Beauden Barrett to exploit, but that needs to be seen to be effective before the tournament starts. The clock is ticking loudly on Williams' rugby career, and this game on Saturday will be very important in terms of what sort of role he's going to play over the next few months.

33

THE WORST CROWD EVER

Westpac Stadium, 27 July 2019
(55 days to the Rugby World Cup)

ALL BLACKS	**16**
SPRINGBOKS	**16**

THERE ARE ABOUT 10 MINUTES to go in the test match, and a fight is threatening to break out. Not out on the Westpac Stadium field, mind you. It's three rows in front of our media box positioned high up in the stands. We're safely enclosed in our glass case at the very back of the stadium, in a tight bank of seats and desks that seems miles away from the pitch. The All Blacks are leading 13–9, and struggling their way to what seems like an unremarkable win over the Springboks.

The two men, clad in the ubiquitous Kiwi uniform of black puffer jackets and beanies, are staring each other down while another is trying to talk them out of it. Eventually it simmers down when one is convinced to swap seats. Who knows what they're arguing about, but it's one of the few times in the whole game anyone in the crowd has actually shown much interest in anything other than sitting still and looking unimpressed. For all the talk of this being another edition of the great All Blacks versus Springboks rivalry, the crowd has remained as flat as a pancake throughout the game.

Maybe it's because the weekend before I was in Buenos Aires, where people actually give a shit about making some noise every now and then. Honestly, I swear I can hear the reserve players talking to each other from up here, and we're a long way back considering Westpac Stadium is a cricket ground as well. To be fair, though, there hasn't been much to get excited about. The game so far has been an unspectacular affair. The much-vaunted experiment of having Beauden Barrett and Richie Mo'unga on the field at the same time hasn't really done much except show that Barrett should probably be back at first five. He's set up the only try of the game so far, to Jack Goodhue, by busting down the touchline and feeding the ball back inside for the mullet-haired centre to streak away and score.

Interestingly, Barrett has taken the kicking tee as well. This is the same ground where he shanked the ball all over the place the year before and ultimately cost the All Blacks the game, given that they outscored the Boks six tries to four.

But the main thing we can see is that both sides are plainly holding an awful lot back. Hansen and Erasmus clearly have an eye on what will transpire in September rather than here, and it's meant that the test has been one of defensive strategy rather than attacking tactical brilliance. Time and time again, the ball is kicked downfield. The Boks are trying to bait Barrett into running it back and getting isolated, but he's wise to what they're up to. Besides, he's just too damn good to let that happen to him anyway. Not long after the tense stand-off between the two blokes in front of us, the score stands at 16–9.

All the All Blacks have to do is hang on to the ball. The crowd can sense they'll see a familiar end to this game with the forwards setting up pods either side of the ruck and then waiting for the final hooter to go, but that's not what happens. For some reason, they try to run the ball in for another try, and lose it. The Boks take over, win a penalty and bang the ball down to the All Blacks' 10-metre line for one last roll of the dice.

Off the lineout they work the ball across field. The All Blacks' defensive line holds, but the Boks have cooked up something to finish the game. It all looks so innocuous, as if they can't make a dent, then suddenly the ball is swept back across the park and recycled perfectly for replacement Herschel Jantjies to whip out to Handre Pollard. Willie le Roux has been essentially walking behind the play for its entire build-up, with the intention of making the All Blacks forget he's even there. All of a sudden he flies onto a short ball from Pollard and creates an overlap for Cheslin Kolbe, because Mo'unga has to come in and make a tackle. The little winger burns towards the 22, and chips ahead. Jantjies motors up the middle and leaps over Aaron Smith—which would be a comical competition of elevation between the two smallest men on the field were it not for the gravity of the situation—grabbing the ball and scoring close to the posts.

The game ends in a draw, but you wouldn't think it by the way the Boks are celebrating.

Pollard steps up and slams home the conversion. The game ends in a draw, but you wouldn't think it by the way the Boks are celebrating. It's not that they've just saved themselves from defeat, but that they've struck the last psychological blow before the teams meet again in Yokohama. They stride off the park, heads held high. The crowd, in such a malaise for the entire match, is almost completely silent. Wellington has now had only one All Blacks win in the past four test matches it has hosted.

'WHAT'S IT LIKE TO LOSE a game 16-all?'

That's the first question levelled at the All Blacks staff in the press conference. It's meant to be a joke, but like all perceptive humour it cuts close to the bone. The home side blew that game, whichever way you look at it. But does it really matter?

Rassie Erasmus and Steve Hansen more or less confirm that, given the nature of the game, neither of them are actually that fussed about not winning. Erasmus continues his (admittedly genuine) charm offensive by praising the All Blacks effusively and talking up their World Cup chances. He and Vermeulen leave yet another impression that the Springboks are undoubtedly the team that has the most respectful rivalry with the All Blacks.

Hansen has engaged in a bit of phony war talk about the importance of pre-World Cup fixtures, with the usual lines about only being focused on the next test, but his demeanour suggests he really can't be bothered with that right now. In fact, neither can the media. It ends up being the shortest post-match press conference I can remember, and no one is complaining too much when none of the Springboks even bother to show up to the individual-player interview session (which would usually be treated as a serious breach of protocol). Hansen's just glad it's over, and they can move on to defending the Bledisloe Cup.

It's finished and we're out the door for another walk through the travesty that is Wellington after an All Blacks test, or what could be described as any other Saturday night on steroids. On Lambton Quay a guy's verbally abusing a woman, who I'm guessing is his partner, while being held back by his friends. Puddles of vomit pool just metres away from the central police station. A girl urinates in the Chaffers Street supermarket carpark while her friends film it on their phones and laugh. Just around the corner, an ambulance loads a passed-out man onto a gurney. All that and I don't even go down Courtenay Place after dark. For a city that likes to think of itself as some sort of arts and culture centre, this scene is a telling reminder of what it really is, no matter how much window-dressing is applied.

At least there's some atmosphere, though. A bit of that in the stadium would've been nice.

34

HELL IS OTHER PEOPLE

Perth, 7 August 2019
(44 days to the Rugby World Cup)

THE GREAT SOUTHERN LAND STRETCHES out below the plane as we break through the clouds a week and a half later. Out in front of us lies Perth, Australia's western outpost and host for the first Bledisloe Cup test of the year. Michael Cheika is down there somewhere, quietly waiting for his opportunity to strike back at the All Blacks. Well, quietly by his standards anyway.

It's slowly started to sink in that what everyone would regard as the last complete All Blacks performance was the last time they played the Wallabies, way back in October 2018. Take out the gimme games against Japan and Italy, and they've only scored four tries since then as well. While the win against England can be classified as a gutsy performance, the New Zealand public are hungry for a hiding to put their minds at ease. This weekend should provide it, you'd think. The Wallabies haven't been up to much so far this season, getting thumped by the Boks in Johannesburg and then squeaking out a win over the Pumas in Brisbane. That last result probably says far more about the Argentinians than anything else—it seems like the Jagaures' success in Super Rugby hasn't really translated into the test arena just yet. In fact, the Pumas have actually been terrible ever since the Jaguares project was launched. Since 2016, their win record isn't even 20 per cent.

While the win against England can be classified as a gutsy performance, the New Zealand public are hungry for a hiding to put their minds at ease.

Besides, the Aussies are missing their biggest name player. Israel Folau, the guy who I confidently predicted would look right at home in the All Blacks, hasn't been seen on a rugby field since May and it's all his own fault. The devout born-again Christian (who was raised Mormon) couldn't help himself on social media again, sending out a post on Instagram condemning gay people to hell. The first time he did it, way back at the end of 2017, Folau found plenty of support from people saying that any censure for the offence he caused was an infringement of his free speech.

This time, not so much. Folau also included drunks, adulterers, liars, fornicators, thieves, atheists and idolaters in his list of folks headed on the downstairs escalator when they die, which alienated about 99 per cent of all rugby fans. Rugby Australia went through with its promise to terminate his contract immediately, and within a couple of weeks Folau found himself unemployed. His last game to date was for the Waratahs against the Blues at Eden Park. Since then he's been perfect headline fodder for the voracious Australian press, who have latched onto him from both sides. On one, he's getting torched for basically anything he does in the wash-up of the homophobic comments, especially when he asks the public for their financial support in his upcoming legal battle to get his contract paid out. On the other, a far more insidious force is muscling in on him in the form of conservative right-wing pundits who have found the perfect martyr for their cause.

Folau seems none the wiser, and quickly loses the modicum of support that he had the first time around. His wife, Maria, the current star player in the Silver Ferns netball team, gets dragged in as well. They're made to look like money-hungry charlatans by the time his appeal goes public. It's estimated his legal costs will top $3 million, which seems like an extraordinary amount to part with for just not being able to say sorry. However, the challenge for Rugby Australia is even bigger: if the case drags on and Folau wins, it could completely cripple the sport. CEO Raelene Castle, the former head of Netball New Zealand and the Canterbury-Bankstown Bulldogs, is under severe pressure to get this over and done with. Put quite simply, the Wallabies need a good-news story, fast.

Add on the not-so-insignificant fact that the test this weekend is being played in a city that isn't exactly enamoured with the sport's governing body, Folau saga or not. Perth is still pissed off about the Force being cut from Super Rugby, and is about to show the rest of the country just why they shouldn't have been. Just down the Swan River, within sight of the mighty skyscrapers bedecked with the logos and names of the great primary industries that have made this area such a boom town, sits the most modern and impressive stadium in the world.

It's there that the All Blacks' season is going to take a dramatic turn.

THE WEEK HAS BEEN A tense one for the team, too. The fact that they're not playing well isn't lost on the players, staff and, most of all, Steve Hansen. An embargoed team list isn't sent out, as it normally would be, meaning an annoying early wake-up at 5am to process the information when it's made public. The Thursday press conference is an exercise in surliness from the All Blacks coach, who delivers a string of uncharacteristic one-word answers to the questions thrown at him regarding the selections he's made. The main one being that Hansen has finally caved to Ardie Savea's excellent form and put him in to start a test at blindside. Then there's going to be another look at Beauden Barrett and Richie Mo'unga trying to work together to ignite the All Blacks backline.

Savea's elevation to the starting side is a pretty huge one, but it's not because he doesn't deserve it. On the contrary, he's probably been the most consistent player in the entire side across Super Rugby and the test season so far. It does, however, confirm that both Vaea Fifita and Shannon Frizell aren't up to the task of filling Liam Squire's boots. This has meant that Hansen's only option is to do away with a rigid adherence to playing a big blindside who is more of an extra lock. Squire was prominent in the lineout and tight work, and his ball-running ability was a serious bonus. With Savea, that's been flipped on its head. The Hurricane ended up playing most of the season at number 8 in Super Rugby, so the general consensus was that he'd force Kieran Read to shift to 6. During the press conference, though, it's becoming increasingly obvious that the numbers on their backs won't really mean anything.

Savea's workhorse role for the Hurricanes has elevated his status from cult hero to out-and-out test-match game changer. His form during the end-of-year tour changed the minds of plenty who thought him too small to be an effective test loose forward. Since then, Canes coach John Plumtree has signalled just how important Savea is by blatantly breaking the All Blacks-imposed sanctions on how many minutes each test player can spend on the pitch. Savea routinely starts and finishes every game, and is the bullocking force that gives the Barrett brothers and Ngani Laumape the space to finish off. If you ask anyone in the capital, Savea isn't just the first name you put down on the All Blacks' team sheet but an overwhelmingly popular choice to be captain and probably prime minister as well.

Not that we're getting any of that sort of enthusiasm out of Hansen. He doesn't even raise an eyebrow at the cheeky spread the hotel has put out for the media: lamingtons and pavlova. While we were waiting, it had the intended effect of triggering a series of conversations about just who invented what, which led on to which country owned Phar Lap and whether or not it was a good or a bad thing to claim Russell Crowe. The Aussie media are keen to try to poke Hansen for something, anything to give them a headline, but he's not budging today. That's not unusual, but he certainly seems more tense this week.

The Aussie media are keen to try to poke Hansen for something, anything to give them a headline, but he's not budging today.

It doesn't get any more relaxed when the players come in afterwards. The man of the moment, Ardie Savea, looks as uncomfortable as ever sitting at the head table and being the centre of attention. He breathes deeply and searches for the right words to some pressing questions, with hands clasped together in front of him, causing his broad shoulders to protrude towards us. It's a defence mechanism—they're the same parts of his body that will slam into the opposition in a couple of days' time. It wasn't that long ago that we were all talking about a different member of his family, and you get the feeling he wishes we were more interested in his brother Julian again.

That story is dead, though. Sorry, Ardie, but the focus is on you now.

35
CRAIG THE UBER DRIVER

Perth, 9 August 2019
(42 days to the Rugby World Cup)

'G'DAY MATE, YOU HEADED OVER to Fraser's Restaurant in Kings Park?'

'Yeah bro, I'm kind of in a hurry, too. I know traffic is shitty this time of morning, but if you can get me there quickly I'll be pretty grateful.'

'I'll see what I can do, mate. You late for work?'

'Yeah. Over here from New Zealand to cover the Bledisloe Cup test on Saturday night. There's always one decent screw-up when you're covering a test week. Well, at least there's always one for me. The Wallabies are staying at a hotel called the Fraser Suites, but are having their morning press conference at a place called Fraser's Restaurant, which I've just discovered is at the other end of town. Naturally I've mixed the two up and it's starting in like 15 minutes.'

'Gotta warn you, mate, this town is pretty fucked when it comes to traffic. They change everything around here without telling anyone—it's a pain.'

'You a rugby fan at all, mate?'

'Nah, not really. Played football me whole life, it's the big one out here. In the middle of the park as a ruckman, best place for a short bloke like me.'

'It looks like fun, I have to admit . . .'

'It messed me up.'

Silence, while I try to figure out something meaningful to say, and fail.

'Huh?'

'It messed me up. I got so many concussions I can't even remember what I'm doing these days. Head hitting the ground, fighting, that sort of thing. Hard grounds around here, these ovals. You get out on the piss afterwards, wake up feeling like shit the next day and you think it's all the booze. Then I got a hangover for a month, and I knew something was wrong.'

'When was this?'

'Back in the '90s. No one gave a shit back then; I got back out on the oval anyway. Never thought it'd be a permanent thing.'

'What do you mean?'

'These days, well, I drive people round in this because it gets me out of the workshop. I've got a small mechanic's business over in Northbridge, but some days I'll be working on something and completely forget what I'm doing, just like that. Brain gets . . .'

'All foggy? Like it's full of cement?'

'Yeah mate, just like that. You know what it's like?'

'I've played rugby my whole life. Stopped counting how many times I'd had my bell rung after about a dozen.'

'Yeah, so you know what it's like. You said you're a journalist, right?'

'Right.'

'You ever write about it? About what happens when the big boys who'll play tomorrow night get whacked in the head?'

'Yeah, a few times. No one wants to talk about it, though. The bosses don't want it to be an issue that'll, you know, stop people from playing or watching.'

'If I'd known what it was going to do to me, I never would've played.'

'Fuck.'

Silence. The car turns onto Fraser Avenue. Up ahead is the restaurant I should've been at half an hour ago. We stop, and I open the door.

'Keep writing about it, mate. Someone out there will listen and it'll probably do them a world of good. Hope no one gets hit in the head on Saturday night.'

He's not the only one in the car forgetting things on a regular basis. I walk off without my tripod, and only realise after Craig has driven back down the road. Luckily he spots it before he turns onto the freeway and drives it back up to me. The conversation and the subsequent demonstration that my brain isn't working the way it should this morning make me think about just what this game has done, and will do, to the health of those of us who play it.

Like I'd told Craig, I've been concussed more than a few times in the 25 years I've been playing. They've all been different—sometimes you see stars, sometimes you just go to sleep straight away and wake up as if nothing happened. The worst one didn't even affect me at the time of the hit, but it led to me feeling like I had a hangover for the next two months. Getting a scan on your head is even less fun. You have a lot of time in a hospital waiting room and MRI chamber to wonder just how bad the last painful blow was and what the image of your brain will show up.

Forget player drain, eligibility or how a global test season might be structured– someone taking the game to court for chronic traumatic encephalopathy is what World Rugby is probably most scared of.

And I'm not alone. Concussions are taking top-level players out of the game more often, and sometimes for good. This is because of the heightened precautions that are in place, and a less macho attitude about admitting that you've had your bell rung. If anything, the number of guys sitting out for concussions is a positive thing, because the people most affected by it are taking it seriously. But it has highlighted that if the game of rugby needs to be worried about anything, it's that this is only going to be turning into a bigger and more visible issue. Forget player drain, eligibility or how a global test season might be structured—someone taking the game to court for chronic traumatic encephalopathy is what World Rugby is probably most scared of.

The problem they face is that you can't fundamentally make rugby any safer without eliminating what it essentially is. Reducing tackle heights is one thing, but that's not going to stop players hitting their heads on the ground or accidentally clashing them with someone else's. All they can do is increase the punishment for players who are seen to be putting others at risk.

But it's a contact sport. The whole point of rugby is that it's risky.

36

THE RED CARD

Optus Stadium, 10 August 2019
(41 days to the Rugby World Cup)

WALLABIES	**47**
ALL BLACKS	**26**

TO GET TO PERTH'S NEW, $1 billion Optus Stadium, you need to walk across the nearby Matagarup Bridge. It's been especially built for the purpose of providing sports fans a direct link over the Swan River to the huge, punchbowl-shaped arena. The Matagarup is impressive enough on its own, with giant steelworks stretching up to the sky to form the shapes of the black and white swans that are the symbol of the state of Western Australia. The local tourism board took us out on the river during the week, extolling the virtues of the area and the stupendous wealth that's literally coming out of the ground around here.

From the bridge, you can peer up and see the massive sheets of glass that clad the upper deck of the stadium. They're there to enhance the fact that, once the sun goes down, Optus becomes a spectacle all on its own. We got to walk out on the turf during the captain's run, out to the spot that is usually the centre circle for the two AFL teams that call it home. The West Coast Eagles are defending their 2018 premiership here every second weekend in front of 40,000 to 50,000 people; in between that, the Fremantle Dockers get to run out to much smaller crowds. The locals say that the Dockers are the 'ugly stepchild' of the AFL, which is apt given that they play in purple guernseys and were named after a pair of pants associated with fat American men.

There's a statue standing tall when you step off the Matagarup. It's Neil Elvis 'Nicky' Winmar, and he's pulling up his top and pointing at his stomach—or more accurately, his skin. Winmar is a local Noongar Aboriginal man, who defiantly made the gesture in 1993 in response to racial abuse from Collingwood fans.

The locals say that the Dockers are the 'ugly stepchild' of the AFL, which is apt given that they play in purple guernseys and were named after a pair of pants associated with fat American men.

The lower half of the stadium has been contrived to appear like the local geographical features—brown and red. It makes it look like a giant basket but, when you enter, it suddenly transforms into an oval-shaped coliseum with lush grass. It's complete with large fabric awnings that stretch out to shade the crowd, just like two millennia ago when they'd be thrown bread in between watching men slaughter each other. Right now, though, the sort of entertainment is a lot less fatal but equally serious. In fact, Scott Barrett is about to find out just how serious.

WE'RE HIGH UP IN A plush new media area. This is the newest stadium in the world, and therefore everything about it is better than anything we've experienced before. We look out at a sea of 61,000 fans. Every seat had a gold Wallabies flag attached before they opened the gates, but only about half of them are getting put to use during the game because a huge number of All Blacks fans are in attendance tonight. Both sides make their way out to the field through a corporate bar area, which I walked through half an hour before. An All Blacks fan was already getting kicked out for being too drunk, and made his displeasure known to anyone in the vicinity with a set of ears.

Well into the game, the score is 13–12 to the Wallabies, and it has to be said that they deserve their slender lead. The clock is ticking down to half-time and they press towards the All Blacks' line. Michael Hooper, all arms and legs when he gets the ball, goes down in a heap clutching his head, and referee Jérôme Garcès, the man who was at the centre of the All Blacks' dramatic escape at Twickenham, wants to see why.

The replays come in, and it's not good for the younger Barrett brother. Like Sonny Bill Williams two seasons earlier, he's driven his shoulder into Hooper's head. The fact that the Wallabies captain was falling in a tackle isn't going to help Barrett, though. Every level-headed All Blacks fan is distraught but accepting of the decision when Garcès reaches into his pocket and pulls out a red card. Scott leaves the field with his hands on his head, Christian Lealiifano kicks the subsequent penalty, and the All Blacks will have to play the entire second half with 14 men.

If there was any belief that the All Blacks could match the effort of their undermanned 2017 counterparts, who almost pulled off a victory against the British & Irish Lions, it evaporates 10 minutes after the break when Lukhan Salakaia-Loto and Nic White score in the same corner. White's try comes courtesy of a powerful run by Samu Kerevi, who ironically bumps off Beauden Barrett with a shoulder to his head. The stadium lights up every time the Wallabies cross the line, and the player who has scored gets the lights focused on them as they saunter back to halfway. Even though Beauden gets one back, the Wallabies aren't going to let this one slip. They score three more tries, and no one in the press box can believe what they're seeing. They reach over the desks and ask me about record scores against the All Blacks. When Reece Hodge scores in the sixty-ninth minute, I tell them that's the most ever conceded against the Wallabies. When Kurtley Beale strolls through to score under the posts, I tell them that's the most ever.

The crowd stays until well after full-time, belting out John Farnham's 'You're the Voice'. I turn and head for the lift that will shoot us straight down to the press conference room, which is located inside the bar area where the teams walked out. I'm joined at the lift doors by a large man with a very smug look on his face. It's Phil Kearns, and he's nonchalantly checking his phone while it buzzes incessantly with messages. The former Wallabies skipper, who memorably pulled the fingers at Sean Fitzpatrick when the Australians snapped the All Blacks' 50-match unbeaten streak in 1990, glances at me and can tell just by sight that I'm a New Zealander. He's still in good shape for a guy his size, and looks an awful lot younger than his 52 years.

I feel like reminding him that the Wallabies haven't held the Bledisloe Cup in 17 years, and that the results this decade between the two sides stand at 23-5-2 in favour of the All Blacks.

'What'd you make of that?' I ask, trying to break the tension. He looks up, takes a deep breath and stares at me.

'We'll take it, mate,' is his scarcely believable yet completely Australian response. I feel like reminding him that the Wallabies haven't held the Bledisloe Cup in 17 years, and that the results this decade between the two sides stand at 23-5-2 in favour of the All Blacks. But that's a stupid idea—Kearns is from an era when the Wallabies would routinely beat the All Blacks and sometimes quite heavily. So for him this is simply the current team living up to the standards his generation set. We step into the lift, and after a bit more fidgeting with his phone, he can't help himself.

'Mate, even without the red card we would've smashed you.'

That's more like it, Kearnsy. Rumour has it he wants to be the next CEO of Rugby Australia, and right now that sort of brash attitude wouldn't go amiss for a game that has to compete against rugby league, football and soccer just to get on TV. The lift doors open, and there's an explosion of noise from the bar that we have to walk through. Kearns strides out to a cheer from the waiting crowd, while we squeeze past into the press conference room.

37

BACK TO SQUARE ONE?

Optus Stadium, 10 August 2019

KIERAN READ HAS THAT STRANGE LOOK on his face again, the one he gets whenever the All Blacks lose. Perhaps it's because it means the expectation built up by a streak of wins can at least ease a little bit. He's smiling amicably as Hansen runs through his list of things that went wrong in the previous hour and a half.

Aside from the red card, there was also the fact that the All Blacks were actually quite awful for most of the game. They could rely on a few touches of brilliance that saw them score 26 points, but it's not going to fool anyone. Once again, Beauden Barrett has had a pretty impressive game—but that's more due to the fact that no one else around him is even worth mentioning. His combination with Richie Mo'unga has once again failed to ignite. Patrick Tuipulotu, who we have all surmised will be starting next weekend no matter what because Scott Barrett will definitely be suspended, was essentially invisible when he came on off the bench. The ruck defence was embarrassing, with Marika Koroibete managing to score a try that would've looked right at home on a lower-grade high-school field.

It's a series of long-drawn-out explanations. While Hansen was short and to the point during the week, he knows that the more he can chew up time answering questions about tactics and refereeing, the less chance there is of fielding any about panic and what exactly the bloody plan is. While all this is going on, Gregor Paul from the *New Zealand Herald* is sitting behind me typing out a column that will set keyboards ablaze everywhere in the rugby world. He accuses Garcès of being a clown; a throwback to when the *Herald* dished out the same treatment to Warren Gatland. This is probably not going to help if Garcès is called on to officiate the All Blacks in the World Cup final.

However, one of the usual post-match trio does have a pretty distraught look on his face. Ian Foster, so often the bit-part player in these press conferences, is quite clearly running through the implications of just what this result means for his heavily documented All Blacks coaching aspirations once Hansen retires. The boss and the skipper can actually take the loss, despite the heavy nature of it, because both of them are out of the picture once the World Cup is over. For Foster, this one goes on a CV that he's presumably going to hand over to NZ Rugby during the summer, and it's not something he'll be looking forward to explaining.

Beauden Barrett comes in and tells us that his brother is distraught as well, and that he's not a dirty player. On the evidence of what we've seen in Super Rugby, though, that's an opinion you could probably feel free to disagree with. Scott has been penalised at least three times this season for shoulder charges, though he hasn't been sent off.

It's the first time we've spoken to Michael Cheika and Michael Hooper post match since Yokohama. Their week has been pretty relaxed right up until kick-off, with the only notable media-related incidents being Cheika having to fend off allegations of a probably imagined feud with Hansen, and a rather ill-judged question by a young local journalist about quokkas. The poor guy obviously had no idea that back in 2007 the Wallabies had found themselves at the centre of a scandal involving the friendly marsupials who live on the nearby Rottnest Island, when a couple of drunken players tried to see how far they could throw them. While it got a chuckle out of everyone else in the room, Cheika simply stared the journalist down and sharply told his players 'Don't answer that question' when Nic White half-opened his mouth in response.

While they're obviously in a lot better mood, it's not quite the champagne-soaked atmosphere we were expecting after a performance that phenomenal. Cheika launches quickly into addressing the red card, all but saying that if he'd had his way Barrett would never have left the field. There's a tinge of what Kearns said in the lift in what he's saying, because he knows that while they probably would've won anyway, it's placed an asterisk alongside this result. Every time the All Blacks' heaviest loss will be brought up from now on, it has to be tempered by the fact that the Wallabies had a numerical advantage.

Hooper gives us all the impression that he definitely wasn't milking it when he hit the deck after eating Barrett's shoulder. He wears a classic thousand-yard stare reminiscent of someone who has been in heavy combat, and clearly looks like he's feeling the effects of a delayed concussion. However, when he's called upon to speak, he snaps into action like the private-school-educated man he is. Belief, teamwork, never had a doubt this group was capable of this, et cetera.

While they probably would've won anyway, it's placed an asterisk alongside this result. Every time the All Blacks' heaviest loss will be brought up from now on, it has to be tempered by the fact that the Wallabies had a numerical advantage.

But it is obvious that Cheika and Hooper know they've done something quite dangerous. They've given the All Blacks a serious point to prove next weekend at Eden Park, a place that has been a Wallabies graveyard for 33 years. The All Blacks are clearly taking this one exceptionally seriously as well, as evidenced by their conduct the next day. We are due to fly out at 1.40pm local time, so the regular press conference is originally scheduled for 9am. After the loss, it's pushed out to 11.15am. We gather at the hotel and set up, but Hansen is a no-show. The clock ticks over to 11.30, and we realise that if we don't leave now, we might be stranded in Western Australia. We rush out the door to a waiting car, leaving Hansen inside with his secrets.

38

THE
PRESSURE

**The Heritage Auckland, 13 August 2019
(38 days to the Rugby World Cup)**

THERE'S A STORM BREWING IN Auckland. The heavens have remained open for the entire time we were away in the sunny climate of Perth, and a steady torrent of water washes down the steep streets that the Heritage perches between. Despite the cold and rain, it feels nice to be back on home soil. Every day I park my car at the Les Mills carpark, make no attempt to go to the gym and tell myself that I'm not ripping them off because I pay a weekly membership fee that more than covers the cost of an inner-city park.

One of the few sound bites you'll get from the All Blacks that actually offers some insight into how they operate comes when they talk about the Heritage. It's often just a few words, but whenever it's brought up, the grand edifice is referred to as 'the second home'. It's where the All Blacks assemble when they're named, where they have their biggest press conferences, and where they convene before jumping off overseas. It's also obviously their base when they play at the ground where they've experienced the most success in the past 30 years. Eden Park is about a 10-minute bus ride up Hobson Street, then through to Kingsland. It's no Lensbury, with its secluded surroundings and ambivalent locals. It's no Disneyworld either, thankfully. The Heritage is slap bang in the middle of Auckland city, a place where the All Blacks can feel like they're the centre of attention—because every time they stay there, they are.

If there is belief in Australia that the Bledisloe Cup may be changing hands this year, it's reflected in the number of media sent over for the next week in Auckland. There's also a Japanese film crew, which has presumably come over to shoot some stuff for the World Cup. This is the biggest media contingent since a cast of thousands arrived for the Lions tour a couple of seasons ago, so it's standing room only when Steve Hansen lumbers in to talk through his selections for the crucial second Bledisloe Cup match of the year.

> **The Heritage is slap bang in the middle of Auckland city, a place where the All Blacks can feel like they're the centre of attention— because every time they stay there, they are.**

And man, he's got a lot to talk through. Eight changes, in fact. Gone are Rieko Ioane and Ben Smith, and in come George Bridge and Sevu Reece. The double-swap out wide shaves the test experience in those positions by 102 caps. Patrick Tuipulotu is in for Scott Barrett, who is suspended for four weeks. Sonny Bill Williams will pair up with Anton Lienert-Brown in the midfield, because Jack Goodhue is out injured. Owen Franks is dropped, replaced by Nepo Laulala. Hansen lowers himself down onto his throne, takes a big drink of water and says let's go.

It's not too much of a surprise when the question comes about whether the senior All Blacks have actually been dropped, as opposed to being rested. The last All Black to feel the full public fallout of a dropping was Julian Savea. However, Hansen's answer can be interpreted any way the press wants.

'Obviously we'd like Ben, Owen and Rieko playing better, but we've made decisions because we've got to find out more about these other people in big pressure-cooker situations, and you don't get much bigger than this one—it's why we've got so many people here this week. We've got two exciting wingers and we need to see them play.'

Hmmm, okay, but Hansen has been saying all year that the Bledisloe is the second-biggest priority after the World Cup. Dropping Ioane would have been understandable, as despite scoring a try in Perth he hasn't actually done anything in an All Blacks jersey so far this year, and not much more in a Blues one, either. Ben Smith, though? We'd all presumed he was there to be the actual fullback when Beauden Barrett would come into the line and work his magic. Both are gone, though, admittedly replaced by one guy who had a pretty fine debut against Argentina and another who never seems to do anything wrong.

So instead of saying that the pair have been dropped, Hansen has mashed it up with the fact that Reece and Bridge need game time in a big test. He's painted himself into a bit of a corner on this one, and everyone in the room knows it.

It's not too much of a surprise when the question comes about whether the senior All Blacks have actually been dropped, as opposed to being rested. However, Hansen's answer can be interpreted any way the press wants.

It has only just dawned on most of us that this test on Saturday will mark a serious milestone for Hansen. It's his one-hundredth test in charge of the All Blacks, second only to his predecessor Sir Graham Henry. It's highly likely Hansen will have a 'Sir' added to the front of his name sometime in the future—if the All Blacks win the World Cup, it may be as early as the New Year's Honours list. Not that he claims to care about either the milestone or the impending honour. He hasn't even thought about it, he says.

THERE ARE BIGGER THINGS TO worry about this week, because this is the most pressure the team has been under in Hansen's entire tenure as coach. If anyone needed any more evidence of that, the scene that greets Kieran Read at the Friday captain's run at Eden Park leaves no doubt.

Read strides up to his position near the eastern tryline to be greeted with a technological octopus. Dozens of outstretched arms clutching phones and recording devices reach out towards him, while forming a perfect circle on the ends of that arc are the camera crews where I've managed to squeeze my rig right in the middle. I'll get a great shot, but working alone means I have to fight extra hard to get a word in because I'm bloody miles away from the All Blacks captain.

Read strides up to his position near the eastern tryline to be greeted with a technological octopus. Dozens of outstretched arms clutching phones and recording devices reach out towards him.

Read puts his hands on his hips and surveys the scene. He's done this many, many times before, but the look on his face this time means he doesn't need to say much to get across just how important this game is. As usual, it's a string of non-answers and clichés, but he does give away one bit of crucial info. He says 'we're hurting right now' because the Wallabies have taken a serious hack at the All Blacks' pride. I pipe up from the back.

'Skip, you said the All Blacks are hurting. Is that where you want to be a month out from the World Cup?'

'There are going to be things you look back on and say, well maybe that helped you and that didn't help you,' answers the All Blacks captain, which is about as close as you'll get to an admission in front of that many journalists that they've got a few things wrong in a World Cup year.

Read takes a breath and then slides back into the regulation 'we're only focused on this week' talk. That's enough for today, though. The talking stops. The next time we'll hear from Read is when he's either holding the Bledisloe Cup or handing it over to Michael Hooper.

39

WHAT HAPPENS WHEN YOU MAKE THE ALL BLACKS ANGRY

Eden Park, 17 August 2019
(34 days to the Rugby World Cup)

ALL BLACKS	**36**
WALLABIES	**0**

A LOT OF WORDS GET USED to describe the All Blacks—so much so that they kind of lose a bit of meaning. Ruthless. Tough. Rampant. Dominant. But probably the most overused is 'emphatic'. There've been so many 'emphatic' All Blacks wins that it's difficult to remember all of them off the top of your head. But there is one that stands out above all others.

At the decaying carcass of Athletic Park on 6 July 1996 the rain hammered in from the south, feeling like it had flown all the way from the South Pole. The Wallabies never stood a chance that day, and made it worse by not even facing the All Blacks' haka. They were soaked before the game even started, then spent the next 80 minutes wishing it'd just been called off. The 43–6 scoreline is probably the most famous in Bledisloe Cup history and, given the strength of Australian rugby at the time, came as a complete shock.

This performance by the All Blacks can safely have the word 'emphatic' attached to it without fear of hyperbole.

Tonight at Eden Park sees that sort of shock play out again, and this performance by the All Blacks can safely have the word 'emphatic' attached to it without fear of hyperbole. If Phil Kearns were here, it's highly unlikely he'd be sauntering over to share a lift ride with any New Zealand journalists afterwards. The difference between the All Blacks and the Wallabies is only one point away from that famous hiding in 1996, which Kearns played in—and they never once looked like winning tonight. From Christian Lealiifano sending the first kick-off out on the full, to who else but George freakin' Bridge scoring the last try, this entire evening belonged to the All Blacks.

Every single question from last week was answered. Every. Single. Question.

The Beauden Barrett and Richie Mo'unga combo has its best outing yet, mainly because Mo'unga is allowed to run the show fully. Barrett sits back, content to play the traditional role of fullback instead of chiming in at first receiver constantly like he has done for the past two games. In fact, Mo'unga has easily his best game in an All Blacks jersey, despite the uncharacteristic miss of an easy penalty at the end of the first half. Patrick Tuipulotu stands up and puts in a huge shift to make up for whatever the hell he thought he was doing last weekend in Perth. He's long got by on reputation alone, so to see him hurling his big frame into rucks and tackles is immensely reassuring. Brodie Retallick will hopefully be back, but Tuipulotu demonstrates that his big-game ability very much exists and can be called upon when required.

Bridge and Sevu Reece both end up on the score sheet. In addition, Bridge's defensive work sees him create the first try with a tackle that dislodges the ball from Reece Hodge's hands. He then turns provider with a stunning break and perfect pass inside for Aaron Smith to score. Sevu Reece, meanwhile, looks dangerous every time he gets the ball. Right now, you have to wonder whether Rieko Ioane and Ben Smith are actually going to make it back into the starting XV.

But perhaps the biggest question to be answered was that of just how important Sonny Bill Williams is to the All Blacks' game plan. The big man has one of his most influential games in a black jersey, stabilising play in the midfield and then launching himself onto a pass in the forty-fifth minute to score a try that effectively kills off any faint hopes of a Wallabies comeback. Williams was always going to be on the plane to Japan next month, but this display will at least provide some positive evidence to present to any of the blowhards out there who seem unimpressed with anything SBW does.

All of that, plus the fact that the All Blacks don't even concede a point—which proves that their defensive structure is entirely effective when they get it right. There was a lot of talk last week about having the right attitude going into the match, and it rings true if that really is the only thing different between this game and the last one.

Emphatic.

40

'NOT ON
MY WATCH'

Eden Park, 17 August 2019

STEVE HANSEN, IAN FOSTER AND Kieran Read are taking their sweet time to come out and talk to us post match in the Eden Park press conference room. It's now 10.30pm, an hour and a quarter since full-time. Cheika and Hooper have come and gone, despite the fact that they were supposed to be the second lot in. What started as excited chatter among the 30 or so of us in the room has now dissipated into a series of yawns and angry tuts at how long this is taking. Keyboards tap as those who have to file straight away craft something to pack around the quotes we're so desperately waiting for. Which in itself is ironic, considering how much we all joke about how we can predict what they're going to say anyway.

While the All Blacks have dominated on the field, it hasn't been such a great night for NZ Rugby. For a start, we were squeezed into secondary media boxes because the main one (which takes pride of place bang on halfway) had been converted into a VIP lounge for some sponsors. Some serious miscommunications also occurred, the first of which was that no team sheets were given to us. While it didn't cause any headaches, it certainly elicited a few grumbles. Then, no one told us the prime minister was showing up to make a presentation at half-time. From our now substandard view of the field, it was hard to even make her out.

Every now and then, Joe Locke pops his head through the door and apologises for the lateness. The team are socialising with the prime minister, which is somewhat hard to believe considering that if she'd really been in the All Blacks' changing room for that long she'd be hammered drunk by now. Then the word is they're socialising with the Wallabies, which makes more sense but also doesn't explain why the captain and coaches can't duck out and let the others share a few beers and stories with the Aussies.

The clock ticks past 11; we're now well behind schedule. The venerable Phil Gifford is here, as he always is when a big game is on at Eden Park, but even he's run out of stories to tell from his time as an All Blacks insider back in the '80s and '90s. I'm actually feeling like drifting off to sleep when Hansen, Foster and Read finally stroll in. Read's in his suit rather than the sweat-soaked jersey and shorts he usually wears. There is a palpable look of vindication on all three men's faces, especially Foster's. It's not smugness, or even relief. They've kept us waiting, and maybe that is the message to all of us who wrote columns in the previous seven days doubting just where this team is at. *Don't doubt us, motherfuckers. We know what we're doing.*

Before they even answer question one, the performance, coupled with a steely gaze of determination on the task ahead, tells us basically everything we needed to know anyway: this is the sort of game the All Blacks are taking to the World Cup. They've clicked into a team that has the ability to score a lot of tries, and defensively hold a rival to zero.

As well as that, it's also noted that this will be Hansen's last-ever defence of the Bledisloe Cup, a trophy that the All Blacks have held long before he even became coach—16 years in fact. All year he's been banging on about its importance, and he utters a quote about why winning this game means so much to him: 'It's just a nice feeling to be able to say "not on my watch".'

THE LATE PRESS CONFERENCE MEANS a late night for all of us. I finally get to bed at 2am after writing what effectively amounts to an apology for comparing the team to its 1991 counterparts earlier in the week.

Of course, there's another press conference in the morning, back at the Heritage—this time, though, there are nowhere near as many of us in attendance. What amounts to about half a dozen are surprised when Hansen bounds into the room on time, which leads to an awkward wait because the press officer hasn't shown up yet. Hansen can't go on the record without him present, so we twiddle our thumbs and wait—again.

When we finally get under way, Hansen talks through the game now that he's had a chance to look at a replay. There's more about how pleased he is with the players who stood up, both the new boys and the ones who had a point to prove. Then he makes his most important statement about how the past two weeks have affected the team. While this could be an opportunity to get angry like last year in Rome, what he says is just as poignant a reflection on exactly what the pressure the All Blacks face means.

'The day that New Zealand rugby doesn't have the external scrutiny like it does, then the game is not where it was. People care and have high expectations, and those drive the internal expectations as well,' says Hansen.

'It's irrelevant whether it's a good thing or a bad thing. It's constant and it keeps you honest. The day that New Zealand rugby doesn't have the external scrutiny like it does, then the game is not where it was. People care and have high expectations, and those drive the internal expectations as well.'

It's an acknowledgement, at least to me anyway, that what we do as the media is crucial to the way the team performs. If we didn't do our job, Hansen and the All Blacks probably wouldn't have theirs. It's nice to hear him at least flirt with the idea of admitting it.

41

THE BIG DAY

**Eden Park, 28 August 2019
(23 days to the Rugby World Cup)**

THERE'S A SLIGHT CHANGE OF scene for this All Blacks World Cup squad announcement. Last time they did this in Parliament, with the then-prime minister, who liked to be photographed with as many All Blacks as he possibly could. In 2019, though, we're in a familiar space—in fact, the room that Steve Hansen waited so long to come out of the last time we were at Eden Park.

They've cleaned up the long changing room, flanked on either side by cubicles into which the All Blacks can fit their broad shoulders. A few of the spaces are adorned with the new jersey specifically designed for the tournament. A table full of finger food runs down the middle, which is good because the room is absolutely crammed with media. There are around 60 of us, with a dozen cameras and the NZ Rugby comms people bustling about and making sure that everyone is in the right place. We take our seats, anticipating the 31 names that are about to be read out.

That's the weird thing, though. This squad, unlike the one named back at the Ponsonby clubrooms, should be pretty straightforward. The only real question marks are whether Liam Squire has decided he wants to play for the All Blacks again, and whether Ngani Laumape will somehow force his way in. Everyone else has had their ticket punched after the last test, really. But Hansen has one more twist for everyone to talk about before the day is out.

He ambles in, along with Ian Foster, Grant Fox and Brent Impey. The chairman takes the podium again and, to my ears anyway, mangles the Māori and Polynesian greetings, again. The three Barrett brothers are named first, then we wait for the list to get to L so we can learn Laumape's fate. Except there's a notable omission before we get to that.

There is a bit of a gasp. The inside word was that Squire had made himself available–after all, he's been in devastating form for Tasman in the Mitre 10 Cup.

Owen Franks is gone. Turns out his absence from the last Bledisloe Cup test wasn't a warning; it was the aftermath of a last chance in Perth. Eyebrows lift around the changing room as Impey names Nepo Laulala, then Atu Moli—both replacements for Franks and confirmation that Laumape indeed hasn't made it. Then Retallick, Savea, Smith, Smith . . . then Ta'avao. There is a bit of a gasp. The inside word was that Squire had made himself available—after all, he's been in devastating form for Tasman in the Mitre 10 Cup. Those are our talking points, and Hansen's explanation around the Squire situation is, well, pretty intriguing.

Apparently, Squire is indeed keen, but will only be used as a replacement player if there's an injury. What's gone from being a potentially do-or-die decision is now somewhat of an after-thought for Hansen, who is clearly happy with the new combination of Cane and Savea on the side of the scrum. It does say a bit about the supposed planning that's gone into the squad, though. We all thought there was a back-up plan for everything worked out well over a year ago, whereas this proves either that Hansen is not rigidly stuck in his ways and is open to the sort of form fluidity that emerges in Super Rugby, or that he's got lucky with a stopgap solution that seems to be working right now.

Franks, though, that's a big one: 108 tests' worth of experience will be watching the World Cup at home like almost every other New Zealander.

Part of that equation is Luke Jacobson, who has now become the dictionary definition of timing your run to perfection. The 22-year-old has been on the field once in an All Blacks jersey, and will reap the reward of being as close to Squire as Hansen can get. His Super Rugby form has trumped the test auditions put in by Vaea Fifita and Shannon Frizell, with the latter now ironically set to battle for a place in the Tasman Mitre 10 Cup squad with Squire.

Franks, though, that's a big one: 108 tests' worth of experience will be watching the World Cup at home like almost every other New Zealander. He'd started his test career a decade ago and won two World Cup finals, with the 2011 one the last time an All Blacks front row had started and finished a test match. He's so long been part of the team furniture that his lack of form has probably gone unnoticed by most of the public, because it certainly has by the media. The truth is, no one really knows much about propping other than props, and they're in short supply as pundits. Besides, the All Blacks scrum was generally considered to be hitting all its KPIs so far this season—indeed, one of the few bright points to come out of the Perth disaster was that for an entire half a seven-man pack managed to not only hold parity but also sometimes dominate their opposition.

But mobility was the key to Franks' exclusion, which means that the long-standing joke about him never scoring a try in an All Blacks jersey is actually now an accurate reflection on why he's on the outer. Joe Moody, who came out of nowhere to play a big role in the last World Cup campaign, now finds himself the most experienced prop with 40 caps.

It shows also that Hansen has no time for sentimentality. Four years ago, five long-serving All Blacks used the tournament as a backdrop to riding off into the sunset after the happy ending at Twickenham. Franks has signalled that this season in New Zealand will be his last, and will link up with his brother Ben at Northampton after the World Cup. Now it'll be after the Mitre 10 Cup.

A sensationalist headline later that day claims that Franks has 'broken his silence' on the issue, which is a tad overblown given that it's only been a matter of hours since he was dropped.

'I'm well aware as a professional athlete, and especially an All Black, that your time in the jersey isn't owed,' he says.

Hansen seems to be in a pretty good mood today. He throws in a few jokes, including a genuinely funny reference to *Weekend at Bernie's* when describing Fox's traditionally mute role during these announcements. A queue forms in front of him for one-on-one interviews, so I sit back and smash the food table. Eden Park always puts on a good spread.

The 2019 All Blacks Rugby World Cup squad	
Hookers	Dane Coles, Liam Coltman, Codie Taylor
Props	Nepo Laulala, Joe Moody, Atu Moli, Angus Ta'avao, Ofa Tu'ungafasi
Locks	Scott Barrett, Brodie Retallick, Patrick Tuipulotu, Samuel Whitelock
Loose forwards	Sam Cane, Luke Jacobson, Kieran Read, Ardie Savea, Matt Todd
Halfbacks	TJ Perenara, Aaron Smith, Brad Weber
First five-eighths	Beauden Barrett, Richie Mo'unga
Midfielders	Ryan Crotty, Jack Goodhue, Anton Lienert-Brown, Sonny Bill Williams
Utility back	Jordie Barrett
Outside backs	George Bridge, Rieko Ioane, Sevu Reece, Ben Smith

42

THE CITY
OF THE
FUTURE

**FMG Stadium Waikato, 5 September 2019
(15 days to the Rugby World Cup)**

ALL BLACKS   92
TONGA   7

HAMILTON HAS FINALLY GOT Lime scooters. Test week is dominated by locals tear-assing around on them, and, given the main narrative around the test this weekend against Tonga, their reputation for being exceptionally unsafe is a bit worrying. That's because the only real thing anyone is concerned about with this game is that the All Blacks can all get through it uninjured before they fly off to Japan on Monday. There is probably just as much chance of one of them busting an ankle due to a Lime accident as a Tongan tackle.

So it's not very reassuring when, on the way to the Thursday press conference, Anton Lienert-Brown and Richie Mo'unga zip past me along Victoria Street.

But it does set the tone for what ends up being the most light-hearted and friendly time with the All Blacks all year. After Hansen comes and goes, adding a few more bricks to the wall he's building around his plans for the next two months, Ryan Crotty and Codie Taylor take the hot seats at the Ibis hotel. For Crotty, this Saturday will be the last time he runs out in an All Blacks jersey on New Zealand soil. When he's reminded of that fact, it becomes really obvious that it will be hard for him to say goodbye to the All Blacks. You can actually hear him gulp when he answers.

'My family will be coming up, so it means a lot. Playing for the All Blacks, you see what it means to a lot of other people, your success. I'm getting a bit emotional talking about it.'

Crotty is a popular guy among the media. He's articulate, friendly, and able to convey the drudgery of what the All Blacks usually say in a Michael Hooper-type way of fooling you into thinking he's saying more. The past couple of years have been eventful ones for him, to say the least. Crotty has become a key man in the ongoing concussion conversation, as he's been knocked out and got back up again more times than anyone would like to see. He's had to field constant questions about whether he should be playing at all, let alone where he sees his place in the always congested midfield picture. But he takes all of them in his stride and battles through his injuries. He's named to start at second five for the Tonga game in what was supposed to be a full-strength

All Blacks team, but which has had to make do with a few players having to cover some injuries.

One of them is the Lime scooter-riding Mo'unga, who has done some damage to his shoulder in the last test. It means that Josh Ioane is named on the bench, and this time his old man only has a short drive down from Pukekohe rather than an 11-hour flight to another continent to watch his son finally take the field as an All Black.

It's all smiles and jokes at the All Blacks' hotel. While there is humour in the Tongan camp as well, it's more of a gallows kind. We're waiting for the Tongan team to come out and train at FMG Stadium Waikato, and they're preceded by their coaching staff, which includes former Wellington and Hurricanes assistant Richard Watt. He comes from the Poneke club, the same as Dane Coles, and shares the All Black hooker's passion for telling it like it is. Without even asking for an interview, Watty comes over and plants his hands on the railing in front of us.

It's all smiles and jokes at the All Blacks' hotel. While there is humour in the Tongan camp as well, it's more of a gallows kind.

'What a fucking week boys . . . what a fucking week. We got ourselves a starting hooker from Facebook!'

Watt is referring to Suia Maile, a 24-year-old roofer from Christchurch who has been rushed into the squad to cover for injuries. After asking around, the coaching staff were given

Maile's name and assurance that he'd been in good form for his Shirley club side. He'd been uploading videos of his highlights, and these clips have proved good enough for head coach Toutai Kefu, Watt and the others to fast-track Maile into the team. A fortnight ago, Maile was nailing roofs on houses in the bitter Christchurch winter, but on Saturday he will be marking Codie Taylor and playing against the All Blacks in what will be his first-ever first-class game. Josh Ioane has been in the All Blacks system for months now, sheltered from any potential domestic game that might cause him unnecessary risk, and is a fully contracted player not even in the Rugby World Cup squad. If there's anything that shows the difference between the haves and the have-nots of world rugby right now, this is it.

All week we've been hearing about the physicality that the Tongans would bring—a very lazy generalisation that's been bandied around a lot and isn't really grounded in any truth.

Then there's the scoreline that the All Blacks actually rack up. It starts with a Sevu Reece try, features four more from George Bridge, and doubles to Ryan Crotty and Ben Smith. Just to make sure all the players saying goodbye to New Zealand get an appropriate send-off, the skipper gets one as well. All week we've been hearing about the physicality that the Tongans would bring—a very lazy generalisation that's been bandied around a lot and isn't really grounded in any truth. The truth is, Tonga never stood a chance in this game—just like every other time they've ever faced the All Blacks. The 80 minutes that plays out in Hamilton is no more than a glorified training session, and it ends with the All Blacks voluntarily dropping down to 14 men. Crotty leaves the field after they've used all their substitutions, which they probably could have done at half-time considering they were up by 54 points.

One move they do make at half-time is to give Beauden Barrett a rest. It means Josh Ioane gets an entire half to show New Zealand that things will be in capable hands if disaster strikes in Japan, and he doesn't waste any time doing so. He sends the second-half re-start high into the airspace above the lush pitch, which is badly misjudged by Tongan lock Sam Lousi. It falls into the arms of the flying Bridge, who scoots away to score his second try. Lousi, perhaps with that in the back of his mind, lays out Ioane later in the half with another poor bit of judgement in the form of a shoulder charge, and gets a yellow card.

It's the first time the All Blacks have played an afternoon game in New Zealand for eight years. There are a lot of children and families in attendance, and the atmosphere is an awful lot more upbeat than the funeral-like settings of the Wellington and Auckland tests. However, things quickly revert to form when it comes to the post-match interviews in the stadium gym that's been converted into a press conference room. In a shambolic turn of events, the schedule is brought forward, backward and then reversed in order—much to the chagrin of the cameramen who have discarded their tripods in anticipation of the players arriving.

However, the first man in is Ioane, who is on the verge of tears when he speaks about having his family there to watch. Bridge once again chuckles his way through describing another afternoon of having everything fall his way, and is asked twice if he'd had Marc Ellis's record of six tries for the All Blacks in a test in the back of his mind. Considering that Bridge was only a matter of months old when that record was set, he answers no and it's entirely believable.

One man who is in no mood for jokes, though, is Steve Hansen. It's kind of a shame after the relatively fun week we've had that it becomes clear he just wants to get on the plane and get the hell out of here. His answers are terse, and he admonishes a couple of journos for what he perceives to be substandard questions.

'I'm pretty disappointed with some of these, because you could answer them yourselves,' he snaps. 'Ask us something invigorating for the fans to read.'

Yeah, easier said than done, coach. Anything we do say that does stray from the usual line of asking about the game is generally met with a sigh and a dismissal. Today he's dismissing pretty much everything, despite the fact that the All Blacks have won by 85 points. The good vibes, which were in short supply in the room anyway, evaporate entirely after that and we plod out the remaining time before the coaches depart. But Hansen does leave us with something: admitting he's happy with where the All Blacks are at two weeks out from the World Cup. The next time we'll talk to him will be in Tokyo, so hopefully he's in a better mood.

43

THE STATE OF
THE UNION

**Eden Park, 8 September 2019
(12 days to the Rugby World Cup)**

THE NEXT DAY, I'M BACK in Auckland and wandering across the Bond Street bridge that spans the Northwestern Motorway. An electronic sign reads: EVENT TODAY EDEN PARK. Usually, it's followed by EXPECT DELAYS, but they haven't bothered to switch that bit on because it wouldn't be true. While the All Blacks will fly out to the World Cup tomorrow, the lack of the sign's second line is more or less a microcosm of what sort of shape domestic rugby is in these days.

The event in question is a Mitre 10 Cup game between Auckland and Canterbury, the two most successful unions in the country. Between them they have won the national provincial championship, in all its guises, 31 times in its 45-year history. They played what is regarded as the greatest Ranfurly Shield game of all time in 1985. Last year, they combined for a thrilling final at Eden Park that went to extra time and saw Auckland win in front of a big crowd.

This used to be a fixture that would draw in at least 30,000 to Eden Park and generate articles and discussion in the weeks, if not months, leading up to it. But here we are with a handful of supporters mostly wearing their local club colours.

The reason the crowd was so big? The union flung open the doors of Eden Park and made it free entry, knowing full well that charging people to get in would result in an embarrassingly empty stadium for the provincial game's supposed showpiece. That's not the case today, and it's underscored by the fact that a fair number of the game's attendees are able to get a park on Reimers Avenue which hugs the only stand that's open today, the northern stand. When I make my way around to the media box, the echo of the few thousand who are in bounces off the completely deserted southern stand. It feels like they are playing the noise through the loudspeakers.

This used to be a fixture that would draw in at least 30,000 to Eden Park and generate articles and discussion in the weeks, if not months, leading up to it. But here we are, sitting in the biggest stadium in the country with a handful of supporters mostly wearing their local club colours. That's something of a sad sight, because if the rep scene is looking unhealthy, at club level the game is on its knees. There are fewer and fewer players coming through to replenish the playing stocks at the grassroots level, despite the fact that the profile of secondary-school rugby has never been higher. If anything, though, the glorification of what essentially amounts to advertisements for mostly private schools has somewhat set back the development of anyone who hasn't been earmarked for higher honours by the time they're 15.

Tellingly, the vast majority of those schools are in Auckland. The arms race that exists in first XV rugby finally had its first official off-field flare-up earlier this year, when the 1A competition members refused to play powerhouse Saint Kentigern College on the basis that they'd been unfairly stripping playing resources. It led to St Kent's pulling out of the boys' schools national competition and entering the co-ed one instead. The model that is being run by these schools is now having an obviously negative effect on numbers: boys' and girls' secondary-school rugby teams within Auckland fell from 225 in 2013 to 188 in 2017, and 181 in 2018. North Harbour had 92 secondary boys' and girls' rugby teams in 2014 and 64 in 2018.

The drop-off rate after players leave school is the biggest pain point for rugby. It's meant that club rugby at premier level has often been a farcical mess and, below that, grades are drying up. College rugby is on a fast track to becoming like the exploitative American NCAA (National Collegiate Athletic Association) model, where only the top players are being looked after before being spat out into a professional environment that can't accommodate all of them. And rugby's governing body either can't, or won't, do a thing about it.

EARLIER IN THE SEASON, I had hauled my weary body into the College Rifles RFC clubrooms. It's a well-run club in the heart of Remuera. It owns its own grounds, which have been converted from a muddy paddock to state-of-the-art synthetic grass fields. There's a gym, two covered training areas, and the rooms upstairs are festooned with memorabilia of its rich history.

The club was busy—there had been a few home games on, so there were plenty of polo-shirt-clad men of varying ages parked up on barstools and draining jugs of beer. Rifles is a nicely presented club, with plush carpet and a slick new interior makeover, but the scene that day was essentially a replica of every other club in the country at that particular time. Late Saturday afternoon, the time when beer tastes its best. Up on the wall is a TV that updates the Premier grade scores. It'd been a good day for our Prem side. A record one, in fact—they'd beaten East Tamaki 126–3. But Rifles weren't alone in the one-sided results department. Ponsonby had thrashed Waitakere 61–7; Eden pasted Te Papapa 79–14; Marist strolled to an 80–0 win over Mt Wellington. The only score that was remotely close was Suburbs' 26–12 victory over Grammar TEC. While you can put this down to a quirk of the draw that pitted all the haves with the have-nots in one afternoon, it demonstrated in stark relief the absolute disparity that exists in club rugby right now.

Go lower down the grades, and it made for even bleaker reading. My team plays in the First grade, which is actually the third senior men's grade after Premiers and Premier Development but was somehow renamed 'First'—presumably to make us feel better. The irony is that there is no open senior men's competition after First grade. Three open men's grades in the largest catchment area in the country.

Impey breathlessly admits that the Crusaders won't be changing their name, and apparently were never going to, in the wake of the 15 March terror attacks.

Not long after that lopsided weekend, I'm listening to Radio Sport in my car. NZ Rugby Chairman Brent Impey is on the air with host Jim Kayes, and what he's saying pretty much sums up why the game is in this parlous state. Impey looks, sounds and most probably thinks exactly the same way every other man in his position has across the history of the organisation. First, he breathlessly admits that the Crusaders won't be changing their name, and apparently were never going to, in the wake of the 15 March terror attacks. In a long, rambling and obviously unprepared statement, Impey says it came down to money and contracts, and that changing the jersey design would be too costly. He then completely contradicts this by saying that the logo will in fact change next season, which means the jerseys and merchandise will all need to be changed with it.

Kayes presses him further about the decision, but Impey veers off into talking about digital revenue and broadcasting, then inadvertently downplays the quality of content on the official All Blacks website—to which Kayes is a contributor. But this diversion probably reveals more about the current state of affairs than Impey intends, as the preoccupation with money soon has him answering a question about the health of the game at the grassroots level.

'You've got tradition versus changing society on one hand. The other conflict you've got is that professional players need money. Only 0.4 per cent of players are professionals, against the other 99.6 which is the community game,' Impey says.

This is the bit where I'm expecting him to actually admit there's a problem. But instead, it's just another trailing, 'So, ummm, yes, ummm . . . everybody wants more.'

The All Blacks fly out to Japan in the morning, but while they may come home with a World Cup, there is another huge battle looming to simply save the game they get paid so well to play.

It's frustratingly obtuse, especially when Impey then overtly admits that Auckland is the biggest problem area, and something they should be doing is encouraging new ethnicities to play the game. That's probably a good place to start in Auckland, but there is no mention of whether NZ Rugby will actually do anything about it.

Now I'm sitting at Eden Park, where the problem used to be empty seats but is now entire empty stands. Provincial rugby is getting the same treatment that club rugby has had ever since the game turned professional, and it's time to face the fact that the trickle-down economic model NZ Rugby is running is simply serving to make the rich richer.

The All Blacks fly out to Japan in the morning, but while they may come home with a World Cup, there is another huge battle looming to simply save the game they get paid so well to play.

PART THREE
THE CUP

44

WE ARE WHERE OUR FEET ARE

Yokohama International Stadium, 21 September 2019 (first World Cup pool match)

ALL BLACKS	**23**
SPRINGBOKS	**13**

THE GAUDILY COLOURED, OVAL-SHAPED PIECE of synthetic material wrapped around a tightly trapped pocket of air leaves the boot of Beauden Barrett and travels high into the sky above Yokohama International Stadium. It reaches its zenith and tumbles down, end over end and into the waiting arms of Willie le Roux, who is immediately swamped by a tide of black jerseys on his 22. And just like that, after all the waiting, planning and preparation, the All Blacks' 2019 Rugby World Cup campaign is officially under way. There are 30 players and a referee on the park, 63,000 in the vast stands surrounding them, and millions watching around the world. The only thing the All Blacks care about for the next 80 minutes—indeed the next six weeks—is where that ball goes next.

There have been a few changes at the stadium since we were here last October—for starters, the copious amounts of World Cup signage and a doubling of the staff patrolling the long corridors. Security has been beefed up too—our faces are now scanned on entry. Makes sense, given that New Zealand's prime minister is here, sitting not that far away from us in one of the luxury boxes that hosted hungover past rugby players in their jandals last year. (Japanese Prime Minister Shinzō Abe attended the opening match last night between Japan and Russia, wearing his team's jersey; Vladimir Putin presumably watched it on TV from the Kremlin.)

Jacinda Ardern took time to visit the All Blacks during the week, out at their training base next to the gigantic construction site of the swimming complex for next year's Olympic Games. She whipped in and out in a diplomatic car, and wished Kieran Read and the team good luck. There was one memorable picture taken of her talking with Sonny Bill Williams, with the midfielder towering over her with his gigantic arms resting on his hips. It makes sense that they would have a one-to-one—Ardern's electorate is Williams' home neighbourhood of Mt Albert in Auckland and she's actually a rugby league fan anyway.

But the week that led up to the game wasn't just photo opportunities and hobnobbing. Williams himself was the centre of the first big load of bullshit to be dumped on the public regarding the All Blacks at the World Cup, with a journalist back in New Zealand claiming he was on a plane home a week out from the first game. While it's not too much of a stretch for that to actually happen, given Williams' propensity to get injured, the problem was that it wasn't actually rooted in any fact. The 'story' even went on to claim that Ngani Laumape was already on the way over.

Laumape had been on everyone's radar anyway after he starred in a dramatic Mitre 10 Cup escape for his Manawatū side. He scored a hat-trick as they rallied to beat Southland, which rekindled incredulity about him not being in the All Blacks. Even given the tissue-paper standard of defence that he was up against in that competition, it's unlikely the argument is going to die down. Especially if Williams does get hurt and plays poorly. Right now, though, Williams is sitting in one of the plastic seats of the bench with number 23 on his back. Ryan Crotty and Anton Lienert-Brown are out in the middle of the park, concentrating on what the ball will do next amid the frenzied roar of the crowd and the muscular attention of the Springboks.

Rassie Erasmus wound up the mind games during the week with some attempts to talk about the refereeing. The match is being controlled by none other than Jérôme Garcès, the man who sent Scott Barrett from the field in Perth. Barrett has served his suspension and is back out on the field, so he can begin to make amends with the Frenchman immediately. The Boks coach claimed that the era of the All Blacks potentially benefiting from marginal refereeing decisions—due to being the best side in the world—should theoretically be over.

'Whilst I've got a lot of respect for South Africa and particularly Rassie, I don't agree with what he's doing,' Hansen told us in the vast press conference room the day before the game. 'He's trying to put pressure on referees externally and they're under enough pressure already. They don't need us coaches doing what he's doing. You can get emotional about that and think that they're picking on you and not on the opposition. We've done it ourselves. At the end of the day, referees try to do the best they can do. Yes, they don't always get it right all the time, and we've suffered from that just like other teams have. It's a big game—we just need to let the ref get on with it and prepare for it himself.'

The Boks coach claimed that the era of the All Blacks potentially benefiting from marginal refereeing decisions–due to being the best side in the world–should theoretically be over.

While that message was clearly intended to get into the officials' heads as well, there's someone else sitting in the stands near us who definitely has a lot going on upstairs right now. From the ecstasy of being selected for his first World Cup, Luke Jacobson has come crashing back down to earth after being ruled out of the entire tournament before a whistle has even been blown. He's aggravated the concussion symptoms that kept him out of so much of Super Rugby, which is extremely concerning for the 22-year-old's playing future. Shockingly, he admitted that last year he'd had headaches for four or five months. Jacobson hasn't returned home just yet, though, because he's not medically fit to fly on a plane.

Taking his place is Shannon Frizell, who is sitting in Jacobson's spot on the bench. The Tongan-born Tasman Mako player certainly looks the part of a bruising loose forward, yet comes in with an asterisk next to his name because Hansen really doesn't have anyone else to call. Vaea Fifita and Dalton Papalii have both managed to get injured in the interim, which rules them out. And, according to Hansen's own words at the original team naming, that spot should belong to Liam Squire. This odd turn of events was purportedly explained by Hansen in one line of dialogue earlier this week, when he said that 'it was too early' for Squire to join the team as a replacement, which didn't sound altogether convincing. (The sad part of all this is that sitting half a world away is Brad Shields. He hasn't made it into the England squad for the World Cup, beaten out by the likes of Sam Underhill, Tom Curry, Billy Vunipola and Courtney Lawes. Had he stayed and taken his opportunity with the All Blacks, there's every chance he'd be on the bench or maybe even out on the field in a black jersey right now. He's about as close as you can get to a like-for-like replacement for Squire, so it just goes to show that you never know what you're leaving behind when you head offshore. His story is far from over, though: it is possible he will add to the handful of test caps he has already earned for his adopted country.)

The All Blacks haven't exactly been all that convincing with the media in general this week. They've pulled some vintage moves when it comes to media disruption, one example being the numbers allowed to attend an event at a local shrine—we're told there's room for only five of us, but then roughly ten times that number of local media show up. Plus, the day Ardern comes to visit results in a totally unapologetic hour-long delay, and we have no access to film her interactions with the team. Their security isn't exactly at military precision just yet, though—thinking I was running late to the training base in Tatsuminomori Seaside Park, I simply breezed through a gate and onto the field before voluntarily giving myself up when I noticed there were no cameras around yet.

Shannon Frizell certainly looks the part of a bruising loose forward, yet comes in with an asterisk next to his name because Hansen really doesn't have anyone else to call.

While the All Blacks can do what they like out at their training base, press conferences are a different story. They're now under the control of the World Cup organisers, who expect a great deal more out of the pressers than the guys are used to. They even have an official sitting next to them at the table directing the questions and making sure it runs almost double the length of a regular session, mainly for the benefit of the mostly English travelling media.

One thing the All Blacks coach says on the Friday is a reiteration of something we've been hearing all year, though. In reaction to yet another question about the long-term prospects of the All Blacks in the tournament, Hansen calmly states that the team 'are where our feet are'. It's a phrase that first came out of Sonny Bill Williams' mouth earlier on, leading us to believe that it was something he'd made up specifically. But then it kept getting repeated as a way to replace the very tired 'one game at a time' rhetoric, and it sounds an awful lot better. By now, Hansen is saying it often—in fact, he drops it in three times during the press conference.

THERE'S NO DOUBT ABOUT WHERE the All Blacks' feet are in the first 15 or so minutes of the opening game, anyway. They're back-pedalling as the Springboks pick up where they left off in Wellington in July, dominating possession and territory. Handre Pollard strikes first with a penalty, and even from high up in the stands you can sense a feeling of panic extending all the way to the opposite hemisphere, as New Zealanders immediately start projecting worst-case scenarios. But then something happens that turns the tide of the game completely.

Sevu Reece, who has retained his spot along with George Bridge on the wing, hasn't had the happiest time of it so far. He's been smashed a couple of times by a willing Boks defensive line. A kick goes over his head as he's caught out of position and it rolls towards the touchline 10 metres away from the All Blacks' tryline. If it goes out, chances are the Boks will settle in for a sustained period of residence in the All Blacks' half. Knowing that, Reece elegantly tips the ball back over the plane of touch while dancing ever so close to the line. He regathers it beautifully and flicks it back to Beauden Barrett, who launches a massive touchfinder all the way down to halfway. That kills off the South African period of dominance and, not long after, Bridge makes them pay even more dearly.

As the All Blacks enter the Springboks' 22, the ball is spun into midfield where Beauden Barrett is waiting. Bridge sees what could happen next, so instead of calling for the pass he points Barrett towards the tryline—Pieter-Steph du Toit has come flying up out of the line and left him a huge gap to run through. All Bridge needs to do is keep up, so when Barrett is caught by Eben Etzebeth he collects the ball and dives over to score the All Blacks' first try of the tournament.

While his dive over the line needs work, it's one of those glorious moments All Blacks fans will remember for a long time.

Three minutes later, though, it's another Barrett heading to the line for his moment of redemption. The last time Scott Barrett interacted with referee Jérôme Garcès, he was wearing an extremely distraught look as the Frenchman produced a red card in Perth. Now, he's regaining his feet to see Garcès blowing a clarion call on his whistle with his arm pointing straight up. Scott Barrett has just run 30 metres to score under the posts off a break by Anton Lienert-Brown, and while his dive over the line needs work, it's one of those glorious moments All Blacks fans will remember for a long time. It gives the All Blacks a 14–3 lead, and that will be ultimately all they'll need.

Sonny Bill Williams comes off the bench for Ryan Crotty in

the second half, and as he removes his jacket and heads across the astroturf-covered athletics track towards the field the people in the stand closest to him roar, and it's infectious. Pretty soon the whole stadium is abuzz, which is probably the most enthusiastic reception Williams has received from a crowd since his time in the NRL. In fact, the entire reception the All Blacks are getting compared with the drab atmosphere of Westpac Stadium and Eden Park should really be putting New Zealand fans to shame. There is no doubt right now that the Japanese see the All Blacks as the team to aspire to, and they're letting us hear it with deafening chants and roars when the ball is swung onto attack. A healthy number of South African fans are in attendance too, but so far the loudest they've got is singing during the haka.

For all the worries, dramas and frustration leading up to the tournament, the All Blacks have pulled out a completely All Blacks-like performance.

Noise or not, though, we've seen this game play out before. In fact, it's starting to look an awful lot like the last time these two sides played at a World Cup back in 2015. That day, while the Springboks kept themselves within a penalty goal of the lead for the whole game, it was clear from start to finish that the All Blacks were never going to lose. After the double-punch by Bridge and Scott Barrett, the rest of the game plays out the same way. Even though du Toit makes up for his bad defensive read with a try after half-time, the All Blacks simply sit back and wait for Faf de Klerk to launch yet another box kick. While the Boks have a ton of attacking talent in their backline, it's being nullified by the defensive reads of the All Blacks and solid form under the ball. The bench comes on, does its job, and before you know it, it's 23–13 with only minutes to play.

For all the worries, dramas and frustration leading up to the tournament, the All Blacks have pulled out a completely All Blacks-like performance. They walk off the field and under the stands, another day at work done. One down, six to go.

45

HOME AWAY FROM HOME

Ōita, 25 September 2019

WHEN WE STEP OFF THE plane and look around it's hard to believe just how beautiful this island is. But Kyushu was where it was all supposed to go down if someone hadn't figured out how to make an atomic bomb. If Operation Olympic had actually gone ahead in November 1945, Kyushu would be known as the site of one of the bloodiest battles in the entire history of the world instead of a laid-back tourist spot full of spa pools and friendly locals.

Olympic was the first part of the plan the Allies were to carry out in order to capture Japan, using Kyushu as a staging base to finish the job in 1946 with another massive landing code-named Coronet. Of course, it would've taken a lot longer than that, with optimistic estimates suggesting that it would take until 1947 at the absolute earliest to win a ground campaign which would've been a race to capture as much of the country as possible before the Soviet

Union did from the north. If that had been the case, it's more than likely that Japan would've been split in two and become the Cold War flashpoint that ended up happening to Korea. Given the rabid anti-communist tendencies of the Japanese both pre- and post-war (even more so than the Americans), there would've been another—probably bigger and potentially nuclear—conflict than the one that happened just across the Korea Strait.

Instead, Kyushu felt the full force of atomic weapons when the southernmost city of Nagasaki was hit by a plutonium-based nuclear bomb nicknamed 'Fat Man'. It was ostensibly done to end the war, but in reality it was probably more of a statement to the Russians—who had declared war on the Japanese the day before and were about to sweep through their northern Chinese territory—to stop right where they were. Of course, the Soviets didn't know that the Americans had just used up the second of only two bombs they actually had, so the first big bluff of the Cold War was on before hostilities even officially began.

Right now, though, no one seems overly concerned with geopolitics and savage history because there's a different kind of cold war going on between coaches. While press conferences with the All Blacks in Tokyo have been mostly straightforward affairs with a noticeable lack of many local journalists, down in Ōita things are quite different. Like Perth, there is a ton of local interest in the team and how the region can leverage the attention they're going to get from around the world in the next few weeks. Steve Hansen was noticeably underwhelmed when first asked about what he was looking forward to during the team's stay, which was a shame considering he'd actually been in a pretty good mood following the match.

In fact, everyone has been. It very much feels as if the aftermath of the Springboks game is one of relief more than celebration, and Hansen goes so far as to admit that the All Blacks have had the toughest game of the weekend. It was definitely the most intense, given that the only other really big match-up, between Ireland and Scotland, turned out to be a dud. Our old friend Joe 'Eyes of Ice' Schmidt made his first statement of the tournament, helped out by some wet weather in Yokohama that played right into the Irish game plan of choking the life out of their opponents. The Scots— who are really only good for one game a year, and have already played it back in their outrageous 38-all draw with England during the Six Nations—had no chance. Knowing full well that they might meet Ireland again at the business end of the tournament, the All Blacks staff keep a good eye on the game, but Ian Foster can't help but chuck in a pointed comment on the 27–3 Irish win.

'One team came to play, the other one to defend.'

It very much feels as if the aftermath of the Springboks game is one of relief more than celebration, and Hansen goes so far as to admit that the All Blacks have had the toughest game of the weekend.

The result is a bad one for the Scots. They also have Japan and Manu Sāmoa in their pool, and on the evidence either of those two games could result in a loss that will send them crashing out of the tournament. Right now, the dream scenario would be that the All Blacks get set up for a rematch with Japan in the quarter-final at the venue where they met back in November 2018.

As we waited for the baggage to come out, the ground crew sent ahead a giant plastic sashimi plate on the conveyor belt to a decent amount of mirth from the tired travellers.

But that possibility feels like a long way away yet. Between now and then, there are three weeks of essentially opposed training runs masquerading as tests against Canada, Namibia and Italy, so the focus is on figuring out something interesting to talk about and getting the All Blacks to comment. We were greeted in Ōita with a regulation bit of wholesome Japanese humour: as we waited for the baggage to come out, the ground crew sent ahead a giant plastic sashimi plate on the conveyor belt to a decent amount of mirth from the tired travellers. I took a video of the makeshift sushi-train and posted it on Twitter. Frustratingly, it ended up being the most engaging bit of social media content of the tournament (over 1000 likes and retweets), which hopefully says more about Twitter's algorithm than my ability as a rugby pundit.

IT'S HOT IN ŌITA, UNCOMFORTABLY SO. It only takes a stroll of about a hundred metres from the station with a backpack on to start feeling the sweat drench my t-shirt. Humidity is right up there, too, so we feel for the All Blacks when we stand on the sideline and watch them get into their work at training. The field is tucked away up on a hillside in Beppu, which is geographically the Hutt Valley to Ōita's Wellington. Beppu is known for its geothermal activity, and is a sister city of Rotorua. The siblings share that same sulphuric smell which permeates that air, but it's unlikely that it's filled the nostrils of the All Blacks too much because they've holed themselves up in their hotel even further up the hill. While they can enjoy the stunning view of the town and the bay, it makes sense that they only make their way down to train.

In stark contrast to Tokyo, where there are a million things on and the Rugby World Cup pool stages are just one of them, Ōita is gripped by the tournament and its responsibility as a host. Everywhere you look, there's some form of rugby-related advertising or artwork, and construction is happening in earnest on a fanzone near the main station. While Japan's win over Russia in the opening match could be described as a bit scratchy at best, red-and-white hooped jerseys are very much in fashion among the citizenry of Ōita. Good scenery, tourist attractions, rugby-mad locals. There is a long time between games for the All Blacks, so it's nice to be in a place that resembles what at least some of New Zealand wants to think it's like.

Not that it seems like many young people are actually interested in the Rugby World Cup back home, though. Being in our All Blacks bubble means it's a bit of a shock to see that, two days later, thousands and thousands march on Parliament to protest against inaction on climate change. They're vilified by a large section of people their parents' age, presumably the ones who took what ended up being the very wrong side when the Springboks showed up to play some rugby in 1981.

There is more to life in New Zealand right now than the All Blacks, and it's good to be reminded of that. Especially because it's another week before their next game.

46
THE COMPANY MEN

Ōita, 27 September 2019

'RUGBY MAN! YOU ARE rugby man?'

He reaches over and grabs my bicep.

'You are big man! You drink with me!'

He waves his two colleagues over, who are dressed impeccably in expensive-looking suits. I've been in this bar for all of about five seconds, but Ōita on a night out is probably the easiest place in the world to make friends right now if you are a New Zealander. The friendly conversationalist introduces himself as Tanaka-san—he and his two workmates are blowing off some steam after a hard day. Unfortunately, his compliments about my arms are about the extent of his English. From what I can tell, they're sales reps for a brewing company that I'm presuming is Suntory, because the giant conglomerate is responsible for basically everything drinkable in Japan, and also runs its own Top League side with the uniquely Japanese name Sungoliath.

The trio, led by Tanaka-san, racks up a line of drinks and some barely decipherable conversation. They're so hammered they just talk to me in Japanese anyway and I shrug and nod my way through what I'm guessing are questions about the All Blacks. These are Japanese company men, who work hard and drink hard. There's a second group firing up at the other end of the bar, and every now and then another bunch of suits staggers past out front on their way to the train.

They're very, very loud. When I say that, I mean in comparison to what the rest of Japan is like in public, so they're actually about the same volume as a group of guys in a pub in Auckland. Japan is a country divided up into places where you're quiet and respectful, which is around 99 per cent of it (bear in mind that you're not even allowed to talk on your phone on trains, for fear of disturbing others—which is actually a good rule), and bars where the locals can cut loose and get absolutely destroyed. The night before, I watched a drunk company man carefully step off the train and then, thinking his hard work was all done, waltz straight into a pillar. I have no idea if what is transpiring in front of me is the ritual I've heard of where company underlings are encouraged to drink as much as possible and tell their bosses what they really think of them, but Tanaka-san seems to be on good terms with his colleagues so maybe he's got nothing to get shitty about tonight.

Up on the TV, the England versus USA game is going on, and it sucks. It opens with former Blues first five Piers Francis taking out American fullback Will Hooley with a very suspect shoulder hit to the head, and that's about all that's worth talking about in the first half. In the second, American openside John Quill metes out a far more obvious shoulder charge and rightfully gets sent off. The irony is that Quill's victim is Owen Farrell, the English playmaker who has made a habit of launching shoulder charges himself. The difference between Farrell and everyone else is that the referees have also made a habit of collectively blinking whenever he does it, so the sight of him laid out on the turf after eating Quill's shoulder cranks social media up to full noise within seconds.

What good is a suspension when someone's already been knocked out?

The biggest narrative of the World Cup so far has been illegal contact with the head and how it's being dealt with. Quill is the first man to get sent off in the tournament, but he's already the fifth to end up getting suspended. Reece Hodge, the All Blacks' nemesis in Perth, will miss the rest of the pool stages for a high shot on Peceli Yato of Fiji. It's meant that every marginal tackle is being dissected in minute detail, and legal frameworks have become required reading. Michael Cheika has already blown his top over it, memorably stating that 'people are starving and they're [World Rugby] flying a QC over'. He's right about the overkill, and it makes me think about my conversation in Perth with Craig the Uber-driving ex-footballer. What good is a suspension when someone's already been knocked out?

Tanaka-san is now doing his rendition of the haka, which

is terrible, though he finishes with a pretty good pūkana then gestures to the whites of his eyes, which leads me to believe he understands the real point of the traditional expression. We slam back another whisky, which is helping us tolerate the dirge-fest on TV immensely. They grow bored quickly, though, and start talking baseball as it is almost play-off time in the Nippon League. The nearby Fukuoka SoftBank Hawks have clinched a place in the amusingly named Climax Series First Stage, and that is of far more importance to the men than some nothing game of World Cup rugby. To be honest, I'm more interested in the baseball right now, too—at least afterwards they won't be talking about red cards.

Bars are for being rowdy. Streets are for being quiet. Trains are for catching a bit of shuteye when you can.

Tanaka-san and his friends bid me good evening after a few photos, then cast themselves into the night, a train ride, and a probable early start back on the grind again tomorrow. One of them will probably fall asleep on the train, but that's to be expected. Bars are for being rowdy. Streets are for being quiet. Trains are for catching a bit of shuteye when you can.

A COUPLE OF DAYS LATER, after everyone had written off Francis's chances of playing any further part in the pool stages, there's a shock. He escapes any formal punishment when his case is heard by the judiciary. England can clearly afford some decent lawyers because the mental gymnastics required to understand the ruling are formidable, to say the least. They somehow manage to lay a bit of the blame on Hooley, with the ruling in part saying:

> The committee decided that there was significant and sufficient mitigation to be found:
> - in the sudden change of height by the USA player immediately before contact. It was only at the time of that sudden change that the clear line of sight factor (against mitigation) came in to play and could become of relevance; and that line of sight factor, therefore, was somewhat limited in its application, and the weight to be given to it;
> - in that the player, being in control of the tackle, attempted to avoid the opponent's head by making a definite attempt to change his own height and his body position . . .

It appears that the RFU have just made a mockery of any claim World Rugby has made about protecting player welfare. There's one law for the rich and one for everyone else in this game, but if you've spent enough time following Pacific Island rugby there's nothing new there.

47

THE RISING SUN MELTS THE EYES OF ICE

Shizuoka Stadium, 28 September 2019

IN THE MEANTIME, THE ALL BLACKS are flying under the radar. Despite bursting with enthusiasm, Ōita is a long way away from the rest of the action, so the media pack down here is pretty much all New Zealanders, a Brit and a Frenchman, and some local TV crews. All the other stuff going on suits the team just fine. There were very few disciplinary issues with the win over the Springboks (save for a marginal high shot by Kieran Read, which is quickly forgotten), and it feels like a lifetime ago now. They simply eat, sleep, train, repeat. Even the headlines back home are more focused on the fortunes of the other teams, and after tonight one of their main rivals will be plastered all over the papers for all the wrong reasons.

Jamie Joseph was a no-nonsense player back in the 1990s. His career spanned the amateur era of extreme violence and the quick transition to professionalism, and it encapsulated aspects of both. Joseph's demeanour on the field for Otago was ruthless and direct, best summed up by a try he scored in their epic but ultimately fruitless Ranfurly Shield challenge against Canterbury in 1994. The blindside flanker carried four defenders over the line with him to score the opening try under the posts, before wrenching free and shooting an intimidating glare at the men he'd just made fools of. After playing in the 1995 World Cup, Joseph's journey led him to Japan's established professional competition, where the Wild West of eligibility laws made him a Japanese test player by the time of the next tournament. When he retired, he moved into coaching, memorably guiding Wellington to lift the Shield he never got the chance to hoist as a player. And after that feat he mocked those who chose not to appoint him as Hurricanes coach by moving to the Highlanders and defeating the capital-based side in the 2015 Super Rugby final.

In 2019 he is still as big and imposing as when he was smashing people on Carisbrook. But now he's the Japanese coach, having taken over from Eddie Jones following the Australian's heroics with the national side in 2015. However, Joseph's got bigger goals on his mind than just masterminding one big upset at this World Cup, especially since he's got home-ground advantage. After their first-up win against Russia, the Japanese turn their sights on Ireland. The game is at Shizuoka Stadium, but while it's awash with red-and-white striped jerseys, there's a healthy dose of green in attendance as well.

Of course, we're down in Ōita when the biggest upset of the tournament happens. After weighing up whether to watch it at my hotel, I drag myself down to the fanzone near the train station. It's been a long day of heading up to the All Blacks' hotel and back in the stinkingly humid conditions. It doesn't help that when I get to the fanzone I discover that it's a long, enclosed marquee with no air conditioning housing around two thousand people. Spirits are high during the national anthem, dampened by Ireland's two first-half tries, but on the rise again when the Brave Blossoms close the gap to 12–9 at half-time. Something is brewing here—we can feel it. The Irish look rattled and tired; perhaps the Shizuoka heat is getting to them.

Kids are hoisted on their dads' shoulders, couples embrace and hope, even the bar staff are screaming at the giant screen at the front of the room.

On Joseph's orders, the Japanese launch an all-out assault in the second half. They dominate possession and territory, and score a go-ahead try. In the fanzone, people are on their feet and cheering wildly. I'm trying to capture as much of it as I can on video, and am rewarded with some beautiful shots of the local fans scarcely believing what they're seeing. Kids are hoisted on their dads' shoulders, couples embrace and hope, even the bar staff are screaming at the giant screen at the front of the room. Japan never look like losing from then on—if their 2015 victory over the

Springboks was a high-scoring thriller, this one is a grinding battle of wills befitting of Joseph's mantra as a player. They triumph 19–12 and immediately we attempt to get our heads around the fact that the All Blacks may well end up playing Ireland in a semi-final anyway.

JOE SCHMIDT'S STAR HAS FALLEN a long, long way since the Irish beat the All Blacks for just the second time ever. In fact, the one platitude he was getting all of last year has quickly been passed on to the coach who just beat him. Now headlines call for Jamie Joseph to be the next All Blacks coach, and even Steve Hansen agrees—well, sort of. When I ask him on the Monday if Joseph has the goods to succeed him, he says yes but points out that it's not worth taking his view into consideration because he has nothing to do with the selection process. While that caveat isn't exactly helpful, he does make the very good observation that just because Joseph has recorded this one big result, it doesn't mean that he wasn't a very good coach before.

Hansen also can't help but take a very subtle dig at the Irish when discussing the All Blacks' upcoming game against Canada. One of the most common things you'll hear any of the players or coaching staff say is how they take things one game at a time, and how they respect their opposition equally, no matter where they stand in the world rankings. This week is no exception, even though Canadian rugby is in an absolute shambles right now. Their men's programme has gone backwards at a great rate of knots this decade, and their only test win this year was against Chile.

'We have to respect the opposition, no matter who they are. You saw what happens when you don't the other night,' he tells us, obviously referring to the flat Irish performance in Shizuoka.

The sun has risen on the tournament after a week in the dark over tackles and refereeing, and it couldn't have come a moment too soon.

Meanwhile, Joseph has a far blunter message for Schmidt and his team, saying: 'We have been preparing for this game for a hell of a lot longer than the Irish have. We've been focusing on today for the last year at least, and probably subconsciously the last three years . . . and Ireland have been thinking about it since Monday.'

There's that direct approach that Joseph carried onto the field back in the day. If somehow the draw conspires to send Japan into a quarter-final with the All Blacks, it will be gigantic. The sun has risen on the tournament after a week in the dark over tackles and refereeing, and it couldn't have come a moment too soon.

48

HAKA, REVISITED

Beppu, 29 September 2019

SOMETHING HEART-WARMING HAPPENS IN THE last All Blacks press conference before the Canada game. A British journalist brings up the haka with TJ Perenara in a thoughtful and respectful way, leading the halfback to give a long, thoughtful and respectful answer. The haka has been a big talking point for all the right reasons since the win over the Springboks because, in a throwback to the performance last year in Rome, Kieran Read has again taken a role as kaea (leader) but has split the duties with Perenara.

As the team formed their wedge-shaped niho (formation), both men stayed on their feet while the rest of the All Blacks dropped to one knee for the rendition of 'Kapa o Pango'. It was fitting that they chose this haka against the Springboks—after all, the All Blacks' biggest rivals were given the honour of facing it for the first time ever in 2005 (tellingly, that was also the year of a British & Irish

Lions tour, but they chose the Boks as the more worthy recipient). Read and Perenara stayed upright in the back row, harvesting the mana from their troops, before the captain strode forward dramatically, slammed his knee into the turf and slapped his left hand onto his tense right forearm. From there, Perenara took over, calling the team to its feet and commanding the final ultimatum to the opposition across the turf before the game began.

While the All Blacks captain has been a bit reticent on the issue, perhaps choosing to save the story for another time, Perenara is more than happy to delve into the relationship and the preparation put in by the pair over the haka.

'KJ [Read] has been doing a lot of work on his role as a kaea and his pronunciation of Māori words. The work he's been putting in, I think's been awesome. He's the leader of our group, he's the leader of the team. When he steps up and leads haka I think the mana it gives our team . . . to see a non-Māori go through the processes to learn why he's leading haka and doing it the way he performed it . . . that's special to me not even as a rugby player, not even as a teammate. As a Māori, to see someone of non-Māori descent go through these steps, I was pretty proud.'

Perenara spent the day after the last Bledisloe Cup test in Auckland visiting the Ihumātao land protest in Māngere, which raised awareness of the issue among a great number of Pākehā rugby followers who normally wouldn't have it on their radar. Now he's working together with the leader of one of the most celebrated groups of men in the country to bridge a gap in understanding of Māori culture.

Asked whether he is a 'student' of the haka, Perenara gives a response that many Māori, especially those who grew up in urban environments and have had little or no connection with their whakapapa, can relate to.

'I grew up with haka, but I don't know everything about it. I'm currently on my journey in speaking te reo Māori as well and my journey with Māoritanga. I know that I don't know everything about it and I know there's people out there that are more educated than me. My ability to grow in this space is something that I pride myself on as well.'

Asked whether he is a 'student' of the haka, Perenara gives a response that many Māori can relate to.

Once again, he's touched on a pretty topical subject. The Māori renaissance has been going on for a good few decades now, and the idea of those rediscovering their connection to their culture is well summed up with the use of the word 'journey'. While the rates of those learning to speak te reo are increasing, it is still a daunting prospect for many Māori who see themselves as having missed out on learning the language when they were children. Becoming a part of Māoritanga takes more than just learning words and communicating, but Perenara has shown that he's willing to put in the effort. More than that, he's brought his Pākehā friends along with him on the journey.

49
THE SAD PARADE

Ōita Stadium, 2 October 2019

ALL BLACKS	63
CANADA	0

ATU MOLI STANDS IN FRONT of us in the harsh glare of the fluorescent lighting underneath Ōita Stadium. The area has been set up to feed the players past groups of media—first the press, then radio, and finally the TV cameras. It's a big loop, resembling a red-carpet event where the players emerge from one door and end up going back out the way they came. Like the rest of the All Blacks players and coaching staff Moli has discarded his tie and unbuttoned the top couple of buttons of his dress shirt, but he is still looking decidedly uncomfortable in his team blazer. Whoever decided to make them out of wool probably deserves to lose their job, because it's currently around 31 degrees and the humidity is 100 per cent.

Moli is leaning on the railing that is separating us from the players in a long room temporarily carpeted with astroturf. He has just played 80 minutes in that heat at prop, but can still flash us a smile complete with the trademark nifo koula, or Tongan gold tooth. He got to watch Angus Ta'avao go for a rest at 20 minutes and Ofa Tu'ungafasi leave after 50.

Moli and the rest of the All Blacks have spent an awful lot of the previous hour and a half walking back to halfway and catching their breath.

'To be honest, I was wrecked at half-time,' says the former head boy of Marlborough Boys' High. It's somewhat of a miracle that Moli is even standing in front of us at all, really, because a year ago he might not have even had a left leg. He took a knock in the first Super Rugby game of 2018 when playing for the Chiefs, which quickly escalated into a compound haematoma that caused him to miss the rest of the season and potentially end his career. At one point, amputation was being considered. However, Moli recovered thanks to four operations that left a scar so huge that pictures of it carried a graphic content warning on news websites.

To be fair, today Moli and the rest of the All Blacks have spent an awful lot of the previous hour and a half walking back to halfway and catching their breath. They've run in nine tries against the hapless Canadians, and the only reason Richie Mo'unga didn't convert all of them is because the first was a penalty try. In all, it's been a good evening for Steve Hansen, but in the post-match press conference he and Ian Foster looked like they were going to melt in their suit jackets as well. KPIs were met, no one got hurt, the management of the players went smoothly. There were a few more handling errors than normal, but that's mainly due to the fact that the All Blacks had the ball for 30 per cent longer than in a regular test. The humidity made the ball slippery with sweat; indeed, most players were soaking in their own perspiration after the first 10 minutes. They're not alone: up in the media box it turns into a battle of endurance to sit through the sticky atmosphere, so the final whistle is greeted with a decent degree of relief.

All three Barrett brothers started in a test for the first time ever, and all three scored tries. It's not without a bit of comedy though: Scott butchers an easy run in by dropping the ball; then on the last play Beauden is embarrassingly gunned down after making a break that on any other day would have ended in an easy try. In between those, though, Rieko Ioane scores in his first game in ages, Brad Weber comes on and scores two, and Sonny Bill Williams puts in an incredibly dominant display in which everything he does ends up working like a charm. His kick-through lays on Beauden Barrett's try, then his powerful run and flick-pass look like something from his league days as he sets up Rieko. Ardie Savea was trumpeted by NZ Rugby for his brave decision to wear protective goggles for the game. But after his injection off the bench late in the second half, the goggles last all of 30 seconds before Savea rips them off and throws them away.

The match was always going to be a hiding. Despite Hansen's

claims about not taking their opposition lightly, the truth is that the All Blacks knew little about the Canadians and it didn't matter. The press pack played a game during the week, counting how many times each player and coach would mention Tyler Ardron, who is both the Canadian captain and lock for the Chiefs—so therefore the only player in the Canadian team that any of the All Blacks have played either alongside or against. We got up to eight by game day, which is supposed to equate to how many beers we're each going to drink on the first official Tyler Ardron Appreciation Night.

The players, most of whom we don't even know, simply walk past and give us a rueful look as they know we're only there to talk to the guys who just whipped them.

Not that there's much interest in Ardron or his teammates after the final whistle. Once Moli is gone, the Canadian players who have been chosen for media duty pop out of the door one by one in their very smart-looking red blazers and ties. They scored no points on the field, and now they're getting no love from any of the journalists, either. World Rugby has mandated that 10 players from each side are made available for media opportunities post match, but for the Canadians, that's about eight too many given there are only a couple of their journalists here. The players, most of whom we don't even know, simply walk past and give us a rueful look as they know we're only there to talk to the guys who just whipped them. The most memorable highlight for the Canadians was the generous swapping of jerseys at full-time, and joining the All Blacks in a lap to thank the Ōita crowd for packing out the domed stadium.

While that's a tad depressing, the All Blacks are in high spirits. Beauden Barrett is happy to joke about his faux pas just before full-time and is full of praise for Mo'unga's game. Ioane is all smiles after his return, but it doesn't hide the fact that it probably isn't going to be enough to get him ahead of George Bridge and Sevu Reece. We pack up and leave the sweaty stadium, down a long tunnel that looks like something from an American prison's death row.

Outside it has started to rain and there's a long drive back on a bus to the train station. Because of a bit of a mishap with hotel bookings, I then have to sit on a train for another hour and a half up to Kitakyushu, where I stay in a hotel surrounded by pachinko halls and brothels. Then an early wake-up call to jump on a bullet train north to Tokyo.

There's no time to waste, either. This is where the All Blacks are going and their next match is only four days away, so the anticipation among all of us and the people back home is . . . oh wait, it's against Namibia.

50
GODZILLA
ROAD

Shinjuku, 3 October 2019

I'M LUGGING MY BAG THROUGH the seething mass of Shinjuku station the day after the All Blacks' win over Canada. It's a subterranean hive, the busiest railway station in the world and a labyrinth of tunnels, platforms and gates. I've got to the point where I can nonchalantly breeze my way past the greenhorned gaijin who frustratingly clog up the Japan Rail inspection point, always staffed by two people in smart grey uniforms complete with officer-style caps. I push my way past the fat Americans or inevitably complaining Brits, flash my 21-day pass (it is the most valuable thing I have on me, costing around NZ$900, although is strangely just a bit of card with my name handwritten on it) and then continue upward towards civilisation.

Navigating my way to the colour-coded Yamanote and Chuo lines that will take me to the places I need to visit on a regular basis has become a part of everyday existence I don't even need to think about anymore. Next, the portal to my home: exit B13. Up the stairs and out into the explosion of colour and noise. This is Tokyo, this is where I live until the All Blacks go home—with a World Cup or without.

I turn right, right again, and join the throng moving past the flashing lights that stretch skyward. Shinjuku is an entertainment district, packed with bars, restaurants and gambling establishments. It has a population density of 18,000 per square kilometre, packed into the high-rises that cast a shadow over pretty much everything along the streets. Vast electronics stores take up half a dozen levels each in the buildings, and are always busy. Crows the size of cats claw at the rubbish left out by bars for collection and squawk loudly. Anime images of scantily clad girls are everywhere, grabbing your attention with vibrant colours. I cross the main street to head to where I'm staying, look up, and see the great monster that rules Shinjuku.

This is Tokyo, this is where I live until the All Blacks go home–with a World Cup or without.

High above, atop the massive Toho IMAX cinema complex that dominates the Kabukichō, a block that was completely rebuilt post-war after being razed to the ground by the B-29s, is Gojira. Better known as Godzilla to us Westerners, he casts his baleful eye across us puny humans going about our daily lives below. Commanding unconditional respect and awe in the Toho studios' movies that were churned out on a regular basis in the 1950s, Godzilla was originally a manifestation of the fear of what happened to Hiroshima and Nagasaki—an unstoppable atomic monster that destroys cities on a whim—but is now loved here in Japan as a cultural icon.

The bust on top of the complex is of Godzilla's reptilian head, plus a claw is tightly gripping the ledge. The street that he looks down on is named after him, which is ironic considering he has specifically destroyed Shinjuku several times in his 36 film appearances. Godzilla Road is a pedestrian route that's a magnet for tourists, and therefore a magnet for tourist traps as well. The hawkers trying to befriend bumbag-wearing white boys and entice them into ridiculously overpriced bars and strip joints aren't hard to discern, since they're not Japanese. But that hasn't stopped the local ward council from blaring out a warning to gaijin about local 'scams and dishonesty' over a set of loudspeakers along the street. Tellingly, as well as being in English it's been voiced in an Australian accent, which says a lot about who are falling for the promises of a really great night out and girls on tap.

Just past Godzilla's gaze is Cinecity Square. As well as having another image of the legendary monster glaring down on it, it's a meeting place for local teens dressed in the traditional Japanese counterculture uniform of heavy black clothing sporting confusingly translated English slogans. They sit cross-legged in circles on the grey stone pavement, chain-smoking and sipping on beers. Around them are the only homeless people I've seen in the entire country, living rough on sheets of cardboard. The square has very popular nightclubs on two of its corners—the cheesily named Blaze and Warp command long lines of house-music enthusiasts well into the early sunlight hours of Saturday and Sunday. On the other corner is a ubiquitous pachinko complex; then on the remaining one is my home for the World Cup—the APA Hotel.

The APA chain is all over Japan, and it's not just known for providing low-cost accommodation. Its founder, Toshio Motoya, is one of the highest-profile Japanese historical revisionists, and isn't shy about making his guests aware of his extremely questionable political views. Each room has a copy of his book *The Real History of Japan*, which details how he believes that claims of Japanese war crimes during their occupation of China and Korea are all just made up to make them look bad. There's also the monthly *Apple Town* magazine, a Japanese twenty-first-century version of *The Dearborn Independent* (the mouthpiece for Henry Ford's racial prejudices), which contains an essay saying that Japan's only crime in World War II was losing. Just to make sure he's got all his bases covered, Motoya is also an outspoken anti-Semite. On the positive side, the breakfast buffet they put on is pretty good.

I walk into my far-right-influenced hotel, past the tiny bar that is now full to the brim with Englishmen in town for their team's next game against Argentina. More white shirts with roses on them squeeze out of the lift and pass me on their way to the giant Asahi handles that are getting filled nearby, as I head up to my room on the twenty-seventh floor. From here I have an elevated view of the rear side of Godzilla's bust and claws, and the struts and cables that tether the whole shebang to the Toho cinema roof—the ability to see, beyond the myth and legend, the inner workings of the beast so feared and loved by the people.

Maybe that's why the Japanese love the All Blacks so much. They want their heroes to be fearsome but predictable. All Godzilla movies are the same: he rises from the depths, kicks some ass, and then goes back while humanity stands in awe of what just transpired. The All Blacks come here every few years and do the same thing—sparingly enough that it never becomes boring to the thousands who flock to watch them play. They fit the Japanese culture of stoic sacrifice, unrelenting obedience and powerful work ethic. There are parallels between bushidō—the Japanese codes of honour—and tikanga Māori. Plus they wear black, which just makes them look cool.

Maybe that's why the Japanese love the All Blacks so much. They want their heroes to be fearsome but predictable. All Godzilla movies are the same: he rises from the depths, kicks some ass, and then goes back while humanity stands in awe of what just transpired.

The support they've had from the local people has been so good it's making the fans who come to watch the All Blacks in New Zealand look even worse, especially after the Wellington test. Right now, I'm fairly in favour of moving the team to Japan for a while, because All Blacks jersey sales are probably right up there with Japanese ones thus far in the tournament.

Later on, I head back down to get some dinner. On my hotel's corner a large congregation of Russian prostitutes try to make eye contact with anyone walking in and out. A couple of guys in England jerseys are drunkenly trying to bargain with one of them, while the queues grow outside the nightclubs. The streets are now clogged with tourists, staring up and around at the manifestation of Japan that they probably had in their heads when they planned their holidays. Tomorrow, though, we're back to the grind. Out to where the All Blacks are, away from the lights and colour. More press conferences, more conjecture, another week of guesswork before the business end of the tournament.

51
NOT SO HEAVY SITS THE CROWN

Tokyo Stadium, 6 October 2019

ALL BLACKS   **71**
NAMIBIA   **9**

'YOU'RE BETTER OFF BEING THE favourite than the underdog. If we came here and everyone said we've got no show of winning it, well that's a bit tough, isn't it?'

Steve Hansen's changed his tune—180 degrees in fact. In the lecture theatre under Aviva Stadium, he was happy to concede Rugby World Cup favouritism to Ireland. But that was almost a year ago. While the All Blacks have had their ups and downs leading into the tournament, the Irish are on a downward trajectory after their loss to Japan and they may not even have any control over what happens to them next. They're currently in a three-way battle with Scotland and Japan to get out of their pool, plus there's a typhoon on the way that could mean their deciding game is cancelled and they'll go home. If they do come second in their pool, they're on a collision course with the All Blacks anyway. Hands up who predicted any of that.

Hansen is sitting at one end of a ridiculously large ballroom that has been set up for a press conference at the Hilton Tokyo Bay. In two days' time the All Blacks and Namibia could play their test match in here, or even a game of cricket, which would probably be more competitive. Hansen has already admitted that he doesn't know anything about the Namibians, which is refreshing and fair given that the only time he would have watched them play since the All Blacks played them in the last World Cup is in the previous two weeks. We're clustered around his customary desk with advertising hoardings behind it, flanked by the All Blacks' official World Cup signage. His admission that the team is probably out-and-out favourites comes complete with a horse-racing analogy, which he's fond of.

'I think it's way better if you've got a favourite in a race horse than an outsider. Favourites normally win more often than they lose. We have to earn the right to win it, but I think it's a better position than to be seen as someone that can't win it.'

Earning the right isn't really something they need to worry about for their game on Sunday, though. Most of Namibia's side still have nine-to-five jobs back home in south-west Africa and the team has never won a World Cup game in 21 attempts, which will become 22 very soon. The game is back at Tokyo Stadium, the same venue where the All Blacks played Japan last year. One of the men who had a bit of a spotlight on him that day is back in it again.

Hansen has named Jordie Barrett at first five, after both Beauden and Richie Mo'unga are given the day off. The coach tells us that it was a spur-of-the-moment decision that he informed the youngest Barrett brother of last night—a yarn that is quashed once again by good old loose-lips Aaron Smith. The halfback comes in next and admits that Jordie and TJ Perenara were running at 10 for the entire pre-tournament camp in Kishawa, so this move is a long time coming.

> **Hansen has named Jordie Barrett at first five, after both Beauden and Richie Mo'unga are given the day off. The coach tells us that it was a spur-of-the-moment decision that he informed the youngest Barrett brother of last night–a yarn that is quashed once again by good old loose-lips Aaron Smith.**

There is one more big announcement for this one, though. Brodie Retallick is back at lock, after an injury-enforced break of just over two months. He was a casualty of the encounter with the Springboks back in July, which threw a decent-sized spanner into Hansen's plans for the World Cup. There was every chance that Retallick, who had originally banged his shoulder up playing for the Chiefs before having it wrenched again by RG Snyman in the Boks game, might have missed the whole tournament. But, he tells us, the day he knew that wasn't true was when he was in the pool about a month ago in Hamilton.

'I was with my wife, aqua-jogging of all things,' he says hesitantly, so we're unsure which part of that sentence he's actually embarrassed about. 'I got out of the pool and it was pretty much as good as gold. I could lift it above my head and out to the side.'

One of the biggest concerns pre-tournament has seemingly clicked back into place. Retallick has a perfect opportunity to run himself back into some form, too, because this game should be a bit of a walk in the park.

JORDIE BARRETT'S FIRST TOUCH OF the ball is in exactly the same spot as his ill-fated clearance that led to a charge-down and Japanese try last year. This time, though, he strikes the ball downfield cleanly and sets off running after it in the All Blacks' defensive line. While that's a good start for him, somehow the Namibians manage to score first through a penalty. In fact, the plucky Africans do more than just frustrate the All Blacks for the first half-hour of the game; they're actually in it. It's 10–9 after another try to Anton Lienert-Brown, but a few looks are exchanged high up in the media box. The All Blacks have had all the ball and haven't really looked like cracking the defensive line made up of Currie Cup, lower-division French and local amateur players. To their credit, the Namibians are playing exceptionally well, and this 30-minute spell will probably go down as the finest rugby they've ever produced at a World Cup.

Then the cards come out. Already we've seen enough of them in the tournament to make anyone glancing at a TV think they were watching the World Series of Poker, and even the All Blacks aren't exempt from the increasingly long arm of the law. Nepo Laulala gets sent to the bin for connecting with the head of a Namibian player who lowers his body position so that the All Blacks prop has no real choice. Mitigating circumstances, so yellow only. Angus Ta'avao comes on to replace him and stays on the field for the rest of the game, which gives a big indication of how carefully Hansen is treading around any players getting in further trouble or even just creating a debate about foul play.

This is because, due to all of the other dramas around discipline and a looming massive weather event, the All Blacks have flown under the radar somewhat despite landing the favourites tag. Their schedule has meant they can tinker away in these pool games while the other sides face crucial battles for survival—and that's just the way they want it.

After half-time, the All Blacks put the hammer down, running in a bunch of tries against the brave but outmatched Namibians and blowing the score out to their highest total at a World Cup since 2011. If they wanted to quietly go about their business with no one noticing, though, the final act of the game messes all that up. TJ Perenara and Brad Weber find themselves on the field together in a test match for the first time ever, with the former taking over at first five while Jordie Barrett drops to fullback. Perenara had already engineered a try for Barrett, which would have been enough to show astute rugby observers that even a guy out of position in the All Blacks can handle the most important role in the team, but then he breaks down the left wing and throws a stunning offload to George Bridge. The winger is brought down 30 metres out, but Rieko Ioane is there to pop a pass to Weber, who goes over the 22 and slings the ball behind his back to land on the chest of Perenara (who has somehow caught up with the play despite being heavily tackled on his own side of halfway).

It's immediately hailed as the try of the tournament, something only the All Blacks could do. Not only that, but three out of the four men involved in it had come off the bench.

But Perenara still has a lot of work to do. Namibians Obert Nortje and Helarius Kisting can still force him into touch, but he squeezes past both of them and just gets the ball down inside the corner flag. Of course we're going to have a look upstairs because it seems scarcely believable that Perenara has scored. The look on TJ's face says that he doesn't really believe it either, and you don't need to be a lip-reader to make out him saying 'Ohhhhhh maybe? Maybe?' to the teammates who have rushed to congratulate him.

The replays confirm that, somehow, he's managed to get the ball down while staying in the field of play. It's immediately hailed as the try of the tournament, something only the All Blacks could do. Not only that, but three out of the four men involved in it had come off the bench.

While that's all very good, the post-match interview process is less than ideal. Players are pushed past us and it appears that the obvious intent is getting the whole thing over with as fast as possible, which is weird because there are only good things to say. This is also on the back of a Kiwi TV crew being rudely moved on during a midweek training session for no good reason as the team wasn't even on the field yet.

On the train back to the city we're subjected to a loudmouth in an All Blacks jersey telling some Englishmen that 'everybody in New Zealand hates Sonny Bill Williams because he's making rugby too woke'. He looks all of about 18, but I'm guessing he didn't just fly in from the climate-change protests. If he had, he might have some idea of what Mother Nature is sending our way over the course of the next week.

52
THE TYPHOON

Tokyo, 10 October 2019

The destructive power of the typhoons that wreak havoc across China, Japan, Korea and the Philippines has intensified by 50% in the past 40 years due to warming seas, a new study has found.

The researchers warn that global warming will lead the giant storms to become even stronger in the future, threatening the large and growing coastal populations of those nations.

—*The Guardian*, September 2016

UP UNTIL NOW, PRETTY MUCH the only discussions about the weather have been in response to monotonous press conference questions about the heat and humidity. There's only been one mention of a typhoon so far, and that was way back before the first game when a

French journalist asked Anton Lienert-Brown what the All Blacks' plans were if one were to strike during the tournament. Lienert-Brown, who misunderstood the question to mean 'what would you do if one struck during a game?', simply said he'd run away and hide. While it got a few laughs, that was the last we'd heard of any tropical storms until now.

What started as a slightly amusing tale of Irish misfortune and the fact that the typhoon's name sounded a bit like 'Heebeegeebees' has now turned quite serious.

At first, it was predicted that Typhoon Hagibis was going to affect Kyushu, where our friends in Ōita and Beppu would presumably be battening down the hatches. That eventuality would have seen the Ireland versus Sāmoa game affected, which in turn would have had a serious effect on Ireland's chances of progressing through to the quarter-finals. But, as typhoons have a habit of doing, Hagibis has changed course. She's dog-legged north towards Honshu. In her path is Nagoya, Yokohama and Tokyo, and she's predicted to make landfall this Saturday.

The All Blacks are due to play Italy in Toyota City, an outlying part of Nagoya where the famously affordable and reliable car manufacturers are based. England and France are supposed to square off in Yokohama, and we are all based in the capital city. What started as a slightly amusing tale of Irish misfortune and the fact that the typhoon's name sounded a bit like 'Heebeegeebees' has now turned quite serious. Most of us are due to travel straight into the storm's path on a bullet train, but World Rugby calls a press conference for midday.

The news leaks well before then, though: the game is off. Not only that, but we're told to stay indoors all of Saturday. That may not be a choice for a lot of us, as apparently the trains are due to stop running when the wind gets strong enough to blow them off the tracks. Some very worrying videos are posted on social media showing what previous typhoons have done to Japanese cities in recent years. But that's nothing compared with the hammering World Rugby is copping for seemingly not having a back-up plan. After all, there is a reason this time of year in Japan is called 'typhoon season'.

While I'm sympathetic to its course of action, given that no one can control the weather, the governing body does show just how seriously out of touch it is by not even bothering to pronounce Hagibis correctly in its press conferences. By Friday morning, though, it's become a no-brainer. All the Shinkansen bullet train services on Saturday are cancelled, and it's likely all the rest of the overland and subway services will be too, so just getting to the ground would be a logistical nightmare for anyone. People are asking for the games to be played in empty, domed stadiums, but that's pretty unlikely given the number of support staff, TV personnel and various hangers-on that would need to be transported to the new venues as well. Besides, the domed stadiums aren't much better than the open ones, with a Climax Series baseball game at the Tokyo Dome called off that night too.

A press conference that was supposed to be the All Blacks' team naming is now just a joint appearance by Steve Hansen and Kieran Read. It's preceded by what we consider to be some absolute bullshit from the All Blacks support staff, who refuse to move the table the men will be sitting at forward a metre to compensate for the room's terrible lighting. This leads to a stand-off between one staff member and a group of experienced cameramen. It seems to the rest of us stunningly passive-aggressive, and we feel somewhat embarrassed to be New Zealanders.

Italy, who were flogged by 63 points when these sides met in Rome last year, had about as much chance of winning this game as there is of an amicable and popular resolution to Brexit.

Hansen then gives a statement that leads us to believe that the game getting called off doesn't really worry him at all.

'Naturally we wanted to play. It's sad, because it's a World Cup game that not only us but the Italians will miss out on. But more so for the fans. You've got to understand the safety reasons why it's been called off—we'll adapt and we know we're in next week.'

Yeah, well you kind of already knew that last part, Steve. Italy, who were flogged by 63 points when these sides met in Rome last year, had about as much chance of winning this game as there is of an amicable and popular resolution to Brexit. In fact, up until now, the Italians' only real contribution to the tournament has been the one red card that no one at all has any qualms with, when prop Andrea Lovotti was sent for the dumbest move ever in their match against the Springboks. It should really have been two reds, as his fellow prop Nicola Quaglio grabbed Duane Vermeulen's legs and dumped him on his head like some sort of pro-wrestling move gone wrong. Now they're being touted as the victims of some great injustice, because the match was supposed to be long-serving Italian captain Sergio Parisse's swansong. He's played in five World Cups and is regarded as the Azzurri's only quality player, so has good cause to articulate exactly what he thinks about the game getting called off.

'It is difficult to know that we won't have the chance to play a match against one of the great teams,' Parisse says in the Italian press conference across town. 'If New Zealand needed four or five points against us it would not have been cancelled.'

That's pretty hard to argue with, admittedly. The All Blacks could definitely have found themselves in that position if they had lost to the Springboks in the first game. If there was even a chance that they were in danger of not progressing due to the weather, the hot air of outrage from New Zealand would probably have generated a tropical storm from down there as well.

Back at the All Blacks' presser, Hansen brings up a very good point: if the typhoon does significant damage to Yokohama or Tokyo stadiums there are going to be some serious ramifications for the tournament down the track, since that's where most of the business end is going to take place. All of a sudden, we're faced with the possibility of relocating out of Tokyo for the remaining three weeks, which is quite a substantial period of time if you're looking for somewhere to work and hundreds of others are trying to do the same. Right now, if it is shifted, the closest decent-sized venue is Shizuoka Stadium, which is about an hour south when the Shinkansens start running again.

All we can do now is sit tight and hope that the next game we attend doesn't have a minute's silence before kick-off.

Outside, the sky has turned grey and very ominous. The All Blacks are getting the hell out of their hotel in Tokyo Bay, where the concrete seawalls will soon be getting a fair workout from Hagibis. The team is heading back into the city—perhaps the first thing they've done all tournament that has made our lives easier. But, like us, they're going to be staying indoors and keeping a very close eye on what happens outside their windows for the next couple of days.

All we can do now is sit tight and hope that the next game we attend doesn't have a minute's silence before kick-off.

53

WRITERS ON
THE STORM

Shinagawa, 12 October 2019

IT'S JUST GONE 9PM AND there's water pissing in through the window frames. Hagibis is bang on schedule, with winds around 190 kilometres per hour shaking the entire building and rain lashing the city outside. The Shinagawa train station has long since fallen silent, its reassuring clickety-clack replaced by an unnerving silence punctuated by distant warning sirens, messages over loudspeakers to get indoors and the occasional wail of an ambulance. Tokyo is a city of people pacing their apartments, peering nervously out their windows. But now we know what Nature has in store for us, because it's causing the lights to sway back and forth above our heads.

I'm in Newshub's apartment, because I didn't like the idea of staying confined to my shoebox in the APA Hotel by myself for 24 hours. For them, though, it's still a work day, given that there's a newsworthy event happening right outside the front door—especially since the area gets jolted with a 5.7-magnitude earthquake during the evening as well. So, armed with cameras and microphones, that's where we go.

The lobby of the apartment block is full of gaijin whose rooms were too shaky, and they can't believe a group of knuckle-headed New Zealanders are about to venture outside into the fury.

Anchorman Mike McRoberts has joined us and is showing absolutely no qualms at all about walking out into a Category 5 storm. The lobby of the apartment block is full of gaijin whose rooms were too shaky, and they can't believe a group of knuckle-headed New Zealanders are about to venture outside into the fury. The concierge agrees to unlock the doors, but looks very concerned when she realises that two of us aren't even wearing shoes. McRoberts points to a nearby railing and tells Blair the cameraman to get set up right in the teeth of the wind. They grip the railing hard as the wind intensifies, almost blowing them over and into the torrents of water now churning along the street. Shot secured, they beat a hasty retreat to where we've been watching them from under the apartment awnings.

We head back upstairs and dry off. While it's been a little adventure for us, things are far more dramatic around the rest of the country. Floods and landslides have caused havoc, especially across the bay in the Chiba prefecture. Of course, we can't understand the local news updates, so we don't yet know that there is indeed a death toll and injuries. The sheets of rain keep belting down as the most violent edge of the typhoon's epicentre whips around and gives us a parting shot of high winds that once again rock the 31-storey building we're in back and forth like we're on a rough Interislander crossing. On the TV, Ireland are giving Manu Sāmoa a hiding down in Fukuoka despite only having 14 men on the field. Former Chiefs wider-squad member Bundee Aki has been sent off and two Sāmoans have gone to the bin as well. Watching the typhoon out the window is far more captivating.

Then, seemingly as quickly as it arrived, Typhoon Hagibis is gone. While it's not done with the main island yet, it leaves Tokyo and heads north. All we can think is that we're damn happy we didn't have to go to Nagoya for the All Blacks' match, and that there's little chance of the game scheduled at Yokohama Stadium tomorrow taking place. The Rugby World Cup organisers may have needed a distraction from all the red-card dramas that were happening, but this isn't at all what they had in mind. If Japan's game against Scotland doesn't go ahead, the whole tournament is going to be a shit-show.

Across town, the All Blacks are watching movies and relaxing. In the heart of the city the effects of the wind aren't quite as bad, because the buildings are clustered together more tightly than our exposed spot next to the low-rises of Shinagawa. They had an inter-squad hit-out at Shining Arcs on Friday, which probably simulated the intensity of a game against Italy reasonably well.

THE NEXT MORNING, WE'RE OUT at Yokohama Stadium. It's dawned fine without a cloud in the sky, although the typhoon seems to have sent the temperature plummeting out of the low 30s to almost needing to wear a hoodie. We're looking out at the flooded areas around the roads surrounding the stadium, and are thinking that inside the stands there will be substantial damage. Surprisingly, we're not only allowed in by the friendly security staff, but we are unchallenged as we walk right out onto the field. It's looking absolutely perfect, like a pool table. World Rugby is due to make an announcement in an hour as to whether the Japan versus Scotland game is still on, but we can see ground staff busy putting up the posts.

We get what we need and head out, where the streets are already starting to see people in Japanese jerseys trickle out towards the stadium. It's only 9am. The game is confirmed to be kicking off on time at 7.45pm, and will decide who the All Blacks will play next weekend. It will also go a long way towards salvaging the reputation of the tournament, because it will turn out to be the best game of rugby so far this year.

Japan and Scotland switch on the afterburners and thrill the 73,000 who have packed the stadium. Sadly, the encounter is preceded with a moment's silence for the lives taken by the typhoon: by now there are officially 23 dead and 16 missing, with both numbers expected to rise. The Scots, so derided in the past few days for threatening to take World Rugby to court if the game hadn't gone ahead, majestically play their part by running the ball with deep-set backlines. The Japanese counter with their effective short passing game and score three tries to the Scots' one in the first half, with the stars of the show being wingers Kenki Fukuoka and Kotaro Matsushima. Stunningly, despite scoring his fifth try of the World Cup, it's unlikely we'll see Fukuoka's name on a team sheet after the tournament as he's decided to follow in his father's footsteps and go to medical school next year. (Fukuoka is also from the city of Fukuoka, but then again the All Blacks have a white lock called Sam Whitelock.)

Jamie Joseph and his Brave Blossoms have given the Japanese people something remarkable to rally around, and it's truly beautiful to watch.

Another big role that's being played in the game is by referee Ben O'Keeffe from Blenheim, mostly because he keeps his whistle at arm's length from his mouth for most of the time and lets play unfold. It's been a tough few weeks for the men in the middle, with harsh regulations on high tackles seeing them cop a fair share of flak for over-officiousness, but tonight O'Keeffe's job is being made an awful lot easier by a couple of teams that actually want to play a game that people will want to watch. It ends up 28–21 to Japan and the crowd roars, as do countless fanzones around the city. Shibuya crossing explodes with red and white jerseys. Jamie Joseph and his Brave Blossoms have given the Japanese people something remarkable to rally around, and it's truly beautiful to watch.

54
CRUNCH TIME

Tokyo, 15 October 2019

A FEW DAYS LATER AND our expedition out into the typhoon has made it into the international media. A video I made of Mike and Blair battling the wind and rain attracts comments saying how irresponsible the actions were, which makes me wonder what those people think about journalists being sent into war zones and the like. But now it's back to the business of the All Blacks and trying to get an insight into their mindset for what could potentially be their last match of the year this week, and Ian Foster is being exceptionally prickly today.

It's a shame that the pressure is doing this to Foster, a genuinely decent bloke who always deals with the worst time slot of each week pretty well. Tuesdays are too late to be discussing the game just gone (even more so this time because the All Blacks didn't even play) and too early to talk about the team that will take the field in the coming weekend. Foster generally deals with any prying questions attempting to squirrel out a clue around selection with a bit of humour, but there's no laughing today in downtown Tokyo. He's grumpy, short with his answers, and clearly wants to leave. Unfortunately for him, the Irish media have arrived in force and they bombard him with questions around preparation, selection and the fact that Ireland have beaten the All Blacks two out of the last three times they've met. Foster dead-bats everything, gets up and gets out.

Dane Coles and Ardie Savea come in afterwards, with Coles getting visibly annoyed with questions about the past couple of losses to the Irish. After all, he played in both matches and doesn't think much of having to be included in the group of players that dropped a test to the men in green for the first time ever. He knows full well that losing this weekend means going home, and he's 32 years old so this tournament may be the last time he pulls on an All Blacks jersey.

There's a bit of that same realisation dawning on the other players and coaching staff this week. When asked about the fact that this might be his last week ever as an All Black, Kieran Read admits that he hasn't really thought about it at all. Ditto Steve Hansen and Irish forwards coach Simon Easterby, who talk to us later on in the afternoon. Normally you'd treat responses like that with the same regard as any other deflection, but the slightly surprised tone of all of them leads me to believe that they're actually telling the truth. They're all a little bit shocked when the reality dawns on them that this is it—lose and this time next week you'll be walking through Customs trying to figure out what went wrong.

If that is the case, it'll be the first time the All Blacks have had to do that since 2007. Coles was still a fresh-faced 21-year-old who'd just made his provincial debut. Read was still a year away from playing the first of his 124 tests. Hansen was deputy to Sir Graham Henry and in danger of losing his job.

They're all a little bit shocked when the reality dawns on them that this is it—lose and this time next week you'll be walking through Customs trying to figure out what went wrong.

That's not all that's changed since the All Blacks sensationally crashed out of the World Cup in the quarter-finals, beaten 20–18 by France. In 2007 there wasn't the vast coverage of public opinion on social media that there is now, no memes getting shared, and hot takes were confined to old men who had the time to ring up Radio Sport. Just what will happen if the team returns home empty-handed this time will be very testing, given that we're yet to experience a World Cup failure where we get subjected to the sometimes interesting but often just awful views of people who don't follow the game anywhere near as closely as the obsessive types like us.

New Zealand is not a fun place to be after a World Cup loss, even though the morning-after in 2007 was a stunningly fine day in Wellington in which we all got together and drowned our sorrows.

While 2003 was the same, 1999 was probably the nadir of public despair given the circumstances, because 1995 was tempered by the fact that the All Blacks had played outstandingly good rugby and gone down in an epic final. I was too young to remember 1991 properly, but given that the country wasn't particularly noted for its sophistication at the time, it's safe to guess it was pretty shit too.

That's what's on the line: the entire mood of the New Zealand rugby public for the next four years. It could be one vilified play, like the forward pass in 2007. It could be just a massively flat performance, like in 2003. Or they could be like the All Blacks and win, which, despite the absolute ton of talk heading our way in the coming week, they are handily favoured to do.

MEANWHILE, IT'S BEEN CRUNCH TIME in a different area of the game. The biggest story of the World Cup back in New Zealand has been the inability for people to actually watch the game through the Spark Sport streaming service. The game against the Springboks had to get shifted to regular television after a barrage of complaints about the feed cutting out, which unfortunately confirmed a lot of fears about the service—a first for such a big sporting event in the country. On the one hand, a few glitches aren't too far removed from the previous reality of Sky's streaming service, and would be familiar to anyone who'd ever experienced 'rain fade' with their satellite TV system. But on the other, Spark talked themselves up deluxe in the build-up, promising no problems at all, so the switch to regular TV was seen as an embarrassing backdown.

But arguably the biggest loser in this debacle, whoever's to blame, is the game of rugby itself. As seen in the empty stands of Eden Park before I left, it is rapidly losing the interest of the casual fan. Once upon a time you could count on everyone in New Zealand tuning in to watch an All Blacks test, but the simple fact of the matter is that our changing society has other things to do on Saturday nights. Asking people to fork out for a viewing service that may not even work isn't going to sway the minds of those wavering in their interest. It's not being helped by the media astroturfing the very worst of the online comments to make the problem seem a lot worse, either.

But Spark knew what they were getting themselves into—plus it's pretty hard to feel sorry for them when they send out press releases insisting that nothing is wrong, à la Lord Haw-Haw or Baghdad Bob. This is the reality of sports viewing these days, so we all ought to get used to it.

55

HEART BREAKERS, DREAM TAKERS

Tokyo Stadium, 19 October 2019
(Rugby World Cup Quarter-final)

ALL BLACKS	**46**
IRELAND	**14**

> Low lie the fields of Athenry
> Where once we watched the small free birds fly
> Our love was on the wing
> We had dreams and songs to sing
> It's so lonely round the fields of Athenry

IT'S BEEN ALMOST A YEAR since Rory Best was sitting in front of us in Dublin, quipping that leading his side to victory over the All Blacks for a second time felt different . . . but definitely not worse. Now, he's in the same spot a few feet away underneath Tokyo Stadium trying not to burst into tears. The 37-year-old has just played his 122nd and final test. To say it hasn't gone according to plan for the Ulsterman is a gross understatement.

About the only thing that has gone to script for the Irish is the singing. Two hours beforehand, the large and vocal contingent of travelling fans were sitting down to our left at the eastern end of Tokyo Stadium. They should have been even greater in number had it not been for their side's loss to Japan, which has meant that an awful lot of Irish fans have got tickets to the wrong quarter-final. After all, this was a side that was favoured to win the whole thing when tickets went on sale back at the start of the year—so it made sense to think they'd top their group and head into the game on Sunday. There's been a flurry of bartering and pleading by those who have just flown in from the four proud provinces of Ireland. They've swarmed into Shinjuku and up Godzilla Road to the APA Hotel, striving desperately to fix their predicament. The solution seems simple, given that Japan have made it into the game the Irish thought they'd be in, but the locals are in no mood to swap given that they would've bought their tickets specifically to see the All Blacks.

I felt like telling the Irishmen lining the street from Tobitakyū train station to the main concourse of Tokyo Stadium, holding signs pleading for tickets, that it probably would have made more sense if they'd written them in Japanese instead of English, but decided against it. The New Zealand contingent is strong as well, and the All Blacks run out onto the field to see the usual mass of locals in their jerseys. The Japanese fans take it one step further by singing along with both national anthems.

The haka, 'Kapa o Pango', is met with a thunderous rendition of 'The Fields of Athenry' by the Irish fans—just as they did a year ago before their epic win at Aviva Stadium in Dublin. For a second I feel like I'm back there. The song is a lament about a man unfairly prosecuted for stealing corn during the Great Famine and being shipped off to a penal colony in Australia—it might not sound like the perfect fit for a sporting anthem, but there have been plenty of odd tunes that have somehow made it into stands and terraces around the world. Unfortunately, one of them is 'Sweet Caroline', which we've been subjected to as the teams were warming up. The White Stripes' 'Seven Nation Army' is a staple throughout the tournament, as is 'Country Roads' by John Denver.

> **The haka, 'Kapa o Pango', is met with a thunderous rendition of 'The Fields of Athenry' by the Irish fans–just as they did a year ago before their epic win at Aviva Stadium in Dublin. For a second I feel like I'm back there.**

Of course, All Black fans don't have a song, so they just settle for chanting the name of the team and clapping. Two of them somehow get past security into our media area, which is set up on the second deck of the stadium and comprises six rows of 100 seats stretching from each 22-metre line. The pair, complete with face paint, All Blacks jerseys and a fake prosthetic arm for some reason (neither of them is an amputee), simply plonk their very drunken bodies down at one of the desks and pretend that nothing is out of the ordinary. Everyone else, especially the security staff, are too polite or busy to actually do anything about them so they just stay there in one of the best spots in the stadium.

Or maybe it's just because we're nervous. Especially those of us who were in Dublin to watch the Irish slowly drive a dagger into the heart of the All Blacks that night and claim their famous win. Those of us who sat numbly through a press conference getting worried about what might happen to the All Blacks' World Cup chances. Those of us who had to trudge past pub after pub of singing Irishmen down the streets back to our hotels. But, for the second time this year, the All Blacks make us wonder just what the hell we were thinking. Just like the build-up and blow-out that was the second Bledisloe Cup test, the team makes a statement on the field that no one can argue with.

As soon as the game kicks off, the All Blacks grab possession and hold on for most of the first 10 minutes. Passes are sticking, ball-carriers are going to ground facing the right way, and the recycle is going at lightning clip. Aaron Smith is everywhere, the two young wingers are getting involved in everything, and the forwards are surging across the park like a river in flood. Above all, the man who is the most prominent in the middle is one who has a serious point to prove against the Irish—Kieran Read. He was the one left prone on his back while Jacob Stockdale raced away to score the match-defining try. He was the one who had to endure the critique of his form. He was the one who had to front an inquisition from the media funnelling the fears of the public over the All Blacks' chances.

Now he is the one ripping into his work as they surge into the Irish 22. He takes a pass from Smith and smashes his way into Best, putting Ireland on the back foot. Smith flicks it to Sam Cane then, seeing that Best hasn't regained his place in the line after Read's run and Cane's quick ruck ball, scuttles through the gap himself to score next to the posts. Last year Joe Schmidt out-thought the All Blacks; this time it's a case of a snap decision making all the difference. It makes the score 10–0, but the writing is already on the wall for the Irish. The All Blacks didn't come to fuck around tonight—this is utu for last year and probably Chicago as well. It hasn't helped the men in green that their media have spent the week reminding the All Blacks of those two results, as if they weren't thinking about it anyway. The next try can probably be construed as a response to the Dublin performance, too.

Last time the biggest problem was the failure to get anything going off first phase, especially in the midfield. So, from an attacking scrum, Sevu Reece floats in behind the backline (much like Willie le Roux did in the draw with the Springboks in Wellington) and then takes the ball from Jack Goodhue unmarked and in an acre of space. His pass finds George Bridge, who burns past Robbie Henshaw and looks destined to score before he's hauled down by Keith Earls close to the line. Stockdale has got across in defence and tries a blatant professional foul on Smith when he reaches in for the ball at the ruck, but it backfires badly when the halfback simply goes for the big blindside gap that's just been exposed to score his second. There's also a nice bit of symmetry when Richie Mo'unga does an acrobatic move to keep the ball in play off a Johnny Sexton penalty kick, much like Reece's one in the first game against the Springboks.

Tally up all these moments of brilliance and add the intensity of the way the All Blacks are playing, and the game is as good as over after 20 minutes. Everything is going their way—such as how a tackle from Reece on Sexton jolts the ball loose, Mo'unga hacks it ahead and 50 metres later Beauden Barrett is diving on the ball to score in the corner. It's 22–0, and by the time Ireland finally get on the board it's 34–0 thanks to Codie Taylor and Matt Todd. Bridge and Jordie Barrett finish the job off, curb-stomping home another All Blacks revenge mission.

> **Tally up all these moments of brilliance and add the intensity of the way the All Blacks are playing, and the game is as good as over after 20 minutes. Everything is going their way.**

IN CONTRAST TO THE POOL GAMES, the two teams do not join one another for a lap to thank the crowd and there are no on-field jersey swaps. Best, however, is given the treatment he richly merits with a guard of honour. He gives an emotional farewell to an Irish crowd that has mostly remained in shock at what the All Blacks have just done to their team. They regain the volume that drowned out the haka with an ovation for their skipper, whose career has just ended before their eyes. Now he sits in front of us, with a blemish on his cheek that resembles a craggy mountain range. His eyes that were so full of pride and achievement a year ago are misty and he's drawing breath sharply to keep the tears from flowing. It's hit him hard.

'Maybe we focused on this for too long. We forgot to win some of the little battles along the way over the last twelve months. We wanted to win a quarter-final because then it becomes almost a habit, we talked about it years ago . . . with Joe, he helped take away some of the fear factor that the All Blacks held.'

Old Ice Eyes is sitting next to Best, staring off into the distance and looking as cold and frosty as ever. If you can say one thing about Joe Schmidt, it's that his tone remains remarkably consistent as he rattles off a ton of chatter about the loss. Long, long sentences punctuated with a few y'knows here and there and bits of coaching jargon that you actually need to be in his team to understand.

'You've got to make the All Blacks work for everything, and I felt that in the past we'd forced them to do that,' he says.

He keeps alluding to the short week Ireland have had given that they played on Sunday against Sāmoa in Ōita, plus their disrupted preparation thanks to the Bundee Aki suspension because of his red card. Through the walls of the press conference room, though, we can hear some commotion and Schmidt probably can too. It's the crowd still cheering for the All Blacks leaving the field.

'We've got a wonderful group of players,' Schmidt presses on when asked how he feels about yet another Irish World Cup failure. 'They've achieved a lot of things, but making it past the quarter-finals still remains. I'd say heartbroken is how I feel and how the players feel right now. Maybe it consumed us too much.'

Steve Hansen comes in and sits down, flanked as always by Ian Foster and Kieran Read. He starts by offering a heartfelt tribute to Best and Schmidt, which is as classy as Best's words albeit at the other end of the scale. He keeps going, thanking the efforts of his coaching staff, clearly savouring this win as one of the most satisfying. But his most telling plaudits are for the man on his left. Read was immense out on the field tonight, having transitioned from his role as a wide-ranging distributor to a tighter operator who can literally lead his team up the middle, as seen with Smith's opening try. But, just to remind everyone of the skill set he possesses, Read also set up Taylor under the posts with an offload through the attention of two tacklers.

'He's copped a lot of flak from people about his form,' says Hansen, in a direct throwback to his words in Rome last November. 'He's led the team really, really well. I think he's even gone to a higher level during the World Cup.'

Hansen turns and looks his skipper directly in the eye and congratulates him. This is a moment of vindication for both men, but the All Blacks coach is not gloating. There is far too much to be done yet, even though they've booked themselves in for a guaranteed two more games. We're now in Japan for the full duration of the campaign, but hopefully that means we don't have to cover what Hansen bluntly describes as (even after taking a moment to choose his words, then thinking 'Fuck it, I'll say it anyway') the 'loser final'. That's his name for the play-off for third and fourth spots—the game no one wants to play in.

He does have a parting shot for the Irish media before he's done, though. Clearly all the talk about the last two out of three games between the two teams being Irish wins is too good an opportunity to pass up, so Hansen calmly spells out an undeniable difference between the sides, which will still very much be a factor in four years' time.

'It was interesting to hear of how experienced Ireland are. Half of our 23 had played in the knockout of the World Cup and won. That was the difference, wasn't it? I'm not being disrespectful here in saying that, but Ireland's experience was not to win. And we have the guys who actually had experience of winning. And that's why you've got to be careful when you start talking about experience.'

MEANWHILE, BACK DOWN IN ŌITA, the All Blacks' opponent next weekend has been found and they have even less experience than the Irish when it comes to World Cup knockout games. The English have won their first quarter-final since 2007, beating the Wallabies 40–16, with the result meaning that Michael Cheika will be out of a job soon and it's up to him to jump before he's pushed. It also means that the All Blacks will not be crossing paths with the one team that's beaten them in 2019 so far, and it's an ignominious fall for the Wallabies from the heights of the Perth Bledisloe Cup test. Since that dismemberment, their season has lurched from bad to worse, losing to Wales in their opening game of the tournament and now getting torched by the English today.

Something has to change quickly in Australian rugby, but that's a story for another day.

Eddie Jones is smiling, though. He's defeated his old Randwick teammate by tinkering with his side and outsmarting what he knew would be a stubbornly narrow-minded approach from Cheika. But next weekend will be a different story, as he's up against Hansen and the All Blacks, who were able to change their entire game plan on the fly the last time the teams met back in Twickenham last year.

Eddie Jones is smiling, though. He's defeated his old Randwick teammate by tinkering with his side and outsmarting what he knew would be a stubbornly narrow-minded approach from Cheika.

That's not the only throwback result people are talking about, either. The last time the All Blacks and England played in a World Cup knockout game was in Cape Town in 1995, with the English firmly confident of a win based on past form. It ended up being possibly the most important game of its era, when Jonah Lomu more or less dragged rugby into professionalism on his own mighty back. While there is no one of his stature around these days, this rematch is shaping up to be a blockbuster as well.

56

FANS WITH KEYBOARDS

Conrad Tokyo Hotel, Minato City, 22 October 2019

GODDAMMIT. HERE WE ARE, THINKING we've finally got something out of Hansen at a surprise appearance at a Tuesday press conference. He's just produced a withering attack on the state of affairs in the Six Nations, saying somewhat hypocritically that the European Tier 1 nations only care about themselves and that a global rugby season needs to be implemented. It's not exactly blockbuster stuff, because there's no secret that he thought that anyway, but it's far better than the usual early-week deflection of any questions about impending team selection. That's what the headlines will be about, and Hansen even says so.

Except, about 20 minutes after Hansen leaves the room, Eddie Jones decides he's going to steal the spotlight. The English team press conference is across town at the Tokyo Bay Hilton, so I had to make a choice about which one to attend. A quick scroll through

Twitter shows that I made the wrong choice, because Fast Eddie is popping off big time and I really should've known because this train is never late. First come the allegations of spying—carefully worded to not actually allege that the All Blacks did it, mind you. The English are training out at Shining Arcs, where last year we joked about how easy it would be for someone to get into one of the 15-storey buildings next door and have a decent look at what the All Blacks are doing. Turns out someone may well have been doing just that—or they were merely a resident of said building having a look out their window. Or Jones is just full of shit. It's unlikely we'll ever know, but that doesn't stop him going on about spying and how he hasn't done it since 2001.

We like to think we're fairly critical of the All Blacks, but compared with the Poms the vast majority of Kiwi writers are basically just a thinly veiled PR machine.

Jones then claims that the All Blacks' mental-strength coach will be the busiest man in Tokyo this week. Again, that's fucking unlikely considering I share my commute with thousands of people who literally fall asleep on trains given that's the closest they get to free time outside of work. By now, though, he's definitely saying everything with a smile that completely gives it all away. Especially when he comes out with his biggest wind-up: that all New Zealand rugby media are just 'fans with keyboards'.

That last one is quite funny, to be fair, as well as being pretty apt.

We like to think we're fairly critical of the All Blacks, but compared with the Poms the vast majority of Kiwi writers are basically just a thinly veiled PR machine. I can count myself in that camp as well in a lot of the stuff that I write, but I guess in our defence it's kind of hard to get too many juicy angles on a team that has the best winning record in sports and almost prides itself on how little information is given away and how dull its press conferences can be. As well as the fact that if you grow up in New Zealand you're an All Blacks fan first and foremost, as they are our national team. The English press, along with the Irish, well, they're different. They don't have as much sentimental attachment as we do and therefore hunt as a pack. At the end of Hansen's talk, half a dozen of them gather together at the front of the room and discuss what the best angles are so they can all get the most out of what's been said.

There's very little of that collegiality among the Kiwi journalists, even between those working for the same organisations. It's a shame, as a bit of unionisation among us would probably force the All Blacks to become more accessible. If nothing else, it would've saved us from a miserable training-ground experience this morning. It's easily the coldest day of the tour so far, but that didn't stop the media liaison from making us wait half an hour in the driving rain at Seaside Park. It's an intolerable state of affairs, and awful, even by the shoddy standards of the All Blacks.

Our shoes were squelching by the time the team finally arrived, and they immediately started doing their warm-ups as far away as possible. When they finally did jog by, they were instructed to turn their backs to our cameras. The 15 minutes of filming time we were promised turned out to be more like half that, and again we were booted out like naughty school kids who'd missed the bell marking the end of lunchtime.

Out we slopped, nursing the same audible discontent as when we were short-changed by the prime minister's visit. Everyone was grumbling or laughing incredulously at what had just transpired. Again I was approached by a foreign cameraman, who has been to a few All Blacks press events now. He asked me a question that basically sums up the whole situation.

'Why do they . . . ummm . . . hate us? Do they not know what we do for them?'

All I could do was shrug. Eddie was right—we are just fans with keyboards most of the time. We also get treated like shit for a lot of that time too, especially at this tournament. I guess you need to be the sort of actual paying fans who show up to watch the All Blacks in New Zealand: ones who pretend they're having a good time and don't make any noise.

I MAKE IT BACK TO the Kabukichō and the looming figure of Godzilla. It's been a landmark few days—I've even managed to get a bit of sleep on the train myself and am no longer reliant on Google Maps. Dinner can be ordered in Japanese and I slurp noodles louder than the guy next to me. I get annoyed when gaijin get in my way on the train, and even more so when they breach protocol while I'm relaxing in the onsen with other hard-working company men. It's in the traditional naked spa bath that it hits home just how much of what Hansen said today should have made headlines for all the wrong reasons, but will get drowned out by the hysteria over Jones' jokes.

To call out the Six Nations unions for not wanting to give up their competition in favour of a global season is a pretty safe swing from where Hansen's sitting, because everyone in New Zealand sees the UK as a pack of greedy introverts. But when you think about it, it's ridiculous coming from someone involved with NZ Rugby. To ask them to give up what will end up being a sizable chunk of their income each year to benefit the rest of the world makes little sense when NZ Rugby can't even invest in the Pacific Islands. In fact, if it wasn't for the French Top 14, Fiji would barely be able to scrape together a national team at all, because it's that competition that offers the Fijian players a pathway to play professionally and still represent their country (true, it's not perfect, and the French are also the most shameless when it comes to identifying talented young Fijian players as potential future Frenchmen, but at least their pro competition exists as a decent incubator of talent compared with the New Zealand system of pretty much closing the Super Rugby doors on anyone not eligible for the All Blacks).

So, at the very least, it's actually a toss-up between two evils. But the Poms and the French always get the blame from this side of the world because they've got bigger wallets to open. However, while I lie back in the onsen and observe yet another dirty gaijin get into the pool without having washed, it's all starting to hurt my brain.

57
SWITCHEROO

Conrad Tokyo Hotel, Minato City, 24 October 2019

FORGET TALKING SMACK ABOUT GLOBAL rugby seasons and spying. Hansen throws out the biggest mindfuck of all when he names his side to play England, because he's relegated one of his most consistent players and an all-round good-news story to the bench. Sam Cane, who a year ago was lying on a hospital bed in Pretoria wondering if he'd ever play again, is in jersey 20. Scott Barrett will start at blindside, which is a move clearly intended to target the English lineout and in particular hooker Jamie George's throwing. The biggest Barrett brother had a great time disrupting George last year at Twickenham—indeed, if you want to go further back, you could pin a decent amount of the blame for the British & Irish Lions' failure to secure a historic win at Eden Park in the third test of 2017 on George's lineout botches.

It's also a dramatic departure from the one area Hansen has been lauded for embracing midway through the season. Cane and Ardie Savea have been in dynamic form together as left and right flankers, but now we're seeing the All Blacks return to a traditional big man at six to carry the ball and offer another tight forward. If it doesn't work, they can presumably go to plan B, which is Cane—which up until now was plan A anyway. This is a pretty powerful statement, though. Not only has Barrett been in fantastic form since his return from suspension, but it shows that Hansen isn't afraid to shuffle the cards yet again so deep into the business end of the tournament.

If anything, that's what he's been doing all year. The key here is throwing something at Jones and his team that they probably weren't expecting, because there's very little the English can do likewise. Barrett coming in means that, on the surface at least, the All Blacks are going to play a tight game like when they mounted their comeback against the English at Twickenham. Or are they? The All Blacks can still play an expansive game with Barrett there, especially with fresh wingers who the English had probably never heard of last year.

> ## It shows that Hansen isn't afraid to shuffle the cards yet again so deep into the business end of the tournament. If anything, that's what he's been doing all year.

There's a bit more talk later in the week from a far more subdued Eddie Jones, who names his side and makes a switch himself. George Ford comes back in at first five, which raises a few eyebrows given that Ford is not exactly noted for his punishing defence and will be in charge of controlling the channel that Richie Mo'unga and Beauden Barrett will operate in.

'Whenever you play New Zealand,' Jones says, keeping up the tournament tradition of opposition coaches and players never referring to them as the All Blacks, 'your work off the ball is going to be massively important. They like to move the ball around, and George [Ford]'s work off the ball is absolutely exceptional.'

You get the feeling that it's going to be an all-out war up front, and the score is most probably going to progress in multiples of three.

Jones playing that aspect up is just one small part of the equation, though. You get the feeling that it's going to be an all-out war up front, and the score is most probably going to progress in multiples of three.

GAME DAY DAWNS FINE IN Tokyo after a Friday of exceptionally heavy rain. It turns our part of the city into something out of *Blade Runner*, especially given the sleaze and vice around Cinecity Square. There's an old homeless guy in a crumpled suit begging for change at the base of a statue of a lion, muttering endlessly to himself. I fish into my pocket, grab a few coins, and the hand that accepts them is missing the top joints of the little and ring fingers. He looks at me and keeps muttering, and by now I can see he's not wearing a shirt and under his jacket his torso is covered in ornate tattoos. This is a guy with a story to tell, and I'm pissed off I can't understand him because I figure that's exactly what he's doing. He is yakuza, a gangster, or at least was once upon a time.

Englishmen are out in force from early in the morning. Many have just arrived and are toting their luggage along the streets and alleys, some screwing up their faces at the smell from sewer vents whose odour permeates a couple of key intersections. They don't have the fatalistic merriment of the Irish a week before, or the crude provincialism of the South Africans. There's a non-committal look in their eyes, like they know that if the All Blacks show up like they did last week, the Poms can fall back on the excuse that they never thought they were going to win anyway. But if the Poms can pull off a win, expect those same noses inhaling the sickly faecal odour right now to be sky-high with conceit for the next four years. If there's any bloody motivation to win this game, that's it right there. Oh yeah, that and the cricket.

58
FLASHBACK

Eden Park, 23 October 1999

I'M 18 YEARS OLD AND standing, shirtless, on the wooden planks that slope up the old eastern terrace at Eden Park. I have my Wellington College black-and-yellow scarf wrapped around my head and I've painted my face in the same colours. It cost me $10 to be at the NPC first-division final, which features Wellington for the first time ever. My team runs out to a decent reception from the large number of away fans, but I'm blown away by the roar that greets the Auckland side as it's my first-ever rugby game outside of Athletic Park. Wellington have had a break-out season—we've finally managed to not finish sixth in the first division. Just making the semis was rarefied air enough, but last weekend we managed to beat Canterbury on Lancaster Park. Four years ago, they put 66 points on us in possibly the worst Ranfurly Shield challenge ever.

There's about 25,000 at Eden Park tonight, in the hodgepodge of stands that aren't linked up in any way. The middle of the field is tinged with a darker shade of brown from the cricket pitch running diagonally across the ground. Our team is full of what you'd term 'battlers'. We only have one recent All Black and it's Norm Hewitt, who has watched far more tests from the bench than he's actually played in. Cult heroes David Holwell, Jason O'Halloran and Ali Koko are in the backline. Colin Sullivan, known as the 'Flying Pencil' due to his slight frame and high speed, is at fullback. Opposing them is a heavily favoured Auckland side with no fewer than nine All Blacks.

I might be young, but I've been watching the Wellington side long enough to know that they're probably going to lose this game. They always do, but keep you coming back because it's the 1990s and there's really not much else to do in Wellington—plus we're getting a flash new stadium next year down on the waterfront, so it's likely that our reasonably decent home crowds for NPC fixtures will get a welcome boost.

Right now, the World Cup is going on, so the two sides are shorn of their front-line All Blacks for the final, which will become the norm in the professional era. There's been some grumbling about the shine being taken off the game's domestic showpiece, especially since the All Blacks have dominated headlines with their Air New Zealand plane adorned with a painting of the front row. They have breezed through their pool and will play Scotland in a quarter-final on Monday morning, which I'm probably going to miss because we'll be travelling home. I'm not that fussed—there's no point getting too invested in a tournament the All Blacks will probably win easily when my beloved Wellington team is playing their biggest game since holding the Shield. The semi-final, against either Argentina or France, should be a breeze as well. Back at Athletic Park in June the All Blacks put 50 points on the French, so they'll pose little threat. It's all about the NPC right now, though.

Of course, Wellington do lose. But at least they go down fighting, scoring the last two tries in a game that ends 24–18. It leaves me gutted but proud—I love this team and what they've achieved this year, and I can't imagine ever not being there for moments like this. Provincial rugby is the lifeblood of the game I love; it pulses through my veins. I'll follow this team to the ends of the earth, even if they never win anything.

ALMOST EXACTLY 20 YEARS LATER, I stroll into the media workroom at Yokohama International Stadium. It's about three hours before the kick-off of the All Blacks' biggest game in four years: the semi-final against England. Someone has their laptop open and is streaming the Mitre 10 Cup final. It's Wellington against Tasman, a team that didn't even exist back when I first travelled to Auckland to watch the final aged 18. Because of the hype surrounding the All Blacks and their campaign, I'd completely forgotten that Wellington had made it into the final. The game is being played in Nelson and I would struggle to name half the Wellington side, but before I left the few glimpses I did catch of them on TV showed exceptionally sparse crowds at the now ageing Westpac Stadium. The semi-final last weekend against Canterbury looked like it had an attendance of about three men and a dog. This is what provincial rugby in New Zealand is now.

Playing for Tasman today is Liam Squire, who would be on his way out here on the All Blacks' team bus if things had gone according to plan. But they haven't, so that's why Scott Barrett is starting in his blindside spot. Right now, it's hard to gauge whether Squire will ever play for the All Blacks again, but he's having fun out in his red-and-blue Tasman jersey this afternoon. Wellington, like they so often do, play their part as the losing finalists and give Tasman their first-ever bit of silverware.

> ## That's the bottom line—no one can question the way the game is headed because the World Cup belongs to the All Blacks and New Zealand . . . But, as it turns out, not for much longer.

It's a curtain-raiser. The real game starts soon here in Yokohama, with the All Blacks still as strong as ever in the eye of public perception. It doesn't matter to them if there's no interest at all in the game below their level, because if they're the best then that's all that matters. That's the bottom line—no one can question the way the game is headed because the World Cup belongs to the All Blacks and New Zealand.

But, as it turns out, not for much longer.

59
DOWNFALL

**Yokohama International Stadium, 26 October 2019
(Rugby World Cup Semi-final)**

ALL BLACKS	**7**
ENGLAND	**19**

FOR ALL THE TALK WE'VE had to endure, all the thinly veiled, lazy dog-whistling designed to infuriate New Zealanders, the English have finally done it. They've come up with a plan that has sucked the life out of the All Blacks and thrown it back in their faces, leaving the New Zealanders flustered and wondering what just happened.

And the game hasn't even kicked off yet.

Every time the haka has been performed during the tournament, it's had a little bit more of an edge thanks to Kieran Read and TJ Perenara's dual leadership. Fingers hover over keyboards awaiting some new development, but this time they come crashing down due to the audacious English response. We're sitting high up in the stands yet again, gazing down upon a full house at Yokohama

International Stadium, and out in the middle the Englishmen have produced a devilishly simple yet stunningly effective move. They've formed an inverted V, surrounding the All Blacks on three sides. In military terms it would be a pincer movement, but in symbolic terms it immediately wrests attention off the haka itself. They're embracing their role of sneering, confident bullies with scant regard for tradition—indeed, the first reaction is to question whether what they're doing is even legal according to World Rugby's guidelines.

Even if it isn't, there is little anyone can do, although referee Nigel Owens attempts to wave the outer fringes of the English formation back behind halfway. Prop Joe Marler, who has proven himself to be never short of a word in his career, has positioned himself on the very far edge and facetiously shrugs and motions that he can't hear Owens or understand what he's being told to do. The haka is done without the drowning noise of 'Swing Low' this time. Everyone is in a bit of shock at what they're seeing, but that's nothing compared with what's about to happen next.

England pull a switcheroo of their own off the kick-off, with George Ford flicking the ball to Owen Farrell to send over to the opposite side of the field than expected. Even though Aaron Smith clears for touch, the English get the possession they want straight away. The All Blacks' perceived plan to target the lineout is absent first up, with Courtney Lawes winning uncontested ball at two and Ben Youngs sending it to the midfield. After only 50 seconds and two English rucks, the All Blacks are already creeping offside and they're about to be caught out.

Richie Mo'unga is defending one man in, out on the left wing next to George Bridge. Elliot Daly spots that the gap between them is ripe for the picking and goes straight through on halfway. By the time Bridge catches him, the damage is done because Daly has all the momentum and frees a pass to Anthony Watson. The winger, who as a British & Irish Lion was on the receiving end of Sonny Bill Williams' shoulder in 2017, cruises past Jack Goodhue and through Beauden Barrett past the 22 as the clock ticks past one minute. Back the ball goes, over to the other side of the field, stretching the All Blacks thin and opening up what the English plan to exploit next.

There's a perfect exchange of passes between Lawes and Kyle Sinckler that sends Ford sailing past Read. Both men have their arms nice and free to make the ball move, because Samuel Whitelock and Joe Moody both charge in low, which is the way they've been focusing on defending ever since red cards started getting handed out at the start of the tournament. Mako Vunipola rumbles it close to the line, then Lawes again, who has timed his run to smash apart any remaining resistance. They're only a metre short and Manu Tuilagi sees that the openside is indeed very open, picking up the ball and crashing through a Moody tackle to score next to the posts.

Time elapsed: 1 minute, 36 seconds.

Farrell sends the conversion through the posts and the All Blacks, along with pretty much everyone else in the stadium, are wondering what the hell we just saw. Yes, it completely mirrored the start of the game last year at Twickenham, but this time it feels far more composed and clinical. Especially when Tuilagi picks off a Beauden Barrett pass and sends Jonny May away for what should be another try. However, somehow Scott Barrett guns him down and saves the day.

Last time, the All Blacks played a bit of a rope-a-dope. Tonight the English have landed a blow that's floored them in the very first round.

It's insanely confusing, because the All Blacks haven't fired a shot and seem content with passively letting England do what they want with them.

The All Blacks aren't helping themselves, either. The first 20 minutes sees them kick away valuable possession—most notably a bomb into the 22 that May takes under no duress at all for a mark. The resulting lineout drive is attacked by Maro Itoje, who rips the ball away and sets England up on halfway to attack again. It's insanely confusing, because the All Blacks haven't fired a shot and seem content with passively letting England do what they want with them. In another throwback to last year, Underhill runs in to score but it's disallowed—although this time the TMO decision is far more cut and dried as Tom Curry has committed an obvious obstruction in the lead-up. But it doesn't matter. The signs are that if the All Blacks are going to salvage this match, it will take a massive turnaround not only from them, but from the red-hot English as well.

Half-time sees the score push out to 10–0 after a Ford penalty, but really they should be up by 25 at this stage. Steve Hansen has coached 106 and a half All Blacks tests in his career, and now he needs to make the most important half-time speech of them all. First things first—the Barrett experiment has not worked, even though Scott has actually been one of the better performers on the park. The English lineout is humming along nicely, but it's their ball-carriers who are doing all the damage by falling nose to the ground and recycling at lightning speed. Most importantly of all, the defence is absolutely destroying the All Blacks' ball-carriers. It seems as though Beauden Barrett is only ever touching the ball going backwards, and the kicking game has gone from bad to worse. England's, on the other hand, is working perfectly. Bombs go up, get contested and won, and are then followed up with long, raking kicks that are finding real estate more valuable than a Ponsonby villa.

Up in the tightly packed media area, faces all around are stunned. Well, almost all. The last week has seen a steady influx of New Zealand media that have come up specifically for the business end of the tournament, so our contingent has swollen to around forty. The latecomers are too excited about simply getting here to really take on board that something terrible is happening, but we campaign veterans can already tell that the writing is on the wall. I go down and talk to Blair, the Newshub cameraman who braved the typhoon. He asks me what do I reckon.

I tell him the All Blacks are fucked.

IT'S JUST AFTER HALF-TIME AND, whatever Hansen has said, England give the clearest indication that they are not going to make the same slip they did last year at Twickenham. Ben Youngs snipes in to score what should be the match-sealing try, but again it's disallowed by a slight knock-on in the lineout drive that precedes it.

As it turns out the All Blacks do end up benefiting from Jamie George at the lineout. The problem is it's basically the only mistake the English make in the whole game, and it doesn't come through any bit of tactical genius. The English hooker simply lobs a bad throw over his jumper that falls into the waiting hands of Ardie Savea, who dives over from five metres out. That try and the conversion are the only points the All Blacks score in the game. The man who masterminded that statistic is sitting up in the stands and probably feeling pretty vindicated right now. It's John 'The Journey' Mitchell, who has spent the better part of two decades bouncing in and out of coaching jobs before landing the role that finally has him on his way to the biggest prize in the game.

The key defensive plays have been the kick-chase and rush defence, plus the almost psychic ability to target the All Blacks' next ball-carrier. It's seen when Jordie Barrett tries to run a kick back and is eviscerated by Underhill, meaning that his attempt at an offload is fumbled forward by Angus Ta'avao. It's seen when lineout after lineout is won with the All Blacks simply standing around and watching. When Ford and Farrell both direct traffic and move behind the ruck to make sure there are always defenders ready to deal with anything the All Blacks throw at them. When the frustration gets too much and Samuel Whitelock of all people shoves Farrell to the ground after the whistle's blown, getting a penalty reversed.

Mitchell, along with Jones, has out-thought the All Blacks. Many New Zealand fans blame Mitchell for the All Blacks losing a World Cup semi-final, when he was their coach in 2003. Now we can do it again, but happily for him this time he's sitting in the triumphant coaches' box.

Of course, by now that sickening feeling I felt last year in Dublin has been growing in the pit of my stomach. Around the crowd, I can see pockets of All Blacks fans suffering the same pain. It's moving down their arms and making their hands reach up and attach to their head, or cover their faces. It's making them stamp their feet when the ball is dropped yet again, sapping their will and rendering them silent. Most of all, it's wrapping around our hearts and slowly crushing us. The clock moves past the 70-minute mark and England have made it a two-score game that the All Blacks have no hope of catching.

The final whistle goes. The All Blacks gather in a circle in the middle of the field, then Kieran Read and some of the other players walk directly up the tunnel. The World Cup is gone. It is Read's 34th birthday.

60
THE BITTER END

Yokohama International Stadium, 26 October 2019

SO IT DOES END HERE, back in the media room where it all started a year ago. When we waited for Michael Cheika to come in and fire up at a question John Campbell asked. Where Steve Hansen made light of a question about the upcoming test against Ireland, which was ultimately lost. When the All Blacks had completed just another day at work and it seemed like threepeating the World Cup was going to be a pure formality.

The mood is pretty different now, although it is almost comical when the World Rugby press guy announces that the All Blacks 'delegation' is on their way. Even now, just moments after the biggest loss they've suffered in 12 years, I can't help but shake my head at the pomposity. The room is packed, but the feeling among everyone present is that we can't really believe what we've just seen. The English have won by the margin of four penalty goals, yet it might as well have been 50 points. None of us have ever seen the All Blacks get monstered so badly in a test, and after racking my brains for a while the only one I can compare it to was the second-test loss against the Lions in 1993. But that was a far, far different era. This English team has clearly been preparing for this night for a long, long time—but Eddie Jones isn't going to rub it in the faces of anyone, like Jamie Joseph did when Japan beat Ireland.

There were no massive turning points, no dodgy reffing decisions (it took about half an hour for England to even be awarded a penalty), no outrageous French miracles. This was like watching your dad getting beaten up for 80 minutes in front of your entire family.

Quite the opposite. Fast Eddie is now Nice-guy Eddie, overflowing with platitudes and respect for the All Blacks. One question by a local reporter is answered with Jones referring to them as the 'gods of rugby'. Meanwhile, next to him Owen Farrell has an unnervingly focused look on his face. It's as if he knew all along this game was going to go the way it did and now he can just focus on the final. It's admittedly impressive—damn it, they're all impressive. They've just smashed the All Blacks and there is no excuse this time. This was the most comprehensive victory, ever, by a team playing the All Blacks. Just let that sink in. There were no massive turning points, no dodgy reffing decisions (it took about half an hour for England to even be awarded a penalty), no outrageous French miracles. This was like watching your dad getting beaten up for 80 minutes in front of your entire family.

Hansen comes in and delivers a statement praising England. Read sits to his left, still in his All Blacks jersey, sporting a black eye and staring off like Farrell, but towards a place that might have been rather than towards the ultimate prize. Foster is there too, looking the same way he did after the Perth loss. All three men field questions and give honest answers about the way the game went, till Andrew Gourdie asks Read about the team's mindset.

'From the players' point of view, did the team turn up with the right attitude tonight?'

Initially, Read gives a boilerplate answer that would probably fly under the radar. After all, it is a pretty standard question after a loss.

'Yeah, I think we did. You've seen how hard we worked out there. Definitely the boys really wanted it . . . It's a hard thing to take and we're all hurting.'

But then Hansen pipes up, and when he does we all lean forward a little bit because we know something big is coming.

'I think it's quite a disrespectful question to suggest that the All Blacks turned up not being hungry. They were desperate to win the game. Because I asked them at half-time to get hungrier doesn't mean to say they didn't turn up pretty hungry. There's a big difference, and if you want to spend some time outside I'll give you a rugby education on that one. But to turn up and say an All Blacks team comes to the semi-final of a Rugby World Cup with the amount of ability and the history it has behind it . . . that's a pretty average question.'

Emotions were high but there was no need for that, especially because all we ever hear from the All Blacks is how they embrace and walk towards pressure. This, whether anyone likes it or not, is a pressure situation. So walk the fuck towards it and don't lose your rag.

Downstairs, Codie Taylor is choking back tears as he tells of the disappointment. Taylor has been sent out first to face the media in Dublin, Perth and now here, but I'm not sure if it's because he's seen as being better at handling losses or it's just the way the roster has worked. Four years of preparation, he says. It might just be a rugby game but we worked so hard. Dane Coles follows and gives a typically forthright assessment. He seems more philosophical, but he's devastated as well.

There was no need for that, especially because all we ever hear from the All Blacks is how they embrace and walk towards pressure. This, whether anyone likes it or not, is a pressure situation. So walk the fuck towards it and don't lose your rag.

Then comes someone who isn't exactly smiling but has every right to. It's Manu Tuilagi, who scored the try that effectively ended the game almost as soon as it started. We want to know about the response to the haka, but he seems almost embarrassed having to describe it.

'It was to show that we're ready,' he says in regards to the V-formation. 'That we accept the challenge and that we're ready to take the All Blacks head-on. Playing the All Blacks, you can't wait, you can't wait. They're the best team in the world, you have to attack them right from the start.'

As Tuilagi talks, he gives away a tell-tale sign. He's the youngest of the six rugby-playing Tuilagi brothers, yet the only one not to play for Sāmoa—even though his full name is Manusamoa. He's lived in England for most of his life, so he talks with a very unique accent. But maybe it's his Sāmoan heritage showing through when he is the only member of the England squad to refer to their opponents as the 'All Blacks' rather than plain old 'New Zealand'.

However, a reluctance to use the nickname is as close to disrespect as this English team has got, and that's a long way off. The V-formation will be talked about a lot in the coming days, but the haka is designed to elicit a response and the English have finally figured out one that works for them. In the coming days, too, World Rugby will post a video of the V-formation on their YouTube page, describing it as an 'incredible response' and garnering more than six million views, then turn around and fine the victors for doing it.

It's unlikely any of the English team will either notice or care.

61
FALLOUT

APA Hotel Shinjuku, 28 October 2019

THERE'S A GIGANTIC, TERRIFYING CROW perched on the railing outside my hotel room. It's making a cacophony of noise as it beats its wings and surveys Shinjuku. I'm sitting on my bed in my minuscule room, pondering how it's fair to say that the English result has done more than just harm the All Blacks on the field. That's because the reaction from back home, from what I can tell, hasn't been good.

It's not like 1999, when people abused John Hart and his horse. It's not like 2003, when one loss dictated a complete overhaul of the coaching and management staff. It's not like 2007, when one referee's non-call has passed into wider national lore.

No, the feeling this time is that there's a distinct lack of feeling, at least in comparison. Of course, that's not to say that people aren't gutted, it's just that it hasn't ground the country to a halt like it used to. There's plenty of conversations to be had as to why— obviously this hasn't happened in 12 years, and society and the way information is spread has changed almost immeasurably—but

I can't help but draw a correlation between the lack of interest in domestic rugby and the general 'oh well, we did our best' talk about the All Blacks' biggest loss in over a decade. Part of it, admittedly, is that the English completely deserved to win and even the most one-eyed All Blacks supporter would readily admit that.

> **You used to watch the local players develop and grow, hoping they'd get picked for the All Blacks one day, so you could feel like you were part of that story too. I was there when Tana Umaga played his first-ever game for Wellington; I watched on when he debuted for the All Blacks; I almost cried when he led 'Kapa o Pango' for the first time.**

But it's obvious that the game hasn't got the same hold on people anymore. There's less of a weekly attachment to a local team, so therefore less of a personal attachment to the players themselves. You used to watch them develop and grow, hoping they'd get picked for the All Blacks one day, so you could feel like you were part of that story too. I was there when Tana Umaga played his first-ever game for Wellington; I watched on when he debuted for the All Blacks; I almost cried when he led 'Kapa o Pango' for the first time. It's silly and sentimental, but it still cemented my bond with the game.

Rugby in New Zealand is, despite all the rhetoric to the contrary, deeply conservative. Things aren't supposed to change much, and when they do, it's generally with a great deal of angst. For over a decade now, NZ Rugby has been happy to trumpet the fact that as long as the All Blacks are the best team in the world, all is well. But that changed on Saturday night and now they don't have that fact to hide behind anymore. The cracks that have been papered over are going to become far, far more visible in the coming years, like the accusing rows of empty seats around the country.

They need to act, fast.

My loud avian visitor lets out one last blood-curdling squawk, spreads its wings and launches itself off the railing. It swoops down, in between the neon and glass, above the heads of the tourists and locals bustling through the Kabukichō. I watch it arch up around the Toho cinema building next door, around the head of Godzilla. For a moment, the crow is a buzzard circling a carcass.

Godzilla has been defeated, beaten back by an English force that absorbed his power and hurled it back in his face. They went into battle with no fear of the great monster, and now will fight it out for the ultimate prize.

62
THE HALF-EMPTY ROOM

Conrad Tokyo Hotel, Minato City, 30 October 2019

WE'VE COME A LONG WAY since the day we sat down in this room for the first official press conference of the tournament. I've come even further since we were in this hotel in the lead-up to the third Bledisloe Cup game, which was exactly a year and three days and a trip around the world ago. It was a hell of a lot warmer then— in both temperature and mood. Everyone's had a lot to digest since the loss on the weekend, and some of us had a lot to drink in the immediate aftermath. Cameraman Blair and I stayed up until 4am on Sunday morning, drinking whisky on a balcony and debating the merits of boomer rock songs, which almost led to an altercation over whether 'Invisible Touch' by Genesis was a female empowerment anthem or a misogynistic rant by a jilted ex.

It was nice to forget about rugby for a while. I get the feeling a lot of the All Blacks want to as well, but unfortunately they're stuck here for what Steve Hansen has called the 'loser final'. It's against Warren Gatland's Wales, who went down to the Springboks in their semi-final on the Sunday night. It was an awful, awful game, made far worse by the fact that none of us wanted to be there anyway, although it was nice to see the charming duo of Rassie Erasmus and Siya Kolisi get the reward for two hard seasons of rebuilding. It wasn't that long ago that the Boks had the darkest on-field day in their history, beaten 57–0 by the All Blacks at Albany. Kolisi is now in line to be the first black African to get his hands on the Rugby World Cup.

It's not that different for England, though. Just a year ago, Eddie Jones was one big loss away from unemployment. Now he's arguably the most powerful man in the game. John Mitchell's 'journey' is unlikely to sway anyone in New Zealand with a long rugby memory, but right now he's being lauded as a genius in the UK. *The Times* runs an article that quotes Courtney Lawes as saying 'we love him'.

It wasn't that long ago that the Boks had the darkest on-field day in their history, beaten 57–0 by the All Blacks at Albany. Kolisi is now in line to be the first black African to get his hands on the Rugby World Cup.

But all of that talk is for their rooms, which are now teeming with British and South African journalists. Hansen walks into ours and immediately points out that around half the chairs are empty. A big contingent of the New Zealand media has upped sticks and jumped on the daily direct flights back to Auckland, back to a nation that is patting itself on the back for how well it has reacted to the semi-final loss. Apparently we've grown up as a sporting nation.

It is an emotional press conference, and it seems that initial reactions have evaporated and been replaced with an eerie emptiness. It's clear from Hansen and the players that the void will be filled with regret and sadness for the time being, with a long period of reflection coming up. The only real future talk this week has been around Sonny Bill Williams, who is rumoured to be fielding at least two massive offers to return to rugby league as both a player and a coach. But that's a story for later, anyway. Right now, we're listening to Hansen talk about the excitement of getting one last shot at playing rugby this season, because for a lot of the team he's just named, it will be the last time ever in an All Blacks jersey.

Along with Kieran Read, Ben Smith will get his richly deserved send-off as well. Ryan Crotty will crash his way up the field for the last time. Williams will presumably do the same as well, although he hasn't confirmed anything yet. That pair have a decent history together, first playing for Canterbury alongside one another nine years ago. Then there are the guys who might be playing their last game (at least for a while) and don't even know it yet—there will be a new coach and presumably an entirely different approach next season, so there's likely to be a bit of turnover within the current 31-man squad. Some of that might not even be due to the new coach anyway—just ask Damian McKenzie and Liam Squire.

While it is still pretty raw, it's probably fair to look back on that missing duo as a fairly key reason as to why the All Blacks aren't preparing for the final right now. It's not because there weren't adequate replacements for them—on the contrary, McKenzie's spot was taken by Beauden Barrett and Squire's by Ardie Savea, two of the best players in the world—it's that the change threw all the meticulous groundwork that had gone into the All Blacks' game plan just slightly out of whack. The Barrett and Richie Mo'unga starting combination took a while to get going, then showed what it could do against the Wallabies at Eden Park. While it looked great in the quarter-final, it's becoming clear that that game says more about the Irish than about the All Blacks. The English nullified the firepower of both players to a gentle squirt, while exploiting Mo'unga's defensive uncertainty out wide.

Ironically, on the whole, both Barrett and Mo'unga had excellent seasons otherwise, but this experiment to replicate the triple-attack threat with McKenzie starting at fullback will go down as a failure. Many have been pointing out that the All Blacks had been running this formation anyway, with Mo'unga coming off the bench in 2018 and Barrett dropping to fullback, but that was later in the game. The small margins are the ones to be exploited in this modern game, and Jones and Mitchell did just that (with Mitchell showing that he's still very capable of upsetting New Zealanders when he suggests that Sam Underhill and Tom Curry are better than Richie McCaw).

Dane Coles comes in and cracks a joke about England being

rich enough to afford the fine that World Rugby has given them over their challenge to the haka because 'they get paid shitloads'. He's then asked about having his family here to support him, including his father who has battled health problems lately. He chokes up and begins to cry.

63
VULNERABILITY

Nippon Seinenkan Hotel, Tokyo, 31 October 2019

'CAN I ADD TO THAT . . .'

Steve Hansen has piggybacked onto a question aimed at one of his players again, except this time it's not launched with the emotional vitriol from the post-match of the other night. I'd asked Aaron Smith about what advice he'd give to people in New Zealand, particularly young men, about dealing with being down and how to communicate their feelings with their peers. Smith opened up, talking about pain, honesty, All Blacks pouring their hearts out, grown men showing vulnerability. Like Coles and Ryan Crotty the day before, his voice cracks a bit as he says the team care about each other a lot, and explains how they check in with each other. How they had left their team review meeting feeling better for talking together.

Now Hansen wants to give us his thoughts, and we're all ears.

'It is a massive problem in New Zealand. Our biggest one is that we don't give people struggling permission to say they're struggling. They think they have to hide it. As a result of hiding it, it bottles up like a volcano and when it gets too hot it blows. Our job as parents, as work colleagues, is to support people. But first of all you've got to know they need the support, and to know that you've got to know your people. You have to allow them to be vulnerable and it takes a lot to be vulnerable.

'How people react to your vulnerability is either going to allow you to do it again or it's going to shut you down. Giving them permission is the key and just letting them be vulnerable. It's no different in sport, families and work.

'And we've got to do it better than what we're doing.'

Out of everything Steve Hansen has said in the whole year that I've been with the All Blacks—a lot of which I haven't agreed with—this is without question the most important and thoughtful. For these final 48 hours, just as he has been for the past eight years, he is in charge of 31 bodies and 31 minds. They're all hurting right now, probably more than they ever have in their entire careers. Every single one of them feels as though they've let the country down. But life will go on, as long as they can open up to one another and say how they feel, conveying the fact that they're not alone.

As rugby players, we've all been there at some level or another. I've never got anywhere close to playing in a World Cup, but I know what it's like to lose and feel like shit in a changing room with a bunch of blokes who are feeling exactly the same way. You sit, you cry, you talk, you reflect. Then, eventually, you laugh. You talk some more and you start to feel better. Your teammates feel better and you keep going. It might be that night; it might be a week later. But it happens because you open up.

Not everyone has the luxury of being in a unit as close as a rugby team. Hansen has touched on the fact that we're not dealing with our problems the right way—and although he hasn't expressly said it, the way I'm hearing it is that he's talking about men. New Zealand's suicide rate is at its highest level since records began, and the male share of it is 71 per cent. We've sat there and listened to Hansen talk for the whole time leading up to and during the World Cup, and he has touched on this sort of thing in the past. He doesn't always get his words right but today he's nailed it, in the right time and the right place. The All Blacks might have lost, but hopefully someone, somewhere, hears what he's said and it helps. Because whatever you think of Steve Hansen, the All Blacks and even rugby, he's right—it takes a lot to be vulnerable.

A COUPLE OF HOURS LATER, we're at Seaside Park in the media holding room. We're scheduled for 2.45pm, and as soon as the clock hits its last quarter we're told to make our way down the driveway in the beautiful sunshine towards the field. The All Blacks are doing their captain's run under Kieran Read's eye for the very last time.

This one is different, though. As we're guided along the fence and through the thick fabric curtains that obscure the view of anyone wanting to sneak a peek, we can hear a commotion coming from the other side. We're greeted with a beautiful sight: all of the players' families and friends who have travelled to Japan to support them. All the way down the touchline are smiles; kids run around and people catch up and embrace. 'Smiley' Barrett is there, watching with his family as his three All Black sons kick a ball around like they used to in the backyard. Ben Smith's wife wrangles their sons, who are wearing replicas of their dad's jersey. Sonny Bill Williams' family sits on the grass and waits patiently for him to come over.

Everyone is smiling, laughing and happy. These are the men who have let their guard down, who have been vulnerable. Today, they begin to heal.

Then, Read gives the go-ahead. Free from doing their drills and goal kicks, the 2019 All Blacks World Cup squad walk over to the waiting parents, wives, partners and kids. Williams, the most outspoken family man in the entire team, is unsurprisingly the first one to embrace his loved ones. The others follow suit. Dane Coles takes the hands of his sons and walks them out onto the park. Read's parents hug their son, on the eve of the last time he will ever pull on an All Blacks jersey and lead his team into battle. But no one is thinking about that at this moment. Everyone is smiling, laughing and happy. These are the men who have let their guard down, who have been vulnerable.

Today, they begin to heal.

EPILOGUE
SAYONARA,
DOMO ARIGATO

Tokyo Stadium, 1 November 2019
(Rugby World Cup bronze medal match)

ALL BLACKS	**40**
WALES	**17**

STEVE HANSEN FINISHES HIS All Blacks career. He leaves the job after eight years and 107 tests, 93 of them wins. Under his tutelage, the All Blacks won the 2015 World Cup, defended the Bledisloe Cup for his entire tenure, and won The Rugby Championship six times. He's been World Rugby Coach of the Year four times. He will go down as one of the greatest coaches not just of the All Blacks, but in rugby history. Hansen's next move is to head back to Japan next year, where he will take up a director of coaching role at the Toyota Verblitz club. NZ Rugby has indicated that his replacement will be named by the end of the year.

Kieran Read walks off Tokyo Stadium a winner in his last game, too—although it's not the game he most wanted to win. The All

Blacks captain has led his team for the fifty-second time, which is second only to the great Richie McCaw. Read sits third on the list of all-time tests for the All Blacks, behind McCaw and Keven Mealamu. He has also scored 26 tries and is generally regarded as one of the most skilful and gifted forwards to ever represent his country. At age 34, he too will return to Japan next year and play for Toyota in the Top League competition.

Beauden Barrett scores a try and leapfrogs ahead of Grant Fox to become the All Blacks' third-highest points-scorer in tests. He is staying in New Zealand, for now at least, because halfway through the year he announced that he was moving from the Hurricanes to the Blues to take up a four-year contract. He will get an unspecified break in that deal to also head offshore (the rumours are strong that it will be the Top League as well), in what many are seeing as the blueprint for NZ Rugby to be able to retain key talent while allowing players to maximise their earning potential. His brother Scott is committed to the Crusaders through 2020, while Jordie is staying at the Hurricanes—although again that is a flexible deal that allows him to shift teams after 2020.

Dane Coles confirms that his desire to play for the All Blacks remains strong, so he looks set to finish his career in New Zealand with the Hurricanes. His parents, who he described as 'normal people from Kāpiti who got to go to Japan and watch their son at a World Cup', see him finish the season with a win and an ovation from the Tokyo crowd when he was subbed off with a leg injury in the twenty-fifth minute. During his time off training, Coles took his family to Disneyworld.

Sam Cane will stay with the Chiefs and the All Blacks for the foreseeable future. His horrendous neck injury showed no signs of slowing him down throughout the World Cup season, and he has confirmed that he has made a full recovery. Now that Read has departed, Cane is very much in the picture to take over the All Blacks captaincy role full-time.

Ardie Savea has also recommitted to the Hurricanes and All Blacks. In 2019 he became the first current All Black to launch a podcast, in which he discusses wide-ranging issues with his teammates, including mental health. As well as continuing with his professional rugby career, Savea runs a clothing line that donates a portion of its profits to the I Am Hope charity. On the day of the test against Wales, he is nominated for World Rugby Player of the Year.

Aaron Smith, TJ Perenara and Brad Weber look set to battle it out for the top All Blacks halfback spot for the time being. They are all signed through to stay with NZ Rugby and their Super Rugby teams through next season. Perenara's try against Namibia, in which he received a behind-the-back pass from Weber, is voted World Rugby Try of the Year.

Sonny Bill Williams and Ryan Crotty combine for a try, with the cross-code star delivering a vintage offload to send his original midfield partner over. Both men are subbed in the fifty-seventh minute to a huge cheer as Hansen empties his bench. Williams uses his last All Blacks media appearance to call for a Māori or Pasifika coach to be included in the All Blacks staff. Crotty uses his to say that he will genuinely miss talking to New Zealand journalists.

Eddie Jones and John Mitchell's England face off against Rassie Erasmus and his Springboks in the World Cup final. In an upset, the Springboks triumph 32–12. The outgoing Erasmus is hailed by the international media for his (and his team's) approachability and honesty. He gives a memorable quote after the final about how 'rugby should not create pressure, it should create hope. We have a privilege, not a burden.' Captain Siya Kolisi becomes the first black African to hold the World Cup aloft, and the moment is immediately likened to when Nelson Mandela arrived at the 1995 final wearing a Springbok jersey. In 2020 the new world champions and the All Blacks are scheduled to play their one-hundredth test match against one another.

By now, Michael Cheika is no longer the coach of the Wallabies. He resigned shortly after returning home to Sydney, amid reports that he and Rugby Australia CEO Raelene Castle had a strained working relationship. Jamie Joseph is one of the names being bandied about to replace him, but Cheika is adamant that his successor should be an Australian.

In 2020 the new world champions and the All Blacks are scheduled to play their one-hundredth test match against one another.

Warren Gatland has finished his tenure with Wales and will head home to coach the Chiefs. Like Beauden Barrett, he has a clause in his contract to take leave for an entire season and coach the British & Irish Lions for their tour to South Africa in 2021.

Joe Schmidt has also ended his test-coaching career (for now). He announced he was leaving well before Ireland's disappointing exit from the World Cup. However, instead of returning to New Zealand as originally planned, Schmidt and his family will stay on in Dublin.

Sky TV wins the rights to screen rugby in New Zealand for the next six years. It also buys the naming rights for Wellington's stadium, which is a clear indication of its commitment to playing games in larger venues despite crowd numbers dropping. The Wednesday after the World Cup final, it will show live the naming of the five Super Rugby squads for the 2020 season, which begins on 31 January.

The next Rugby World Cup will take place in France. Between now and then, there are 1408 days for the All Blacks to prepare to win it back.

ACKNOWLEDGEMENTS

This book would not have been possible without the support of members of the rugby media, most notably: Nigel Yalden and Elliott Smith (Radio Sport); Ross Karl, Blair Martin, Wuz Armstrong, Tom Bartlett and John Day (Newshub); Joe Porter, Leilani Momoisea and Clay Wilson (RNZ); Jon Hill, Marcus Kennedy, Paora Ratahi and Kirstie Stanway (Sky NZ); Dewi Preece and Matt Manukia (TVNZ); Marc Hinton, Aaron Goile, Liam Hyslop and Joe Pearson (*Stuff*); Chris Reive and Liam Napier (*New Zealand Herald*); Karim Ben Ismail (L'Équipe); Tom Decent (*Sydney Morning Herald*); Rob Kitson (*The Guardian*); Nik Simon (*The Daily Mail*); Ben Smith (*RugbyPass*); Jim Kayes (Newsroom); Lynn McConnell (*allblacks.com*); and Scotty Stevenson (Spark Sport).

Thank you to all the people who are working hard to keep the game going at grassroots level, especially the ones who provided me with the motivation to tell this story.

Much love and respect to the team at Allen & Unwin for having the drive to tackle such a demanding project, especially freelance editor Mike Wagg for all his help and quick turnarounds.

Photography credits

Cover image © INPHO/Dan Sheridan: All Blacks captain Kieran Read speaks to the team after the final test of the 2018 end-of-year tour.

Image on pages 14–15 © INPHO/Tommy Dickson: The All Blacks form a huddle following their loss to Ireland on 17 November 2018.

Image on pages 122–123 © Jamie Wall: Kieran Read speaks to media at the captain's run on 16 August 2019, ahead of the deciding Bledisloe Cup test in Auckland.

Image on pages 250–251 © David Ramos/World Rugby via Getty Images: The All Blacks head through the tunnel to the field following half-time in the 2019 Rugby World Cup semi-final against England.